N E A L - S C

TECHNOLOGY MANAGEMENT HANDBOOK FOR SCHOOL LIBRARY MEDIA CENTERS

BY
LESLEY S. J. FARMER

AND
MARC E. MCPHEE

NEAL-SCHUMAN PUBLISHERS, INC.
NEW YORK   LONDON

Published by Neal-Schuman Publishers, Inc.
100 William St., Suite 2004
New York, NY 10038

Printed and bound in the United States of America.

The paper used in this publication meets the minimum requirements of American National Standard for Information Sciences—Permanence of Paper for Printed Library Materials, ANSI Z39.48-1992.

Library of Congress Cataloging-in-Publication Data

Farmer, Lesley S. J.
    Neal-Schuman technology management handbook for school library media centers / Lesley S.J. Farmer and Marc E. McPhee.
        p. cm.
    Includes bibliographical references and index.
    ISBN 978-1-55570-659-3 (alk. paper)
    1. School libraries—Information technology—Management.
2. Instructional materials centers—Information technology—Management. I. McPhee, Marc E. II. Title. III. Title: Technology management handbook for school library media centers.

Z675.S3F2373 2010
025.1'978—dc22

                                                        2010009301

"To everything there is a season, a time for every purpose under the sun."

To our families for their loving support.

Table of Contents

List of Illustrations

Preface

The mission of the school library program is to ensure that students and staff are effective users of ideas and information, no matter what format, so today's school library media specialist must feel equally comfortable and confident in the world of technology and the world of print. The school community expects that the library will have the resources needed to satisfy their information needs, easily accessible whenever they choose to look for information. With the ever growing variety of educational technologies, managing these resources can be a daunting task. Hence this book.

The idea for the *Neal-Schuman Technology Management Handbook for School Library Media Centers* was inspired by the library media technologies course that the authors now teach at the California State University–Long Beach. No appropriate text existed years ago when Marc McPhee took the course as a graduate student from Lesley Farmer, and no book really addressed the technology management needs of practitioner school library media specialists. When the two discussed how to design their course for future librarians they realized they could fill the gap in technology management literature themselves. Thus, this book represents the collaborative perspective of both a school library educator and a building-level practitioner.

The *Neal-Schuman Technology Management Handbook for School Library Media Centers* specifically targets school library media specialists (LMSs) who are beginning to address and incorporate technology. This book combines these two sets of competencies—technology and management—to provide a basic understanding and practical strategies for library media program success in technology management.

After reading the chapters that follow, one should have an

understanding of how school libraries can best acquire and manage technology. The authors provide numerous scenarios, reference guide sheets, technical tips, and other handouts that can save time and ensure success.

ORGANIZATION

The first chapter provides essential background information about the world of technology management, including its role of technology resources in society and the library, and explains how technology needs to embraced and made manageable by LMSs.

The second chapter focuses on the big picture: planning for technology management. Beginning with assessment, the chapter promotes ongoing, systematic improvement using an action research model. The chapter walks through a planning process, from ascertaining a vision and goals through developing strategies, identifying resources, and monitoring results.

The third chapter focuses on acquiring technology resources, including selection policies and procedures, purchasing equipment and software versus leasing access, recording keeping, and ways to keep technology current.

Technology maintenance and troubleshooting is covered in Chapter 4. This chapter focuses on the care and repair of technology resources, from preventative measures as simple as cleaning the facility to backups and security measures. Tips are given for general maintenance practices, troubleshooting, and servicing.

The fifth chapter deals with managing spaces for technology. Facilities issues are covered, such as technology arrangement, supervision, and power demands. The chapter describes networking issues and specific issues of virtual environments involved in distance education.

Communication issues related to technology management are detailed in the sixth chapter. Beginning with the purposes of communication, the chapter explains how to manage virtual channels for communication, including 'casting communication (e.g., podcasts, vodcasts), Web 2.0 technologies (e.g., blogs, wikis), real-time interaction (e.g., voice-over Internet protocol, virtual realities, videoconferencing), and library Web sites (e.g., integrated library systems, portals).

The seventh chapter deals with administrative issues related to technology management, specifically policies and procedures. The chapter also covers disaster planning and ethical and legal issues related to LMS technology management.

The final chapter deals with technologies that are used for professional development. This chapter identifies ways for the LMS keep up to date using human networking (e.g., participating in professional organizations and learning communities) and via collaborative technology tools (e.g., listservs, RSS). The emphasis is on communities of learners.

A Glossary, list of Resources, Bibliography, and Index follow the final chapter.

Digital technology has put a terrific amount of power in the hands of school library media specialists, but this power is useful only to those who can harness it. The authors hope you will find that the *Neal-Schuman Technology Management Handbook for School Library Media Centers* helps you effectively meld technology into the building-level program. Doing so will help teachers teach better and students learn more.

Chapter 1

Introduction to Technology Management

Generations of new technology can transform society, be it radio, television, or the Internet. Today's biggest technology force is Web 2.0, the interactive Internet. Particularly as students encounter and interact with an ever enriched technology, library media specialists (LMS) need to know about these technologies and determine how to manage those technologies to enrich library media programs in support of the school community. Indeed, as new interactive technologies have given rise to Library 2.0, LMSs need to refine their function as information professionals who manage technology to support student learning.

TECHNOLOGY RESOURCES IN SOCIETY

What is technology? A pencil is technology. A book is technology. If an item has been created by a human, a tool, then it is considered a technology. In today's world, technology is usually linked with power, be it solar or electric. Operationally, one could say that technology is something with an on and off switch. More narrowly, in the digital world, technology is often used a shortcut for the term "electronic technology" or "digital technology." Because this book deals with technologies such as videotape (even though this technology is being phased out), the term "technology" will refer to the broader concept of electronics. Even within this scope, technology consists of a broad range of products, most of which can be found in school libraries, or in library media centers (LMC).

Indeed, technology has always played a central role in libraries, from manmade scrolls to e-books, from handwritten inventories to bar code scanners, from tables to high-density shelving and networked servers. Small wonder since libraries are social institutions that select and manage social artifacts, providing physical and intellectual access to those artifacts. As such, libraries reflect and promote societal efforts and values. Technology is certainly one of those valued entities.

Technology and society have a significant symbiotic relationship. Typically, individuals or a small group of people create technology, but this technology can impact the society at large and sometimes change society as a whole. Not that all technologies are transformational. First, society has to accept them. The U.S. Patent Office is full of examples of interesting but little-used technological inventions. Some technologies are accepted for a short time, such as the eight-track audio tape. On the other hand, the Internet has certainly transformed both economies and research worldwide.

What makes the difference? The advantages of the new technology needs to outweigh other alternatives, be it in terms of saving time, saving money, or providing new or enhanced services or products. Enough people must use it in order for others to develop products or applications supported by the new technology. Scalability also factors into the equation; can the product be manufactured fast enough to enable sufficient numbers of people to acquire and use the item effectively and then communicate their success with significant stakeholders?

Education tends to have greater success in integrating technology when society sees the value of the technology and demands that education incorporate it. On the other hand, when education has used technology that remains within that institution, then that technology tends to fall away. Language labs constitute a good example; although considered a means to provide students with practice and timely feedback, language labs had little application to the outside world. Insufficient numbers of labs were created that were considered cost-effective in other settings. The impersonality of labs and the difficulty of teachers to use this technology to diagnose and intervene in learning precluded their embrace by education. In contrast, the Internet started in the research arena and broadened to commercial usage. Both private and public domains found numerous applications for this technology and saw that education could incorporate the Internet to expand access to information and enhance communication, helping students prepare for the economic world. Particularly as the Internet became easier to navigate, the number of users and the extent of their involvement grew exponentially so that most societal factors were influenced by—and in turn influenced—its adoption and expansion.

Even when new technologies emerge, their older counterparts continue until they are no longer viable. Floppy disks are basically an extinct storage device. Word processing has largely eliminated typewriters. In some cases, the newer technology overlaps but does not replace the older technology (e.g., e-books and print books) so the two can coexist. In fact, their coexistence can help them differentiate them (e.g., font/background modification of e-books versus the tactical experience of print).

The school library media center (LMC) reflects the mixture of various technologies (occasionally archiving some obsolete items such as filmstrips). LMSs realize that the format shapes the nature of information. Therefore, LMSs try to match information sources to learner needs, based on personal learning style preferences as well as the information task. Technology has exponentially expanded the potential access and use of informational resources.

The advent of the Internet signaled the end of the closed universe of the library. No longer could LMSs select all of the materials to be accessed by library users. The library collection became relatively limitless, and it became inclusive rather than selective. Seldom can a student *not* find information on a topic; the issue is more of discerning which information is the best suited to the information task. Consequently, instruction needs changed.

Now more than ever the library may be renamed a media center (the term that this book has adopted), but probably more useful is the reconceptualization of the library itself to embrace a potentially unlimited variety of information formats or knowledge representations, which the library may own or access. In any case, the LMS still provides physical and intellectual access to information and ideas so that the school community can use those ideas effectively.

TECHNOLOGY RESOURCES IN THE LIBRARY: CONDITIONS FOR STUDENT SUCCESS

A core function of the school library media program is resource management, and the rest of the school community depends on the LMS to provide resources efficiently. With the central role that technology now plays in the LMC, management of a myriad of resources becomes an increasingly complex job. Additionally, technology itself has become a central tool in management processes. Therefore, the need for a book that focuses specifically on managing technology resources as part of the school library media program has become paramount. This book is intended to fill that need, particularly for beginning LMSs and other library staff.

The range of technology resources that LMSs may come across while serving in libraries can be overwhelming:

- **Hardware:** desktop computer, laptop computer, tablet computer, server
- **Software:** production-centric resources, learning activities, programming, and networking
- **Peripherals:**
  - Input devices: keyboard, mouse, graphics table, microphone, scanner, probeware, camera, camcorder, SMART Board
  - Communication devices: printer, telephone, Internet, videoconferencing
  - Projection devices: monitor, overhead projector, data projector
  - Storage devices: videotape (largely outdated), audiotape (largely outdated), CD (largely outdated), DVD, flash drive, other portable storage device (e.g., iPod), server
- **Other digital devices:** mobile technology, response systems, voice enhancement equipment, game consoles, photocopiers
- **Internet resources:** World Wide Web, streaming video, videoconferencing, databases, ebooks, 'casting, learning objects, and other online delivery

In addition, libraries use profession-specific management technology, such as integrated library management systems, cataloging software such as MARC Magician, digital collection software, and digital reference software.

WEB 2.0 AND LIBRARY 2.0

The current interest in Web 2.0—the interactive Web—exemplifies societal acceptance and social change. With online collaborative tools such as blogs and wikis, users around the world can easily contribute to the Internet knowledge base. They can share their ideas and express themselves creatively to a worldwide authentic audience. Web 2.0 has democratized information and given voice to the masses. This same strength can be threatening in some areas as the ability to discern the veracity and value of information seems to fall behind its production. Previous editing and filtering processes have been overridden to a large extent in Web 2.0 environments, which the average user might not realize. Basing their decisions on faulty information, citizen may witness disastrous consequences.

With Web 2.0, the library universe has expanded even further. In this environment, school LMSs need to pay attention to Web 2.0, address it, and embrace it judiciously. Web 2.0 can impact collection management, instructional design and delivery, and communication practices. Several general questions arise for each aspect of Web 2.0 resources, such as the following:

- **Access.** How can the school community access Web 2.0 resources? What policies and procedures need to be in place to comply with the Children's Internet Protection Act? Does the LMS need to prescreen or preselect Web 2.0 sites? What control does the LMS have in such decision making or over access issues?
- **Use.** How can the school community evaluate Web 2.0 resources in terms of their quality as well as their usefulness? What is the LMS's role in such evaluation, instruction, and practice? How can curriculum incorporate Web 2.0 resources? What training does the school community need in order to use Web 2.0 resources effectively, and what is the LMS's role in such training?
- **Production.** How can the school community produce Web 2.0 resources? What are the pros and cons of the school

community producing Web 2.0 resources? What special procedures (e.g., parental permission) are needed for minors to produce Web 2.0 resources? What copyright and other regulations need to be addressed, and what is the LMS's role in complying and explaining these regulations? Where and how will Web 2.0 products be hosted and stored? What is the LMS's role in storing and organizing Web 2.0 products?

The Web 2.0 philosophy changes the school library media program. Take collection development, for example. In a print environment, interactivity manifested itself in school community products, such as instructional aids, student work, class anthologies, and bibliographies, products that were created and modified by individuals and groups. In some cases, the LMC's collection included such products. In any case, the LMS (sometimes in collaboration with classroom teachers) generally selected which items to incorporate into the collection. The nature of digital information makes such interactive production and "repurposing" (e.g., the same information reformatted and packaged for a different purpose) easier than ever to do. Nevertheless, the LMS can still monitor and select which digital items to incorporate into the LMC, depending on the access and control that the LMS has to these documents. Issues of file transfer protocols and permissions, storage space and organization, and access methods and permissions all need to be considered. LMS technical management, particularly of processing materials, becomes decidedly more complicated. Nevertheless, the participatory element that Web 2.0 can bring to the LMS offers a window of opportunity for LMSs to empower the library media program by empowering the school community to contribute to its resources and services.

WHAT IS TECHNOLOGY MANAGEMENT?

Within the scope of the school library media program, managing technology comprises several activities:

- Acquiring LMC technology resources, including gaining access and acquiring equipment needed to experience and use digital resources
- Maintaining LMC technology resources in good condition, including servicing them as needed

- Managing physical and virtual spaces for LMC technology
- Providing effective physical access to LMC technology at a distance (e.g., local and distant networks)
- Managing virtual communication channels for LMC communication (e.g., library portals, Web-based databases)
- Managing LMC-related telecommunications and broadcasting
- Developing and implementing policies and procedures relative to LMC technology
- Managing the fiscal aspects of LMC technology

It should be noted that the technologies, be they physical or digital, need not be located within the LMC itself or even on the LMC's server. Rather, the critical question is whether the technology is considered part of the school library media program. Is the LMS responsible?

LIBRARY STAFF ROLE IN MANAGING TECHNOLOGY

Each one of these technologies requires training and time to implement. In most cases, the benefits of technology outweigh the costs and effort. Processing can be done much more quickly, more resources can be accessed more quickly, resources can be tracked more efficiently, and new services can be provided.

A case may be made that technicians should manage LMC technology. After all, such individuals have specific training, such as network management and computer troubleshooting. In general, their focus, their "end," is on the smooth operation of technology. On the other hand, information professionals have as their central goal the effective use of information by their clientele. Information professionals achieve this goal by providing effective physical and instructional access to information. In school settings, LMSs as information professionals have as their "end" student learning. Technology can be a significant means to that end. Because LMSs realize the extent that technology has impacted information, they often tend to be early adopters of technology and try to find ways for the school community to access and use technology in their use of information.

For LMSs to manage technology, they need a solid knowledge

base and specific skills in educational technology. As the National Board for Professional Teaching Standards stated in 2001, "Accomplished LMSs serve the learning community as technology leaders and integrate the latest technologies into the curriculum to enhance learning" (p. 11). With regard to technology management, "accomplished LMSs demonstrate expertise with the technologies for information creation, storage, retrieval, organization, communication, and use, and they are informed about a full range of materials in print and electronic formats" (p. 17).

In 2005, the California Library Association established a baseline list of relevant competencies for library workers:

- Basic operations and troubleshooting of computers and peripherals (e.g., printers)
- Software operations, including operative systems
- Operation of library e-resources
- Awareness of security issues

Professional library staff are also expected to use Web browsers, search effectively, oversee public computers, understand online resources, and instruct users in the use of library online resources.

While LMSs certainly appreciate the work of technology experts and technology-trained paraprofessional LMC staff, it is the LMS who needs to oversee technology management as part of the larger library media program. To this end, LMSs need to be technologically competent and able as managers. The remainder of this book provides the nuts and bolts of managing the ever-changing technology assets.

WORKS CITED

California Library Association. 2005. *Technology Core Competencies for California Library Workers*. Sacramento, CA: California Library Association. Available: www.cla-net.org/included/docs/tech_core_competencies.pdf (accessed June 30, 2009).

National Board for Professional Teaching Standards. 2001. *NBPTS Library Media Standards*. Arlington, VA: National Board for Professional Teaching Standards. Available: www.nbpts.org/the_standards/standards_by_cert?ID=19&x=52&y=8 (accessed June 30, 2009).

Chapter 2

Planning for Technology Management

Technology changes. Curriculum changes. The school community changes. Managing the status quo, particularly in terms of technology, is a no-win situation. In order to manage technology proactively, library media specialists (LMSs) need to plan for the short term and the long term. Obviously, the plan must align the library media program goals with the school community. LMSs should conduct environmental scans, assess student outcomes and factors contributing to academic success, and evaluate the library's current program, school resources, and stakeholders. Fortunately, school library media programs are well positioned to manage technological resources and services and can partner with the school and larger community to that end. LMSs also need to pursue grants in order to advance technology agendas. This chapter offers tips in planning strategically for optimum technology management results.

LMSs also need to evaluate their own effective management of technology. This chapter describes an action research model and details sources of data (e.g., usage statistics—integrated library management system, counters, "hit" history, network logs), surveys, video observation, student work, data analysis, communication of findings, and explains how to act on recommendations. An example technology plan focuses on impact on student learning.

WHY PLAN?

Sometimes it feels as if LMSs spend all of their time responding to others' demands and dealing with a series of crises, particularly when managing technology. Mr. Vegas needs the laptop cart, a data projector bulb just burned out, a desktop crashed, the printer ink ran out, the photocopier jammed. And technology changes all the time, so why plan?

Well, planning ahead can ameliorate some of those crises: scheduling computer use, stocking backup supplies, keeping computers in good condition and configuring them for minimal crashing, and having service numbers readily available. Thinking more strategically, LMSs can routinize desktop refresh and software upgrade schedules, participate on school site and district technology committees to keep in the technology loop, and maintain a list of prioritized technology while keeping an eye on grant opportunities. Then when those unexpected windfalls come along, LMSs can take advantage of them to get desired technology.

At the very least, just as the school tries to plan strategically, so should the LMS. And technology should be an integral part of that planning. Nowadays, most schools or districts need to develop a yearly technology plan. Where is the library media program in that plan? Ideally, LMSs throughout the district should collaboratively plan in order to maximize their impact and ensure equitable service for all students.

ASSESSMENT

Assessment is central to ongoing technology management. How well do technology resources meet the needs of the school community? Are their allocation and maintenance effective? LMSs constantly assess their technology management efforts: "I should have bought an extra flash drive last week," "I need to teach the library clerk how to clear up a paper jam." Planning helps make this assessment more systematic and action-oriented.

Generic Assessment Factors

Assessment basically has three functions:

1. **Diagnostic:** to describe what is happening now and to identify possible needs or gaps
2. **Formative:** to determine the status of resources or actions in progress (how far along is the situation to meeting a goal)
3. **Summative:** to determine whether the goal or objective was met

Within that construct, several questions arise:

- *What* will be assessed?
- *Why* will it be assessed?
- *Who* will assess?
- *How* will it be assessed?
- *Where* will it be assessed?
- *When,* and how often, will it be assessed?
- What will be done with the assessment? How will it be analyzed? How will the results be communicated and acted on?

Assessing Current Library Technology Management

Not only is assessment core to technology management but it may well precede planning efforts, for if the LMS does not know what the current situation is, then determining a direction for action is impossible. Beginning with the library itself, assessment of technology as it applies to management should include all entities that might impact library media center (LMC) management.

First of all, the LMS must determine what technology resources and services now exist. An inventory log (Table 2.1) for each piece of technology can help the LMS keep track of the status of each item and identify possible problem areas (e.g., an unstable computer model).

Maintaining a database and printing out that data (each type of technology having its own page or binder division) enables LMSs to document and communicate management efforts easily. This inventory can also facilitate refresh and upgrade schedules and requests for funding. LMSs should briefly note their other technology management activities, along with other duties performed, on a daily basis. At the end of the day or week, LMSs can classify

Table 2.1
Inventory Log

	Name/Brand/ Model/Version	Serial #	Specs	Date Acquired	Funding Source	Maintenance Log
Hardware	MSI Wind Notebook VR220-004US	334455	1.6 GHz, 1 GB DDR2, 160 GB, Built-in Ethernet, WLAN, Web-cam, mike	11/11/08	PTA	
Software						
Peripherals						
Other devices						
Web resources						

those actions by color-coding them or otherwise making appropriate notations. This process can help when assessing time management to prioritize work. For instance, if it becomes apparent that computer desktops have to be cleaned up daily, totaling five hours a week, perhaps a desktop security management program would be cost-effective.

Several other strategies can be used to assess LMC technology management:

- Digital collection comparison with similar school libraries
- Work flow analysis
- Traffic flow analysis
- Analysis of number and quality of service contacts
- Circulation statistics for equipment
- Content analysis of telecommunications relative to technology management
- Computer (and other technologies) use analysis
- LMC portal and online subscription database "hits"
- Digital reference transaction analysis
- Observation of technology use
- Referrals and other interventions for inappropriate technology use
- Examination of student work to determine physical and intellectual access and use of technology

In most cases, such assessments would be conducted when a more general assessment indicated that some kind of intervention was needed.

At this point in time, technology should be an integral part of the total library media program, not an add-on. Management of technology, therefore, should fold seamlessly into the larger management mix. In assessing the management of resources, how do digital resources compare with print or audiovisual materials in terms of acquisition, processing, storage, and retrieval? In assessing the management of services, what role does technology play in providing instruction and promoting literacies? Does technology work in parallel with other program entities or in tandem? Perhaps some aspect of management is not working well, such as class scheduling; is technology being used, or could its use solve the problem (e.g., online scheduling)? As LMSs assess the library media program as a whole, using a management lens, they can drill down to the role of technology to determine what significant patterns emerge and then leverage them to the program's advantage.

Assessment Linked to the School Community

In focusing on technology management, LMSs use assessment to pin-point which steps along the way of technology resource acquisition and maintenance need improvement as well as assess the management conditions for optimal technology use (e.g., policies, facilities, communication). The Milken Exchange on Educational Exchange defined seven dimensions for assessing the effective incorporation into the learning community (Lemke and Coughlin, 1998), which apply well to technology management issues:

- **Learners.** Is technology managed so that learners can access and use it? Do all learner subgroups, such as English language learners and individuals with disabilities, have equitable access?
- **Learning environments.** Is technology accessible for all school community members, including those with special needs? Does technology management enable users to retrieve technological information easily?
- **Professional competency.** Are LMSs and other school staff technologically competent? Does the LMC staff manage technology effectively? Does the LMC staff use technology to improve their ability to manage technology?
- **System capacity.** Does the library media program demonstrate a compelling vision and clear expectations? Does the LMS's technology management align with the library media program's and school's long-term plan? Does the infrastructure supply capacity to implement the LMS's technology plan? Does the LMS analyze the learning community systematically?
- **Community connections.** Are community partners involved throughout the LMS's technology management plan? Have all potential stakeholders and collaborations been identified and engaged? Is communication clear and ongoing?

- **Technology capacity.** Are technology infrastructure and equipment available to support LMC technology management? Is connectivity adequate to manage LMC technology? Are users satisfied with the way that LMC technology is managed? Are facilities capable of supporting the LMS's management of technology?
- **Accountability.** Have LMC technology management goals, objectives, and benchmarks been established? Are assessment efforts and analysis done effectively? Has LMC technology management improved because of data-driven assessment?

In assessing LMC technology management in light of the school program, the central focus should be student success since this is the mission of the school. What technology factors contribute to that success? In 2007, the International Society for Technology in Education (ISTE) recommended six clusters of technology competencies that all K–12 students should demonstrate. Schools address these competency outcomes through curriculum, instruction design and implementation, and assessment. After each competency listed are ways that LMC technology management can contribute to students meeting those competencies.

- **Creativity and innovation.** LMSs can provide and manage technology resources (including equipment) and production areas for students to create technology-enhanced products. LMSs can create and manage repositories of learning objects and student products.
- **Communication and collaboration.** LMSs can provide and manage collaborative tools and telecommunications channels to enable students to interact and collaborate online. LMSs can provide and manage communication tools.
- **Research and information fluency.** LMSs can provide and manage digital content, access tools, and productivity tools for student use. LMSs can provide and manage learning objects to help students gain fluency. LMSs can schedule use of the LMC to instruct students and provide them with opportunities to practice research and information processes.
- **Critical thinking, problem solving, and decision making.** LMSs can provide and manage digital content including

data sets, access tools, and productivity tools for student use. LMSs can provide and manage learning objects to help students learn these skills. LMSs can schedule use of the LMC to instruct students and provide them with opportunities to practice research and information processes.

- **Digital citizenship.** LMSs can manage computers and networks to minimize inappropriate online use and intervene when users abuse technology. LMSs can inform users of photocopiers, scanners, and computers about compliance with copyright and other intellectual property rights through signage and other communication. LMSs can model digital citizenship through their management practices. LMSs can train and manage student aides to model and coach peers in digital citizenship.

- **Technology operations and concepts.** LMSs can manage technology so that it is in good working condition for users. LMSs can provide and manage learning objects to help students learn technology concepts and operations. LMSs can train and manage student aides to model and coach peers to operate technology appropriately.

For each competency, LMSs can identify which relevant technology management functions they perform, how well they perform them, and the impact of their efforts on student learning. It should be noted that in 2008 ISTE also developed technology standards for teachers, which LMSs can also address as they manage technology.

Of course, LMS management of technology does not exist in a vacuum; it is deeply impacted by the rest of the school, the district, and the community. Therefore, LMSs naturally should examine how technology is managed in other parts of the school. Many sites or districts have technology plans that can serve as guide for assessment. State and national technology assessment models also exist. The following representative tools can be adopted or adapted for local use. LMSs can use these tools themselves as they assess LMC technology management as part of the school's overall technology efforts, and they can share these assessment tools with existing technology committees and administrators.

- International Society for Technology in Education: www. iste.org/Content/NavigationMenu/Research/Evaluation-PlanningResources/Evaluation_Planning_Resources.htm
- National School Boards Association: www.nsba.org/sbot/ toolkit/tpt.html
- North Central Regional Technology in Education Consortium: www.ncrtec.org/pe/index.html
- SouthEast Regional Initiatives Technology in Education Consortium: www.serve.org/seir-tec/techplan/plans.html
- California State Department of Education: www.cde.ca.gov/ ls/et/rs/techplan.asp
- Michigan State Department of Education: www.techplan.org
- Teachnology: www.teach-nology.com/teachers/educational_ technology/tech_plan

School sites and districts are, themselves, impacted by state and national educational initiatives and mandates. For instance, The United States Department of Education (2004) national technology plan recommends the following actions, which can impact the LMS's technology management plans as noted in italics:

1. **Strengthen leadership.** Administrators need training in technology decision making and implementation. Schools need to partner with the community. *LMS can train administrators (or learn alongside them) in the use of technology for decision-making (e.g., use of spreadsheets, project management software).*

2. **Consider innovative budgeting.** Integrate technology into school financing and provide for roll-over funding to support substantial technology acquisitions. *LMSs should participate in site and district budget committees and provide LMS budgets for technology resource allocation.*

3. **Improve teacher training.** Teachers need to know how to integrate technology to improve student learning. *In terms of management LMSs can promote their databases of digital resources and develop a repository of site technology-enhanced learning objects. LMSs can also develop Webliographies of online tutorials and other resources to help teachers learn how to integrate technology effectively for student learning.*

4. **Support e-learning and virtual schools.** Every teacher and student should have opportunities to learn online, and standards need to be developed to ensure high-quality teaching in that virtual environment. *LMSs can locate and develop repositories of learning objects. LMSs need to make sure that the LMC catalog and digital resources are available and accessible to the entire school community on a 24/7 basis. LMSs also need to manage digital-based reference services, or at least provide a means to access such online reference services, in order to guide learners in a timely fashion.*

5. **Encourage broadband access.** The infrastructure should support 24/7 educational use for data management, assessment, e-learning, and digital resources. *LMSs need to support and facilitate broadband access initiatives and make sure that the LMC's resources are accessible via broadband.*

6. **Move toward digital content.** High-quality digital resources should be available and accessible at all times. Teachers need training in their effective use. *LMSs need to acquire and manage educational digital content. LMSs can facilitate in-house production of digital content through the management of production resources and services. LMSs can store and manage those in-house developed digital content for online access.*

7. **Integrate data systems.** Data files should be interoperable in order to optimize assessment, data analysis, and decision making. *LMSs should make sure that the library's integrated management system is incorporated into the school's data systems. LMSs can access and use school data systems and develop additional data sets that can be incorporated into the school's overall data plan (e.g., assessment of student literacy).*

Assessment of Community Stakeholders

The larger community is mentioned in the national technology plan recommendations, and those stakeholders need to be assessed as well in terms of their impact on LMC technology management. In most cases, these entities impact the LMC indirectly, such as a local business that sells school supplies, but the LMS makes some connection with them, as indicated in italics.

- Educational entities (such as other K–16 institutions): *resource sharing, consortium purchasing discounts, joint professional development opportunities, technology management consultation, joint grant opportunities*
- Public entities (such as public libraries and utility services): *cabling licenses, telecommunications consultation, power audits*
- Private entities (such as businesses and religious institutions): *grant and donation opportunities, technology and management consultation*
- Civic organizations (such as chambers of commerce and social clubs): *grant and donation opportunities, technology and management consultation*

In identifying partners, LMSs need to consider the potential group's goals and values, reputation, resources and competencies, and alignment with LMC technology management issues.

In terms of assessing existing partnerships, LMSs should consider the quality of the community partnerships in light of their shared objectives in order to optimize the conditions for collaboration. Some of the general factors to consider include the following:

- **Time frame:** length of partnership, regularity of communication
- **Activities:** quantity and quality of joint activities, degree of interdependence of activities by each partner
- **Degree of partnership:** communication, cooperation, collaboration
- **Impact:** degree to which LMC technology management is impacted

Focusing on LMC technology management, LMSs can take a couple of approaches. LMSs can identify problems in technology management and ask community members for help. Alternatively, if the problem rests with the community, such as power overloads, in which case the LMS would probably contact a site administrator to resolve the problem with the utility company.

Since the school and district's effective technology use involves several stakeholders, LMSs need to assess those entities in order to determine what actions to take either internally or with the help of others. This environmental scan should include the following:

- Strengths of LMC technology management and other aspects of the library media program (e.g., resources and capabilities to serve the school community such as well-trained technical aides)
- Weaknesses of LMC technology management and other aspects of the library media program (e.g., resources and capabilities that hinder serving the school community, such as computer monitors that are hard to supervise)
- Opportunities in the external environment that might impact LMC technology management (e.g., installation of campus-wide wifi system, requirement of a district technology plan)
- Threats in the external environment that might impact LMC technology management (e.g., budget constraints, require-ment of filtering software and other regulations).

By identifying key factors, LMSs can take those factors into account as they plan. LMSs can align their technology management efforts with the school's priorities, emphasizing their program's strengths and seizing on school opportunities.

MAKING USE OF ASSESSMENT

By analyzing the data collected from assessing LMC technology management factors in light of the overall library media program, the school's mission and implementation, and the community situ-ation, LMSs are poised to plan strategically.

What trends or patterns emerge? Each data set tells a story. Accurate data analysis is key in understanding an issue. Data can be categorized based on the assessment question, such as how does computer access impact student performance. A survey can reveal which students have access to computers outside of school: at home, at friends' homes, at an Internet "café," or at the public library or other public facility. Quantitative (e.g., descriptive statistics) and qualitative (e.g., anecdotes) statistics can be applied to the data. Of course, numbers by themselves mean little without a context. What other factors might contribute?

- Has the situation changed over time? Does the time of the day or week factor in?
- Where does the issue occur? Does it happen elsewhere?
- Who influences—or is influenced by—the issue?
- What resources might impact the issue?

Sometimes reading what other people have done in the same situation (reviewing the literature) can shed light on underlying causes and possible solutions.

By looking at the overall picture and considering possible contributing factors, the LMS can interpret the data more fully and pose possible solutions to the problem. At that point, available resources can be identified in order to weigh the costs and benefits of different solutions. Then a decision can be made and acted on. If the LMS can control all of the factors, then an action plan can be developed and implemented directly; the plan should also be communicated with his or her supervisor. If other entities are involved, then the LMS needs to work with them and should get administrative support. In any case, the intervention should be assessed to determine its effectiveness, with this analysis perhaps leading to its modification.

For instance, the LMS may find that one bank of computers consistently crashes. A number of reasons could be at the root of the program: hacking due to lack of supervision, lack of desktop supervision program, faulty power supply. Upon further investigation, the LMS determines that a couple of advanced computer students have taught their friends how to get around the LMC's desktop configuration. After a talk with the computer teacher and the hackers, the problem stops.

In planning proactively, the LMS can schedule time with the computer class to discuss property rights and acceptable computer use. Alternatively, the LMS can turn around the computers so that the screens are all easily visible from the reference desk. The LMS might also consider installing desktop protection software. Depending on whether the LMS wants to spend the time closely supervising computers (an alternative being a computer supervision program at the reference desk), a desktop solution might be the most cost-effective and least laborious.

ACTION RESEARCH

A systematic way to address and solve concrete technology management issues is "action research." This outcomes-based approach is
a form of planning that typically has a short-term time frame. The
research is typically an active participant in the system. The steps
are as follows:

1. Focus on a topic or issue, such as an aspect of technology
   management.
2. Review relevant literature about the issue and underlying
   research about the topic.
3. Develop action research questions.
4. Collect data.
5. Analyze data.
6. Make recommendations and report findings and conclusions.
7. Develop an action plan based on the data and research.
8. Take action.
9. Evaluate the action plan.

Sometimes assessment leads to action research as LMSs analyze
routine assessments, such as annual LMC user surveys or sample
student work, and spot a potential issue. If reviewing a LMC plan,
the LMS may see an area that has been neglected or isn't meeting
a predetermined goal; action research offers a systematic method
of addressing this gap. Alternatively, a schoolwide initiative such
as writing across the curriculum can drive the LMS action research
focus.

For example, a school site might focus on improving student
reading. The following case study illustrates how action research
can help technology management (Powers, 2008):

1. The LMS might manage an accelerated reading (AR) program that supports the school's initiative but finds that the
   program isn't well implemented. The LMS's workload might
   be overburdened because students have to take all AR tests
   in the LMC.
2. The LMS researches factors for successful AR programs and
   finds that motivation and engagement are two significant

factors. The research further indicates that successful AR programs involve the entire school, not just the library media program.

3. The LMS develops three research questions:
   a. How can the LMS improve the management of the AR program?
   b. What motivates students and teachers to use the AR program?
   c. What factors increase engagement in using the AR program?
4. The LMS surveys a representative student and teacher population about their perceptions and use of AR.
5. Survey data is analyzed using descriptive and correlation statistics; open-ended questions were coded and categorized. The LMS found that teacher perception impacted student motivation. When teachers promoted AR through book sharing and let students freely choose reading, students were more motivated and more engaged. The LMS also found that convenience also impacted engagement. If the teacher let the students take the test at any time, students were more likely to read more (although this approach burdens the library media program). Teachers who knew how to use AR data were also more apt to motivate and engage their students in its use.
6. Based on the data and analysis, the LMS recommended that the AR program be installed on the English teachers' computers and that the LMS train those teachers how to manage AR. This report was given to the principal and shared at a faculty meeting.
7. The plan included migrating from a CD- to a Web-based version of AR and training English teachers and students how to use AR. The LMS also wanted to purchase more books that had AR tests.
8. The LMS moved from a CD-based to a Web-based AR program, which was made available on the English teachers' computers. The LMS created an AR management manual and trained the English teachers. She also trained students on test-taking processes and book selection. She spent $2,000 on books and AR tests, based on students' interests.

9. Students and teachers were resurveyed. Standardized reading scores were compared with the prior year's data. LMC use was also assessed in terms of class and individual use as well as circulation records. The LMC technology management workload was also assessed.

STRATEGIC PLANNING FOR TECHNOLOGY MANAGEMENT

Most of the examples so far have dealt with specific issues or problems and have resulted in short-term planning. However, long-term strategic planning for technology management is also useful as it provides an extended goal and direction for resource allocation and an effective service program under the auspices of the overall library media program.

Strategic planning begins with a vision: what is an ideal school LMC? This vision combines the LMS's educational and librarianship philosophy with the library profession's values and the realities and hopes for the school and its community. In 1998 the American Association of School Librarians (AASL) and Association for Education Communications and Technology (AECT) asserted that the mission of the school library media program is "to ensure that students and staff are effective users of ideas and information" (p. 6). How that mission is conceptualized and contextualized at the school site depends on the needs and priorities of the school community. More specifically, the library media program mission needs to align with and support the school's mission. Thus, if the school's charge is to develop creative students, then the LMS should include opportunities for students to generate knowledge and express themselves creatively. Nor should the library media program's mission be developed solely by the LMC staff but should include the input of the LMC's major stakeholders. The vision is then transformed into a statement of purpose, or charge, that summarizes the raison-d'etre of the library media program. This mission drives the ensuing goals and specific objectives, one of which can focus on technology management as a means to achieve the library's media program mission.

To implement the goal of effective technology management, the LMS can draw on existing standards. A couple of standards have already been mentioned: the U.S. Department of Education's

National Educational Technology Plan, ISTE's (2007) *National Educational Technology Standards for Students,* and the National Board for Professional Teaching Standards (2001) NBPTS *Library Media Standards.* Other applicable standards that inform technology management planning follow:

- International Technology Education Association's (2003) *Advancing Excellence in Technological Literacy: Student Assessment, Professional Development, and Program Standards*
- AASL's *Standards for the 21st Century Learner* (2007)
- Bibliographic standards (e.g., MARC, or machine readable cataloging)
- International technical standards (e.g., Open System Interconnection [OSI] seven-layer reference model)
- National technical standards (e.g., TCP/IP, Z39.50, 802.11, OpenURL) established by the American National Standards Institute, National Information Standards Organization, and Institute of Electrical and Electronic Engineers
- State technology standards
- District technology standards

Based on applicable missions, goals, objectives, and standards, the LMS can then conduct a needs assessment to ascertain what gaps exist between the current situation and the target goal. Assessment plays a central role for this task. Only then can the LMS reasonably determine which strategies to use to bridge those gaps. It can be useful at this junction to cluster strategies by technology management functions:

- **Acquisitions:** for example, select subscription databases, migrate to a new integrated library management system
- **Maintenance:** for example, develop a desktop refresh schedule, establish a maintenance schedule to manage desktops (for example, disc scan, clean towers)
- **Facilities management:** for example, provide wheelchair-accessible computer furniture, install a security alarm system
- **Telecommunications and networking:** for example, create online "bookmark" Webliographies via Delicious, learn basic networking functions

- **Documentations and communication**: for example, improve documentation of computer repairs, add an instant messaging function to the LMC's Web site
- **Policies and procedures**: for example, develop a selection policy for subscription databases, develop procedures to address the PATRIOT Act.

While brainstorming numerous strategies to improve technology management can be a useful exercise, the LMS needs to prioritize these strategies based on their significance to the library media program, their timeliness (e.g., a short window of opportunity), their alignment to school initiatives, and the resources available. Earlier identification of school priorities and resources (both allocated as well as potential funding opportunities) helps the LMS decide which strategies are feasible and will be supported by the administration. Having an LMC advisory committee to provide input strengthens the LMS's stance and credibility and helps weave the LMC plan into the school's overall planning strategy.

Once strategies are determined, the LMS can create an action plan to implement it and assess its effectiveness. A simple grid can document and monitor tasks, each column noting the stakeholders, persons responsible, time frame, and progress notes. It is also wise at the beginning to identify what means will be used to assess the action plan's success.

Table 2.2, adapted from AASL's (1999) *A Planning Guide for Information Power*, provides a checklist of factors to consider when developing a plan for technology management.

This table helps the LMS and others involved in planning and implementation to keep track of progress and determine if changes in tasks or personnel are needed. Particularly when one person's efforts or one benchmark impacts another task, timely monitoring and adjustment are vital. If a bottleneck occurs, then action can be taken to resolve or work around the problem.

Both short- and long-term planning offer valuable direction for LMSs as they seek to improve LMC technology management. Short-term projects provide quick visible results that the school community can appreciate and the LMS can build on, and long-term planning provides a sustainable future that can weather the occasional setbacks that occur in education.

Table 2.2
Planning Checklist

Activity	Time Frame	Comments
Preparing for planning process: • Vsion • Steering committee/stakeholders • Needs assessment		
Mission statement		
Goal and objectives (linked to demographics, curriculum, etc.)		
Strategy action plan:		
• Stakeholders		
• What—obstacles, support for ideas, strengths and weaknesses		
• Where—rationale for developing program ideas		
• When—timeline		
• Who will do it?		
• How will you raise awareness about issue/what is your message?		
• Communication tools		
• Assessment (indicators of success and tools to measure them)		
Planning chart:		
• Tasks		
• Person(s) responsible		
• Progress notes		
• Date completed		
Supportive evidence		
Assessment and analysis		
Professional report		

MANAGEMENT PLANNING FOR TECHNOLOGY-ENHANCED LEARNING

A core value and mission in K–12 schools is student achievement, the result of student learning and application of that learning. More recently, education has recognized the role that technology can play in such student success, as evidenced in the U.S. Department of Education's technology plan, ISTE's 2007 student technology standards, and other educational entity documents. How does the library media program support and facilitate technology-enhanced learning, and what management planning needs to be done to ensure that the library media program will succeed?

At its very core, the library media program provides the conditions for technology-enhanced learning: digital resources and other materials, technology-rich environments that are conducive for learning, and skilled LMC staff to help students engage meaningfully in technology-enhanced learning activities through instructional design and delivery. These material and human resources need to be well managed for LMC conditions to function well.

The following two adapted management plans (Stephanie Hall and Jasper Bui, unpublished data), exemplify how LMC management can facilitate student learning through technology.

ABC High School Language Arts Technology Plan

Vision

Technology will be available for every language arts classroom to increase student motivation and achievement and to help meet the Language Arts Standards for the State of California.

Rationale

Language Arts is the one core subject that has technology use imbedded into the Standards for the State of California.

9th and 10th Grade Standards

- Reading Comprehension 2.6: Demonstrate use of sophisticated learning tools following technical directions.
- Writing 1.8: Design and publish documents by using advanced publishing software and graphic programs.

- Writing 2.6: Write technical documents.
- Listening and Speaking 1.7: Use electronic media to enhance the appeal and accuracy of presentations.

11th and 12th Grade Standards

- Writing Strategies 1.8: Integrate databases, graphics, and spreadsheets into word-processed documents.
- Writing Applications 2.6: Deliver multimedia presentations.
- Speaking Applications 2.4: Deliver multimedia oral presentations and, thus, all language arts classes must have access to computers for their students to use.

Objectives and Strategies

- Technology: Our school will provide our language arts teachers with computers and support peripherals to use in the classroom setting, no matter in which classroom they teach.
- Curriculum: Grades 9–12 language arts teachers will enable all of their students to improve their computer literacy by providing them with learning opportunities in their courses to meet all the state technology standards.
- Collaboration: Our administration and teachers will help write grants to fund the technology to make these goals possible. Student groups and parents will volunteer to help maintain the technology.
- Staff development: Our language arts teaching staff will develop sufficient technology literacy to create lesson plans to teach their students how to use technological resources through a "team approach" sharing the information taught in the professional Apple in-services (funding provided) as well as through LMS taught in-services offered once every other month.
- Funding: Our school will develop a bonus program for staff members who win grant funding and who are able to generate funding via the community or other sources. Our administration will commit to annual funding to maintain this technology in the classroom and the LMC.

Staff Development

- Two hours of "buyback time" will be offered to language arts teachers who attend a "iLife '06 Workshop," which is given weeknights at the local Apple retailers.
- Two hours of "buyback time" will be offered to teachers who attend either the "Getting Started" or "Advanced Getting Started" workshops available at the local Apple retailers on Saturday mornings.
- Sixteen staff members will be trained by Apple and will then be teamed up with another 16 as "team teachers"; they will be responsible for sharing what they learned, thus educating all 30 language arts teachers.
- The LMS and language arts teachers will provide future staff development, sharing lesson plans and positive teaching experiences (along with the pros and cons of the technology).

Funding Sources

Our school will apply for a variety of grants, including education grants from U.S. Bank and the National Endowment for the Humanities as well as from local district technology grants. Our school will ask the local community for donations to help offset the remaining amount due on the four-year lease of the mobile cart. For fiscal years 2009–2012,

- the school budget will designate $8,000 per year toward the lease of the mobile lab;
- the language arts department will designate $300 per year toward the lease of the mobile lab;
- the LMC budget will designate $250 per year toward the lease of the mobile lab.

Evaluation

This technology plan will be formally evaluated annually in May by a technology committee consisting of the LMS, principal, language arts department head, and one classroom teacher. Also, evaluations by classroom teachers and students will be given monthly to ensure the computers are meeting the needs of the classrooms. [See Table 2.3 for example objectives, instruments, and measures of evaluation.]

Table 2.3
Technology Plan

Objective	Schoolwide Assessment Instruments/ Evidence	LMC Management Evaluation
Computer and peripheral use	Sample lesson plans, class observations	Inventory, circulation records
Improved student computer literacy	Sample student work, standardized technology test	Class scheduling and planning documents, class observation, repair records
Improved teacher computer literacy	In-service performance, sample teacher documents	Class scheduling and planning documents, circulation, class observation
Technology-enhanced lesson plans	Sample lesson plans	Planning documents, circulation, class observation
Grant awards	Grant application and award documents, bonus program awardees	Grant application information about LMS management
School community involvement in technology maintenance	Volunteer workload and logs	Maintenance and repair records, training records, observation
School financial support	Budget allocation, bonus program funding evidence	Budget allocation

Technology Management Action Plan for the 2009–2010 School Year

TECHNOLOGY ACQUISITION

One Apple Mobile Learning Lab	$25,000
20 MacBook computers and Bretford Laptop Mobility Cart AppleCare Protection Plan	
Epson data projector	$850
Apple Digital Educator Program	$4,600
2-day in-service program for 16 participants	

LMC Technology Management Policies

- Teachers will check out the technology on a rotating basis.
- Teachers will check out the technology for no longer than one week at a time.
- The language arts teachers, an LMC staff worker, and the district technician will oversee technology.
- Students will need to sign a "Technology Use" form prior to accessing the technology.

LMC Management of Technology

- The new mobile computer lab and data projector will be used primarily by the high school language arts classes. The LMC staff will circulate the equipment on a daily basis for use by the language arts teachers, and the equipment will be available on a reservation basis for other classes. When not in use by the language arts department, the equipment will also be available for the LMS to use in the LMC to teach classes and to meet the Library Media Standards for Technology 4.2.
- LMC staff will train student and parent volunteers to do the following:
  — Circulate and check returning equipment
  — Take preventative measure to keep equipment in good operating order
  — Troubleshoot equipment and software problems
  — Help the school community use the equipment and software
- LMC staff will supervise and evaluate volunteer work.
- The LMS will work with the district technical support staff member assigned to service the computers as needed and will work with the local Apple distributor to conduct in-services focused on equipment care.

Middle School Library Management Plan 2009–2010

Introduction

While the middle school library media program has been built on a strong foundation, there are many areas for improvement. The collection contains an ample number of current books that reflect the school's collection and the school population's interests, but there is an ongoing need to weed and replace outdated books. Fifteen reference computers are available, but they, too, are beginning to get old and will soon need to be replaced. The amount of money that the LMC receives from the school's general fund will not be sufficient to replace these resources as they become obsolete.

Students have access to the LMC before school, during school, and for extended hours after school. Students often come to the LMC on their own to pursue their own interests or to work on school assignments. Teachers have the flexibility of sending students to the LMC in small groups or to make an appointment with the LMS to bring in the entire class. Having a full-time LMC clerk allows the LMS to focus on developing and managing programs and curriculum. While a few teachers regularly collaborate with the LMS on developing curriculum, projects, and assessments for student learning, many teachers do not, resulting in inequitable access to the library media program.

Library Advisory Team (LAT)

PRINCIPAL

The principal holds the position and power to support the library media program through budget allocations; endorsement of the program to the faculty, staff, students, and parents; and schoolwide implementation of the plan.

FORMER PARENT TEACHER STUDENT ASSOCIATION (PTSA) PRESIDENT, PARENT REPRESENTATIVE ON SITE GOVERNANCE COUNCIL

This parent is well-networked with parents and provides expertise in public relations and funding while remaining focused on student achievement.

SIXTH GRADE HUMANITIES DEPARTMENT CHAIR

The chair has been supportive of the LMS as a resource for student learning. He is a major catalyst for the implementation of a library media program for all sixth grade students.

Seventh Grade Social Studies Teacher

This teacher collaborates the most often with the LMS. She would be invaluable in developing curriculum and instruction and implementing new ideas.

Eighth Grade Science Teacher

This teacher has shown interest in collaborating with the LMS to provide more instruction in research and technology for her students but has not had a chance to put it into practice. Eighth graders are in fact the ones who use the LMC the least. Having her on the library advisory team would give her more ownership of the program, and she would be more likely to implement any plans for the eighth graders if she were on the team.

English Language Development Department Chair

The English language development program was out of compliance. This chair can help to assess how the library media program has and should support a subgroup of students often neglected by school programs.

Technology Teacher

This teacher provides expertise in technology trends, purchasing, installation, instruction, and use. He provides the LMC, computer labs, and classrooms with the hardware and software for staff and student use.

Library Media Specialist

The LMS will chair this team, helping to guide and facilitate the planning and implementation of the plan.

Action Plan

Goal

The library media program provides a wide variety of information and technology resources necessary for all students and staff to become effective users of information and ideas.

Objectives

The LMS will analyze the collection in relation to the school's needs. The LMS will develop a collection development plan.

TARGET GROUPS

Students, teachers, staff, and administrators

ASSESSMENT

The LMS's collection development plan for 2008–2009 addressed only short-term needs, mostly updating the LMC's collection of print resources without any consideration of electronic media and technology. Furthermore, the collection plan was based on an assessment of the collection that may not have been accurate; a complete inventory performed using technological resources has not been possible because of an out of date automation system and technology.

STRATEGIES

All libraries in the district are in the process of migrating to a new and more powerful integrated library management system that would allow the LMS to more readily and accurately assess the collection. After the migration process is completed in July 2009, the LMS will perform a thorough assessment, using the new automation system to identify the strengths and weaknesses of the collection. Using surveys of teachers and students, the LMS, in collaboration with the library advisory team, will prioritize the needs of the library media collection based on the demographics and goals of the school.

TIMELINE AND PEOPLE RESPONSIBLE

- April to August 2009: LMS trains for use of new integrated library management system.
- July 2009: Migration to new integrated library management system will be complete.
- August/September 2009: LMS performs analysis of current collection.
- September 2009: LMS surveys staff and students.
- October 2009: LMS presents collection analysis and results of surveys to library advisory team.
- October 2009: Library advisory team and LMS develop new collection plan.
- November 2009: Implementation of new collection development plan begins.
- May 2010: Plan is evaluated.

COMMUNICATION TOOLS

- The LMS will use newsletters and e-mails to update the school community on the status of the migration to a new integrated library management system.
- The LMS will use charts and graphs, developed using the new integrated library management system, to communicate the strengths and weaknesses of the collection.
- The library advisory team will develop a concise collection plan and a PowerPoint presentation, including the assessment, goals, priorities, and budgets, to present to other constituents, such as the school leadership team, site governance council, or PTSA.

EVALUATION

The LMS will collect statistics on the use of the LMC and its resources, using September and October of 2009 as a baseline. Statistics should include circulation of target areas of the collection and the number of teachers and students who collaborate with the LMS on research and other projects. The LAT and LMS will develop end-of-year surveys to gather information from students and teachers about the LMC collection, and these surveys will be compared to those collected at the beginning of the year. [See Table 2.4 for an example of a planning chart.]

Table 2.4
Planning Chart

Tasks	Target Groups	Person Responsible	Progress Notes	Date Completed
Goal Objectives: The library media specialist will analyze the collection in relation to the school's needs. The library media specialist will develop a collection development plan.				
LMS trains for use of new automation system	LMS	LMS	In progress	
Migration to new automation system complete	LMS	LMS	In progress	
LMS performs analysis of current collection	LMS	LMS	Scheduled for September	
LMS surveys staff and students	Staff and students	LAT and LMS	Scheduled for September 2009	
LMS presents collection analysis and results of surveys to library advisory team	LAT	LMS	Scheduled for October 2009	
Library advisory team and LMS develop new collection plan	Staff and students	LAT and LMS	Scheduled for October 2009	
Begin implementation of new collection development plan	School community	LAT and LMS	Scheduled for November 2009	
Evaluation	School community	LAT and LMS	Scheduled for May 2010	

WORKS CITED

American Association of School Librarians. 1999. *A Planning Guide for Information Power: Building Partnerships for Learning.* Chicago: American Library Association.

American Association of School Librarians. 2007. *Standards for the 21st Century Learner.* Chicago: American Library Association. Available: www.ala.org/aasl/standards/ (accessed July 2, 2009).

American Association of School Librarians and Association for Educational Communications and Technology. 1998. *Information Power: Building Partnerships for Learning.* Chicago: American Library Association.

International Society for Technology in Education. 2007. National Educational Technology Standards for Students. Eugene, OR: International Society for Technology in Education. Available: www.iste.org/Content/NavigationMenu/NETS/ForStudents/2007Standards/NETS_for_Students_2007_Standards.pdf (accessed July 2, 2009).

International Technology Education Association. 2003. *Advancing Excellence in Technological Literacy: Student Assessment, Professional Development, and Program Standards.* Reston, VA: International Technology Education Association. Available: www.iteaconnect.org/TAA/PDFs/AETL.pdf (accessed July 2, 2009).

Lemke, C., and E. Coughlin. 1998. *Technology in American Schools: Seven Dimensions of Progress, An Educator's Guide.* Santa Monica, CA: Milken Family Foundation. Available: www.mff.org/edtech (accessed July 2, 2009).

National Board for Professional Teaching Standards. 2001. *NBPTS Library Media Standards.* Arlington, VA: National Board for Professional Teaching Standards. Available: www.nbpts.org/the_standards/standards_by_cert?ID=19&x=52&y=8 (accessed June 30, 2009).

Powers, Deborah. 2008. "Accelerated Reader: Motivation and Engagement of Students and Teachers." Master's thesis, California State University, Long Beach, California.

U.S. Department of Education. 2004. *Toward a Golden Age in American Education.* Washington, DC: U.S. Department of Education. Available: www.ed.gov/about/offices/list/os/technology/plan/2004/site/theplan/NETP_Final.pdf (accessed July 2, 2009).

Chapter 3

Acquiring Technology Resources

Technology has always played a central role in libraries. Of all technologies in today's school library media centers (LMCs), the personal computer might be the most significant. As library media specialists (LMSs) acquire digitalized resources such as e-books and subscription databases for their LMCs, simultaneously student demand and need for computer access grows, a trend impacting libraries worldwide. A recent American Library Association (ALA) survey found that only 17 percent of public libraries have enough public access computers to meet demand throughout the day (Clark and Davis, 2009).

As more resources become available digitally and LMSs continue the shift from information providers to teachers of information literacy, the need for computers will continue to grow in school LMCs. Along with computers come myriad other technological devices to support the school's instructional program, such as SMART Boards, digital projectors, and MP3 players. The acquisition of library technology is central to the role of LMS and thus warrants discussion.

Chapter 2 discussed technology planning, including technology assessment and sources of funding for technology. LMSs regularly assess technology in the LMC. Inevitably, many LMSs will go though the assessment process and determine the need for more technology. Thus begins the technology acquisition process. This chapter explores the acquisition of technology resources for the LMC, with a focus on management decisions during the acquisition process. Once the LMS acquires new technology for the library media program, the LMS needs to make users aware of the newly acquired technology. Chapter 6 discusses some technologies LMSs use to communicate with users. The ultimate goal of any technology acquisition is that users will embrace the technology and begin to use it. Otherwise, technology is just another expensive dust collector. Thus, Chapter 7 discusses the circulation of technology and Chapter 4 discusses ongoing maintenance.

EXISTING SELECTION POLICIES AND PROCEDURES

As a first step in the technology acquisition process, the LMS must identify and understand any site and district acquisition and maintenance policies.

In some cases, the school or district centralizes all technology purchase procedures. The LMS makes a request for the type of equipment, and the district selects the specific item. In such cases, the district is likely to have established standards for hardware and software (e.g., speed, storage, features) and even a pre-approved list of vendors. Such districts might also "batch" purchases, such as buying a software program only when a sufficient number of copies are being requested, in order to get discounts.

In some districts, a request for proposal (RFP) needs to be developed for capital purchases such as a lab set of computers. Typically, the RPF cannot identify a specific brand or model, just the specifications. The RFP then goes out for bidding, and the vendor with the lowest bid wins the contract. In such cases, the LMS should research the intended product thoroughly in terms of required and desired features. For example, one brand of equipment may have all of the features wanted, including some features that are unique to that brand. In writing the RFP, the LMS should state the specific features, including the unique ones of that brand; in that way, the desired product is more likely to be purchased. OpenRFP (www.openrfi. com/cfm/si_pd.cfm?PID=6) is a vendor-neutral Web site that guides all types of librarians in the RFP process for procuring software.

In other districts, purchasing decisions and processes rest mainly with the LMS. The LMS is likely to have a library budget, which may have fixed or flexible line item amounts. In such cases, the LMS is likely to spend more time researching possible products and vendors in order to get the best deal. The LMS should probably develop a baseline standard for technology and get it approved by administrators in order to facilitate selection and ensure some measure of quality for library technology. While more time-consuming and perhaps more costly, this selection situation enables the LMS to have more control of the ultimate technology in the LMC.

Selection must consider not only the new product but also how it will be maintained throughout its lifetime. For example, the LMS must ascertain the level of support available at the school site to support computers and other technology acquired for the LMC. Is there a full-time technician on campus? What is the caseload of the technician? What is the average age of existing computers on campus (the older the computers, the more time the technician may have to spend supporting them)? What software solutions has the school site provided to assist the technician in managing the computers? For example, does the technician have imaging software in order to easily restore the hard drives of computers that become corrupted? Are any service guarantee times currently in place? What technologies, if any, are supported at the district level? Without good servicing, the LMS needs to either buy service agreements when purchasing technology, be prepared to maintain the products himself or herself, or assume that broken technology will need to be replaced.

Computer Selection

All of this information will help the LMS determine appropriate technology repair expectations for equipment the LMS subsequently acquires. This may impact purchasing decisions. For example, if it is important to have 20 working computers at all times, and the LMS knows that it could take weeks for repairs to be made whenever a computer is down, the LMS might consider purchasing additional computers that can serve as backups. Likewise, the LMS may consider purchasing an on-site warranty through the manufacturer or a third party to supplement the services provided by the on-site or district technician or lobbying administration for the hiring of more on-site technical support. At any rate, the LMS should conference with any on-site technician as well as site administration, determining expectations for minimum software, hardware ,and on-site warranty options. This is especially true with computers.

Policies for computer acquisition and maintenance will vary from district to district. In some school districts, schools are provided guidelines for purchasing computers; however, the school site is ultimately responsible for making appropriate expenditure decisions. In such settings, the school generally is also responsible for obtaining warranties or for otherwise developing plans to repair and eventually replace computers as they become outdated or damaged beyond economical repair. When the school site is responsible for both the selection and maintenance of computers, the LMS is free to select the computer model and vendor best suited for their LMC.

In some school districts, the individual school sites select and order the computers, but the school district is responsible for the maintenance of computers. When the school district is responsible for maintenance, often there are acquisition policies the LMS must follow related to the maintenance and servicing of computers. Take for example the Los Angeles Unified School District (LAUSD). In LAUSD, all IBM-compatible desktop computers and laptops are ordered through one vendor, who is responsible for delivery and setup of the computers, creating custom restore discs and providing next day on-site warranty service for five years. After warranty expiration, the LAUSD Instructional Technology Division (ITD) is responsible for on-site repair of computers until it is determined that the system is so old that it is not cost-effective to repair (Tortorice, 2008).

In schools where the district is responsible for repairing the computers, it is common for the district to require schools to purchase long-term warranties such as with LAUSD. This provides the school district with a guaranteed time period for which the district will not need to service the computers. In addition, as with LAUSD, it is common for computer choices to be limited to certain brands, models, and configurations. By limiting the choices, the district can efficiently order and stock replacement parts their technicians will need when they service the computers. In addition, when the district salvages a computer, it can reuse operational parts from salvaged computers since other computers in the district will use those exact parts. Salvaging is the process of removing equipment from use when it is determined that repairing is not cost-efficient.

LMSs and technicians base the decision to salvage on multiple factors, including the cost of repair parts, the time or service cost required to repair the equipment, and the expected remaining life of the equipment if repaired. In addition, the replacement value of the equipment should be determined. If the equipment is older, most likely its value will have depreciated significantly. Thus, the same equipment may be available for purchase used at a cost similar to repairing the existing equipment. If the cost to repair exceeds 50 percent of the current cost of the item, the LMS should consider purchasing a newer model. Generally, LMSs can expect a newer model to last longer and perform better. Therefore, investing monetary resources in a new piece of equipment in lieu of repairing often is the wisest use of limited funds.

Internet searches or visit to Web auction sites can help the LMS determine the current cost of the equipment. In addition to reusing and stocking replacement parts, limiting model choices makes it easier to service equipment. For instance, software issues (e.g., viruses, corrupted files, etc.) are a common source of computer problems. Often, the solution is wiping the hard drive and reinstalling the operating system and programs. This can be a time-consuming process. To speed this process, the district or the vendor can create a custom image of that model's software configuration. Investing the time to create custom images makes sense when large groups of equipment share the same hardware configuration. Chapter 4 covers computer maintenance and provides more discussion on imaging software.

Requiring schools to purchase through set vendors can help the district ensure that all computers ordered by schools meet minimum required district specifications. Minimum specifications or "specs" are standard hardware and software requirements. For example, the district may require all computers to run Mac OS X or better, or it may specify that computers must have at least 1 GB of RAM (random-access memory) and have at least 40 GB of hard drive space. When the district has set minimum specifications for new computers, schools generally can order computers with specifications above the minimum but not below. Districts set minimum specifications to ensure equipment will have an appropriate life span. As technology consultant James Oliver (1997) writes, "it is easy to purchase older equipment that may do the job today but will most certainly become obsolete rapidly." This advice was true in the 1990s, and it is equally true today.

Table 3.1 depicts student desktop minimum specifications for new purchases in three sample school districts. Schools or school districts with minimum specifications should review technology specifications yearly, if not more often, and revise as necessary, as advances in technology may justify adjustment of the minimum specifications.

In addition to minimum specifications for new computers, schools and districts often have minimum specifications for donated computers. These specifications may be lower to or equal to the specifications required for purchasing new computers. Thus, regardless of whether the computer equipment is new or donated, it is important that the LMS understands existing policies regarding minimum computer specifications.

In addition to ensuring the computers that schools order meet minimum specifications, the district may also require schools to order though a set vendor in order to negotiate special pricing. Through the pooling of orders, the school district can realize significant cost savings. In addition, the contracted vendor can work with the school district and its schools to provide desired specialized services, such as asset tagging and tracking, computer delivery and setup, custom computer software images featuring district-owned licenses, and restore discs. This ultimately simplifies management of computers.

Limiting school choice to a small selection of computer models through specific vendors provides management benefits. However, this decision can also impact the ability of the LMS to order computers best suited for the existing LMC furniture and building layout. For example, if student computer desk space is limited, the LMS may consider small form factor (SFF) desktops or all-in-one computers due to their small footprint. Or the LMS may decide that purchasing flat screen LCD monitors is most appropriate. All of these options would provide students more desk space for books and other materials. However, if these options are not available through the required district vendor, the LMS may need to consider other possibilities, such as purchasing new student computer desks with built-in holders for the computers.

Table 3.1
Minimum Specifications for New Purchases of Student Desktop Computers

SPECIFICATIONS	Lompoc USD	Mead School District	Hemet USD
Processor	Intel P4 2.0 Ghz	3.2 Intel Processor	Intel P4 3.0 Ghz
Hard drive	40 GB	80 GB	80 GB
RAM	1 GB	512 MB	1 GB
Monitor	17" LCD	17" color SVGA	17" CRT w/ built-in speakers
Ethernet Card	10/100/1000	10/100/1000	10/100
Optical Drive	CD-RW/DVD combo drive or DVD-ROM	48X speed CD-ROM	48x32 CD-RW/DVD combo drive
Windows Operating System	Windows XP, service pack 2	Windows XP Professional	Windows XP Professional
Word Processing	Microsoft Office 2003	Not specified	Microsoft Office 2003 Professional
Ports	Not specified	1 parallel, 1 serial, 2 USB 2.0	PS2 serial port adapter
Sound	Not specified	Integrated into motherboard or separate sound card	Not specified
Keyboard/mouse	Not specified	104-key keyboard and 3 button PS/2 style mouse	Keyboard and optical mouse w/scroll
Warranty	Not specified	3 year parts and labor, 48 hour maximum response	3 year limited warranty
Floppy drive	Not specified	Not specified	1.44 MB floppy drive

Other Equipment

Standards are not just for computers. Consider camcorders, which the LMC circulates to school staff, along with other LMC equipment such as televisions. To display the video directly from the camcorder to the television, the LMS must ensure the camcorder has the right cable to interface with the television. The LMS must ascertain available inputs on the television, for instance s-video, composite, or high definition multimedia interface (HDMI). While all televisions will have one or more inputs, the types of available inputs may not be compatible with the camcorder. If some televisions do not have the required interfaces and staff expect to use the devices in conjunction, this creates additional management issues as the LMS circulates equipment. For instance, the LMS may need to purchase additional cables for each type of input. If such cables are not available, the LMS may need to ascertain the staff member's planned use for the equipment, thus complicating the equipment reservation and checkout processes. In addition, if directions and terminology varies from device to device, the LMS will need to invest more time in staff training.

Another issue to consider with digital camcorders is how users will edit video. The typical high-definition (HD) camcorder records in either advanced video codec high definition (AVCHD) format or high definition video (HDV) format. One popular program for editing video is Windows Movie Maker; however, only the HD version of Windows Movie Maker, which comes with Windows Vista Home Premium or Windows Vista Ultimate, are able to import HD video. Thus, if the LMS is using Windows Vista Business, Windows Vista Home, or any version of Windows XP, Windows Movie Maker will not work for editing HD videos. In addition, users can import only HDV format videos into Windows Movie Maker. Windows Movie Maker does not currently import videos recorded in AVCHD format unless the LMS uses another program to convert the AVCHD format into one compatible with Windows.

On the Mac side, HDV camera downloads can appear jerky on slower Mac systems because the Mac has to convert the HD video into a format that facilitates editing; fast dual-process G5 Power Macs and Intel-based Macs can process downloading in real time. Thus, with older Macs, the user should view the file transfer on the camera's LCD screen and use that camera's buttons to start and stop playback.

Sometimes, one poorly planned purchase can necessitate many more unexpected purchases. Imagine Sam who purchased an AVCHD camcorder for the LMC, intending to use the camcorder to edit booktalks and other video to post onto the library Web site. After a few days of recording, Sam prepares to import the video to his computer. This is when Sam learns he is unable to edit his video in Windows Movie Maker. Sam goes to the store and picks up Pinnacle Studio Ultimate version 12 (www.pinnaclesys.com) based on recommendations from a friend. Sam installs the software; however, it is very slow to a point where it is impossible to successfully edit the video. In reading the specifications on the software box, Sam notices his system does indeed meet the minimum specs for video editing, which is an Intel Pentium or AMD Athlon 1.8 Ghz processor and 1GB of RAM, however his system does not meet the minimum specifications for editing AVCHD video using this program. To edit AVCHD, the minimum specs are an Intel Core 2 Duo 2.4 Ghz processor and 2 GB of RAM (Pinnacle Systems, accessed 2009). Sam discovers that his motherboard is not compatible with the type of processor he needs, so upgrading the processor is not an option. Sam must now decide whether to give up on his goal of editing the videos. Alternatively he may look for another software program with lower minimum specifications, purchase a new computer, or purchase a different camcorder. All require additional expenditures. The lesson is that LMSs should clearly understand standards and specifications for equipment prior to purchasing. Had Sam taken the time to properly research compatibility of products, he would have realized that a non-HD camcorder would meet his need for publishing video to the Web, and Sam would not have needed to purchase additional hardware or software.

Another consideration in the acquisition process is brand and model. For each piece of equipment the LMS may acquire for the LMC, brands and models can vary significantly. Limiting the variety of brands and models on campus for each type of equipment simplifies management on multiple fronts. To start, each equipment brand is often similar in terms of user interface. For example, the on-screen menu of one model of a Panasonic videocassette recorder is likely to resemble a second Panasonic model more than a Toshiba brand videocassette recorder. If multiple staff members throughout the school use the equipment, the LMS may want to consider the same brand when acquiring additional equipment or replacing existing equipment. This can help those who use the equipment, especially users who struggle with new technology. This situation highlights another reason for the LMS to collaborate with the rest of the site staff: to coordinate technology purchases.

When deciding on equipment, LMSs also need to consider the accompanying consumable items. For example, a laser printer uses toner, and an overhead projector uses bulbs. In most cases, the consumable is specific to one model or at most a few models. In limiting the variety of equipment models on campus, the LMS can simplify the process or ordering and stocking necessary consumables. The cost of those consumables can also impact purchasing decisions. For instance, an ink-jet printer may be very inexpensive, but each ink cartridge might cost $20 and need to be replaced within a day (or even an hour for heavy print assignments). Even though a laser printer and its toner cost more, in the long run, they are more cost-effective and tend to be more robust operationally.

Staff training is another concern. Most LMSs create directions and provide training and assistance with using equipment. Alternatively, the LMS may train students or other LMC staff to provide support. Again, in limiting the number of models on campus, the LMS will spend less time creating documentation and training support staff. The LMS might also consider buying a piece of equipment that has fewer functions or is easier to use in order to decrease training demands. Usually, a basic model does the job, although the LMS needs to know what the potential use of the equipment will be in order to acquire one that supports the desired task.

Software

LMSs acquire several kinds of software for the LMC. Again, standardization is important. There can be large differences in software versions, such as with the interfaces of Office 2007 and Office 2003. Additionally, software programs may require system specifications that are beyond the library's current hardware's capacity; if the LMS does not read all of the details for a software packet, he or she may buy the program only to have to return the software or update the equipment. Often, only the most recent version of the software is available for purchase. Luckily, most software companies allow users to purchase the current software and then downgrade to an older version. Additionally, if the LMS has an existing version of a software program and registered it, an upgrade or update purchase may carry a large discount.

LMSs should avoid situations in which software varies from one computer to the next. Consider the situation in which the LMC has 20 computers but not every computer has the same software. In this scenario, the library has acquired Adobe Master Collection CS4, which is loaded on three computers. When Susan comes to the library to finish working on her newsletter using Adobe InDesign (one program in the suite), she finds that many computers in the library are available but not those containing the program she needs. Thus, she must either wait for one of the three computers to be available or politely ask a current user to move to another computer. Either solution wastes time and can create issues, especially if the student needing the computer needs support with her or his interpersonal communication skills. The moral of the story is that the LMS should strongly consider maintaining a standard suite of software on all LMC computers.

Prior to purchasing software, the LMS must determine if the district has established software standards or provides any district-wide software licenses. A license is an agreement providing the user the right to install and use specific software. Licenses can be for one computer or for a set number of computers. In addition, licenses can be for all computers at one physical building or all computers belonging to one institution, such as a school district. Manufacturers may also sell licenses based on the number of users that will use the software instead of the number of computers the LMS installs the software on. If the school district provides a free site license for antivirus software, then obviously ordering antivirus software when purchasing new computers would be a complete waste of funding. As a general practice, LMSs should check what existing site- and district-provided resources such as software licenses exist before making any software purchases.

In addition to district-provided licenses, schools can benefit from educational pricing. Many software companies offer academic or educational pricing to K–12 schools. Sometimes these licenses are available directly from the software manufacturer, and in other cases they come through computer software vendors. When acquiring software, the LMS should contact companies to determine what discounts are available to the school. In addition to published discounts for schools, the pooling of purchasing power can also lead to significant cost savings, similarly to the pooling of purchasing power when ordering equipment. Purchasing consortiums, cooperative purchasing agreements, and piggyback bids are all mechanisms that schools and districts may use to reduce overall acquisition costs. For example, the New York State Association of Independent Schools (NYSAIS) is a purchasing consortium consisting of over 175 member schools. The consortium utilizes the combined power of the member schools to negotiate cost savings on purchases. The idea is that through increased order volume and centralized negotiating and bidding, consortium members realize cost savings that would be unachievable by individual schools alone. In addition, if problems occur, those schools can call on one another for help.

Databases

Subscription databases constitute a growing digital resource that LMSs acquire for the library. Subscription databases are referred to by many different names, including research databases, electronic databases, and online databases. Subscription databases are collections of resources, usually organized around a particular theme. Themes can be content-based, such as a science database, or resource-based, such as a periodical database. In terms of management, LMSs like these digital resources because they have been preselected and indexed for easy and appropriate use, they save space, they are easy to keep current, and they are less likely to be damaged or stolen.

For the LMC user, there are many reasons to use electronic databases. To start, electronic databases provide time savings by allowing users to search more than one source at the same time. For example, when using the Biography Resource Center by Gale Cengage, users can search over 100 different reference sources simultaneously. Electronic databases provide users more ways to access the materials. With reference books, users find information using the index and table of contents; with electronic databases,

SELECTING ELECTRONIC DATABASES

Many electronic databases have similar features. Content, cost, and ease of use thus become major factors in choosing the most appropriate one so that patrons can access and use the database independently to accomplish their information tasks. Content factors include alignment to and support of the curriculum, accuracy and authority of the information, appropriate reading level, and appropriate format (e.g., text, images, sound, video). In addition, the database should comply with ADA (Americans with Disabilities Act) requirements; a few have not met that standard.

Here are guiding questions to use when assessing a potential database. Not only should LMSs test databases in a trial basis but they should have their users try them out as well and provide feedback about the products. Not only does the LMS get valuable information, but users feel they have a say in the purchase and may be more apt to use the product once it has been acquired.

- **Main page**: What features appear on the main page? Is the layout clear and easy to use? Is the text readable, and do visual options exist to accommodate special needs?
- **Help menu**: There should be a link to a help menu. Some help is general, while other is page or function specific.
- **Information/About section for the database**: This may appear in the help or separate section. Use it to find out about features of the database, sources included, and/or potential uses for the database.
- **Navigation**: What navigation tools exist? Are they easy to access and use independently?
- **Keyword search**: Almost every database has a basic keyword search.
- **Advanced search**: Almost every database has an advanced search option that enables the user to narrow a search. Look for drop-down menus, special access point choices, and search tips (e.g., use of truncation and wild cards).
- **Search results**: Usually databases present search results as citations. Some organize results by date, others by topic, category, or type of resource. If results are subdivided, you may need to click on a button to access more results.
- **Printing**: Usually there is a "print-friendly" option to select. Once in a while, the database prints only one page at a time, which can save paper but can also frustrate users.
- **File transfer**: Many databases allow the user to download the document or e-mail it to a specified e-mail address. If users have

limited time to find articles, this can be useful. The LMS needs to decide where the file can be downloaded to: a portable drive, onto the desktop, or to a designated directory for easy removal once the user is logged off.

- **Citation help**: Most databases provide users with help in citing their resources, and users typically can choose from the major citation styles. Sometimes, the citation is at the end of the article. Other times, users must locate and click on a special button.
- **Administrative features**: Many databases can be customized in terms of appearance or default search strategy that can provide accommodations for local learner needs. Some databases include statistical and report functions, which help the LMS analyze database usage.

users typically perform keyword searches in addition to other search options each database may provide. Finally, subscription databases provide portability, allowing users to print or copy and paste information into a word processing program. Most electronic databases also allow users to e-mail articles, which makes it easy for users to research and complete assignments without lugging around heavy books.

LMSs also need to consider technical requirements of subscription databases. What are the system requirements: platform, operating system, amount of RAM, bandwidth, video and sound cards? Can the database be networked locally or remotely? What authentication procedures are available or needed? Most sites select only Web-based products at this point.

In Maryland, all 24 school districts belong to a statewide consortium established in 2002 for online subscription database acquisitions. When the school districts initially formed the consortium, a steering committee evaluated and selected subscription databases based on pre-identified criteria. One important criterion was whether or not the subscription database aligned to Maryland's state content standards. Through pooling of purchasing power, the consortium has saved significant costs for the 24 member school districts. For example, prior to the consortium, Baltimore County Public School District used district funds to provide a subscription database for elementary students. Through the consortium, allocating roughly the same amount of money used to subscribe to that one subscription database for elementary students, the district was able to purchase almost 20 databases for use by all students in grades preK–12 (Bailey and Moore, 2008).

Another digital resource LMSs can offer are e-books. An e-book is an electronic book. As with subscription databases, through the use of e-books LMSs can move beyond limitations in physical library shelving. Each year, e-books gain in popularity. The International Digital Publishing Forum (IDPF) has collected data on e-book sales in the United States since 2002. Their data represents only United States revenues, does not include all publishers, and does not include library, professional, or educational sales. Thus, while the data does not represent the entire e-book market, it does provide a snapshot in terms of trends. In the first quarter of 2002, e-book revenues were roughly $1.55 million. In the fourth quarter of 2008 (the most recent data available from IDPF), e-book revenues had grown to $16.8 million. Overall, their data shows a clear growth in e-book sales that continue to accelerate (International Digital Publishing Forum, accessed 2009).

OWN VERSUS ACCESS/LEASE

Some school districts and individual schools choose to lease technology rather than purchase. Leasing computers is like leasing a house or car. Schools sign a contract and pay a smaller sum each month, quarter, or year in order to acquire needed technology, such as laptops, computers, or even copy machines. Over the course of the agreement, the school may end up paying 25 percent or more than if the school had purchased the item upfront. However, as part of the lease agreement, the school often will receive additional services, including technical support and repair of equipment, setup/installation of equipment, and even staff training. The LMS should consider these extra benefits when weighing the pros and cons of leasing versus owning. Schools benefit from leasing by receiving needed equipment immediately, without taking a large hit on school finances in one fiscal year. Leasing provides schools and districts with a manageable contracted expense that it planned and budgeted. When the lease ends, schools are able to sign a new lease contact. This practice provides schools with a methodical method to ensure older equipment is regularly refreshed with newer technology (Nadel, accessed 2009).

One drawback, in addition to the extra overall cost, is that leasing creates the need for ongoing perpetual expenses. It may also force schools to upgrade to new equipment when the old equipment is still sufficient to meet existing demands. This is because when the lease expires, the school or district returns the equipment to the vendor. The vendor may then refurbish and resell the equipment or scrap the equipment but sell components within the equipment. For instance, the hard drive and the computer's RAM will have resale value. eBay (www.ebay.com) is one Web site where some vendor's resell end-of-lease equipment to consumers. Most leases will have purchase options at the end of the lease, based on the depreciated value of the equipment as stated in the contract, known as the residual value. A school can choose to retain the equipment by paying the residual value of the equipment at the end of the lease.

Leasing agreements for databases, in particular, can be very complex; typical elements include scope, completeness of content, access, confidentiality, sharing, archiving, disability compliance, duration, warranties, and indemnities (Farb and Riggio, 2004). With electronic databases, institutions typically purchase a license to access the resource for a set period of time. (When budgets are flush, subscribing for two to three years can be a significant cost-saving practice.) Schools can purchase subscriptions; however, often district or state funding provides the subscriptions. One challenge with databases is the ongoing cost each database represents. Books are purchased and then available until lost, damaged, or weeded from the collection. Subscription databases, on the other hand, may be available one year and then unavailable the next year if sufficient funding to continue the subscription is not present. The LMC is left with nothing since databases can seldom be downloaded or archived locally. Increasingly, large systems are opting for leasing with an option to buy in order to get backfile ownership.

Schools have the option to lease directly from many manufacturers or through a firm that specializes in such transactions. When leasing equipment, it is important to keep track of all parts, as the school can be charged extra if parts, such as cables, peripherals, cases, software, manuals, and documentation, are missing at the end of the lease. A lease is a contract, so LMSs should understand

and be aware of all parts of the contract. For instance, the LMS can expect normal wear and tear will occur to any equipment leased by the school. The contract should have clear definitions to avoid misunderstandings and unexpected charges at the end of the lease. Increasingly, libraries are considering lease-to-own options in databases as a backup plan when subscription money disappears.

One often overlooked technology access is e-rate. The Telecommunications Act of 1996 promoted universal telecommunications service, including provisions for libraries and schools to get access to these services at discounted rates (e-rate). Depending on the need, such as socioeconomics, libraries and school can get between 20 and 90 percent discounts. Section 706 of the act further asserts that such systems should be accessible to all. However, two steps are needed to get such discounts: the legal entity must the eligible, and a form needs to be completed and filed. LMSs should find out if the school has submitted the required paperwork. The Federal Communications Commission Web site links to several online resources that can help LMSs navigate the regulations to obtain the discounted e-rate. E-Rate Central (www.e-ratecentral.com) is a commercial Web site that provides e-rate services and posts current information.

STARTING OUT RIGHT

To effectively manage LMC equipment, the LMS must know what equipment falls under the library media program, regardless of whether such equipment is physically located or stored in the LMC. Effective record keeping begins during the acquisition process. The first step in effective management is to ask what needs managing. Employees, resources, time, and equipment are all examples of resources requiring management.

For library technology, at the most basic level an LMS new to a school site needs to survey library media program equipment. For instance, the LMS might report that she has 40 desktop computers, two printers, and one scanner. While helpful in understanding the types of technology available in the LMC, such basic information does little to help the LMS effectively manage this equipment.

On a more detailed level, the LMS needs to know the brand, model number, serial number, acquisition date and age of equipment (if purchased secondhand), warranty information (if applicable)—

including a warranty contact and expiration date, storage location of equipment, and responsible staff member. For computers and other equipment, the LMS must know the technical specifications or "specs" of the equipment. For a computer, this will include items such as the speed of the processor and size of the hard drive. Without this information, the LMS will not be able to determine if contemplated equipment and software acquisitions will be compatible.

Without a comprehensive inventory of equipment, the LMS will be unable to make effective management decisions. Take, for instance, a library media program with computers that are five years old. When originally acquired, the school purchased a five-year warranty that is now is set to expire. The LMS has noticed some issues with the computers. One student recently reported the DVD drive on computer 12 will not read discs. Another student recently mentioned the USB port on computer 18 is not functioning properly. Since these issues do not impact the day-to-day use of computers and students are able to use other lab computers, the issue does not seem pressing. These are all issues the LMS could address by utilizing the warranty. However, due to time constraints, the LMS puts off contacting the company for warranty repair.

In this same scenario, imagine additional issues exist that the LMS has not discovered. For instance, a number of DVD drives have stopped reading discs. Four months later, the LMS notices these additional issues and decides to contact the manufacturer for warranty repair. Upon doing so, the LMS learns the warranty is expired. Now imagine instead that the LMS maintains a comprehensive inventory of equipment including warranty expiration dates. The LMS sees the upcoming warranty expiration and is able to set aside time to complete a test of each computer with an expiring warranty. The LMS documents issues and reports them to the manufacturer before warranty expiration. At the same time, the LMS is already working on plans to deal with warranty loss. This may include budgeting money for expected labor and equipment repair costs in next year's budget or a plan to purchase either replacement equipment or a repair contract with a local company.

Marking/Engraving/Labeling

When the LMS receives new LMC equipment, the LMS should permanently mark the equipment with information identifying the property owner (the school or district) by either engraving or marking the equipment with a permanent marker. Clearly identifying the equipment makes it difficult for a thief to resell. This decreases the motivation to steal LMC equipment and thus deters theft. If equipment is accidently lost and subsequently found by an individual outside of the school or district, marking the equipment will increase the likelihood for return. Before marking equipment, the LMS should take the time to test the equipment. This is to ensure the equipment is functioning as expected. If not, often the LMS can return the faulty equipment to the vendor for immediate replacement. However, once engraved or otherwise marked, most vendors will not accept for return items not in their original condition. This forces the LMS to work directly with the equipment manufacturer for warranty repair of the item. While testing, take a moment to play with the new technology and get to know its features.

LMSs should consult district policies for labeling equipment prior to beginning. Depending on the cost or funding source, the school district may have specific policies for how the equipment must be marked. When writing with a marker, it may be difficult to read a black marker on a dark surface, such as a black rolling television cart. For these situations, LMSs Pat Franklin and Claire Gatrell Stephens (2006) recommend that LMSs have a white or silver marker in addition to a black marker. Other suggestions include having a consistent way of marking each type of equipment. This includes avoiding areas users will regularly handle, as this will help prevent the mark from rubbing off. For items containing multiple parts, they recommend that LMSs ensure their labeling also identifies the items as a set. In case components are accidently separated or mixed, this will help LMSs correctly combine the correct parts together with one another.

For multiple copies of the same item, LMSs should also consider adding a sequential number. The sequential numbering of computers and other LMC technology can be especially useful in lab settings. For example, the LMS reports to the on-site technician that one of the LMC computers has a malfunctioning USB port. The

LMS has not sequentially numbered the computers so she instead provides a serial number. Later, the technician arrives to fix the computer but the LMS is not available. The technician searches for the computer with the correct serial number, which takes significant time. Hopefully, the technician identifies the correct computer, as serial numbers can be extremely similar and it would be easy for the technician to make a mistake. On the other hand, if the LMS had sequentially labeled each computer, the technician would have quickly found the correct computer.

In terms of how to identify the computer, the LMS can engrave on, tape on, or otherwise affix the assigned sequential number to the equipment. One solution is to use a label printer in conjunction with label tape to quickly make professional looking labels. Label printers are available as handheld devices or as printers that connect directly to a computer. The latter is useful for library media programs that need to label devices frequently, as it creates the labels faster.

Consider a library collection of 40 Webcams. Each Webcam has a unique serial number in tiny letters. The LMS has recorded the serial number of each Webcam into the database. One day the LMS discovers only 39 Webcams remain; one is missing. The LMS must now determine the serial number of the missing Webcam for the police report. Scouring through tiny serial numbers on the Webcams and comparing to the database to determine the missing serial number will not be a fun or easy task. Among the 39 remaining Webcams, only minor differences, such as one letter or number, might differentiate one serial number from the next. However, what if the LMS had assigned a sequential number to each Webcam (e.g., 01–40); marked, engraved on, or affixed the number to the Webcam; and included this number in the equipment database along with the corresponding serial number?

With such organization, the LMS could quickly line the Webcams up in order to determine the missing number. Using the database, the LMS could then determine the serial number that matches the missing Webcam number. With sequential numbering, if computer 12 needs servicing, the LMS can use the database to look up the serial number of computer 12 instead of accessing the computer directly to locate the serial number. This can be especially useful when library media program equipment is located throughout the school.

To facilitate the checkout process, some LMSs choose to bar-code each piece of equipment and add it to the LMC circulation system. Barcoding is usually a supplement to, but not a replacement to, marking or engraving devices. This is because the LMS affixes bar codes to equipment and thus users can easily remove a bar code, unlike engraving or a permanent marker. When possible, consider placing a second bar code out of user sight, for instance on the bottom or underside of an audiovisual cart. This can serve as a backup, in case a user removes the first bar code or it otherwise falls off the device. If the LMS wants to bar-code all equipment in his or her LMC, the LMS must consider how to deal with equipment that is too small to bar-code. A common strategy is to place such equipment in a ziplock bag, bin, or similar storage container. This allows the LMS to then bar-code the bag or storage container.

One drawback to barcoding is the initial time and materials cost in cataloging every piece of LMC technology. However, doing so allows the LMS to collect usage statistics through the circulation program. In addition, the LMS can track who used the equipment in case of vandalism. On the other hand, even if the LMS knows the previous user of the equipment it will be nearly impossible to actually prove that user vandalized the equipment and thus hold the user accountable unless there is a procedure in place for LMC staff to inspect equipment with the patron at checkout and check-in (similar to how car rental companies inspect rentals both before and after each rental).

Documentation and Registration

When the LMC receives new equipment, it often comes with documentation in the form of paperwork and manuals. In addition, manufacturers often provide CDs or DVDs containing drivers and further documentation. A management plan regarding how and where this information will be stored needs to be in place. The LMS should store this information so it is readily available and accessible whenever needed.

The LMS must know what software initially came with the equipment, what additional software (if any) was purchased for use on the equipment, how many licenses for that software the school owns, and on what equipment these software licenses are utilized.

If the LMS does not track this information, software licenses may go unutilized. Even worse, the LMS may inadvertently violate copyright law if the LMS installs the software on more computers than the license allows.

To store software, LMSs should consider using a large three-ring binder and CD/DVD binder sheets, such as 4 × 4 CD/DVD binder sheets from Fellowes. Each sheet allows for the storage of eight DVD or CDs (four CD/DVDs on each side of the sheet). As the LMC's collection of DVDs and CDs grow, it makes sense to further organize them to facilitate quick access. Use alphabetical index binder tabs to sort the CDs or DVDs by vendor.

Bulky manuals can be stored by filing alphabetically by vendor in hanging file folders or in a three-ring binder using plastic literature sleeves. Often, the same documentation is available online. If the documentation is available online, the LMS may want to consider downloading the documentation and storing it electronically. Purchase orders or receipts are another important piece of documentation. Many technology items purchased for the LMC may come with significant warranty periods. Often, the warranty requires proof of purchase in the form of a dated store receipt. This is problematic, as over time receipts can fade. Thus, LMSs may want to consider scanning receipts for digital storage.

Many times LMSs purchase multiple pieces of the same equipment simultaneously, for instance 40 new computers for the LMC lab. In such cases, the LMS may receive multiple copies of the software and documentation. Forty copies of the quick installation guide can be redundant. In such cases the LMS can discard extra copies, retaining one copy for later use. If the LMS distributes equipment to staff members for use outside the LMC, the LMS can file one copy of the documentation and provide the remaining copies to staff members receiving the equipment for their reference.

Most users will not need the typical manuals that come with equipment, and some may find it inaccessible. Many LMSs instead create simplified directions for each piece of circulating equipment. Often, this includes information on using the equipment specific to that school site. These simplified directions can direct the user to the location of the manual if needed, whether it is stored online, as a scanned file on the school's server, or kept in the library for reference.

When the LMS determines that users will not need extra copies of documentation, discarding this extra documentation can simplify the organization and storage of equipment documentation, which in turn facilitates document management. That being said, it is important to carefully inspect documentation before discarding it. Discard documentation only if truly it is duplicative. If the document contains a unique serial number or proof of purchase, the LMS must retain it.

The same is true with software. The LMC does not need to retain multiple copies of the same installation CD. Just like documentation, it is often available online. Thus, the online copy serves as a backup should some calamity befall the original disc, damaging or destroying it. If the LMS is concerned about the need for backup discs, keeping a second copy of software, either with the first copy or with the documentation can provide additional peace of mind. Before discarding the installation CD for software, the LMS must ensure there is proof that the LMC lawfully obtained the software installed on the computers. The LMS can print out one copy of the standard software configuration for the brand and model number of the equipment if that information is not already included in the documentation or on the invoice. This is typically available on the vendor's Web site.

As LMSs receive new equipment they should register the equipment with the manufacturer. In today's world, most manufacturers offer convenient online methods to register new products. If there is a product recall, such as when manufacturers recalled the batteries in many laptops due to fire danger, being registered is useful, because the manufacturer will be able to contact the LMS regarding the recall. In addition, when the manufacturer releases a new update such as a new software driver for the device, registering provides the manufacturer with a way to contact the LMS. Many vendors require users to register before receiving technical support. Finally, the act of registering can document with the manufacturer the date the LMC first acquired the equipment. As Eric Griffith in *PC Magazine* states, registering is beneficial, as "you stand a better chance of being recognized when the time does come to call for help—and you know that time will come" (Griffith, 2009).

Inventory

Recording serial numbers and equipment information at time of acquisition is extremely important. Small nuances between characters (is that an 8 or a 3 or a B?) become difficult to determine as stickers containing the serial number become worn over time. When the LMS calls in a computer for warranty repair, he or she will need the serial and model number of the computer. In lab settings, identifying which serial number belongs to which computer can be a daunting task. Reporting the wrong serial number for repair can lead to delays and complications.

Recording serial numbers at the time of acquisition provides other benefits. For example, the model number and serial number are often located on the back of a computer, making it difficult to access after installing the computer. Recording the model and serial number when the equipment arrives prevents the need to add contortionist to the list of LMS job skills. LMSs should carefully record serial numbers as it is easy to make a mistake, especially with long serial numbers with only minor differences, such as one letter or number. Serial numbers can be case-sensitive, further complicating matters. As mentioned earlier, the serial number is also required when filing police reports of stolen equipment. If a fire or other calamity destroys equipment, quick access to models and serial numbers of the destroyed equipment facilitates the filing of an insurance claim.

A database program such as Microsoft Access is the best place to store inventory data. A well designed database contains multiple tables to minimize data input. Consider the LMS who orders 40 new desktop computers. All computers have the same model number and brand. In addition, they share the same purchase date, warranty expiration date, warranty contact, vendor contact, and invoice number. When using tables in a database, the LMS can input much of this information once instead of forty times. Thus, using a database saves time.

Another option is to maintain equipment inventory information in a spreadsheet such as Microsoft Excel or to utilize a table, such as with Microsoft Word. While the LMS can copy and paste repetitive information, it must be physically entered into the spreadsheet or table multiple times (once for each computer). In addition, the end product will not be as easy to navigate as a database containing forms for easy data entry. In addition, it will not be as visually appealing as a report generated from a database.

Earlier in this chapter, we provided an example of an LMS who tracked warranty expiration dates and used this information to address problems before warranties expired. Continuing this example, the LMS needs to know which computers have warranties set to expire in the upcoming year in order to inform administration of the need to either purchase new computers or an extended warranty. This is not a one-time activity, it is an annual need. Each year, the LMS will need to provide this information to administration. For instance, administration needs the basic facts: how many computers in total have warranties that will expire, what are the expiration dates, and where on campus the computers are located. Furthermore, the LMS does not want to provide administration with extraneous data. The LMS knows the administration is busy and with a cursory glance might misinterpret the data if not clear and concise. Thus, it is important that the LMS provides only the relevant data to administration, with a more detailed attachment should administration desire additional data.

If using a spreadsheet or table, the LMS must manipulate the data in order to exclude unwanted information. In order to do this, the LMS must first sort the data by warranty expiration date. Next, the LMS copies the relevant data (computers with warranties expiring in the next year) to a new spreadsheet or table. The LMS then needs to remove or hide extraneous fields (such as the acquisition vendor) or rows (such as printers if the LMS is providing information on expiring computer warranties). The LMS must then format the data in a manner that is comprehensible to the administrator. To answer additional questions, such as the location of all graphics tablets, the LMS will again need to sort the data; this time by graphics tablets, then by room number, and then repeat the steps. If this sounds complicated, the point has been made. Using a database, the LMS can create reports once and save them for future use, again saving valuable time.

TECH MOMENT: CREATING AN ORGANIZED EQUIPMENT DATABASE

The Microsoft Help and Support site (support.microsoft.com) provides free step-by-step tutorials on using Microsoft Access. When creating an equipment database for the library media center, the following are good tables to include:

Purchase Info Table

This table contains the basic ordering information for each asset acquired. Create a new record in this table for each different asset type. For instance, enter 20 laptops with the same brand and model number as one entry. However, laptops with different information should be entered as separate records. This table should contain the vendor name, vendor contact information, purchasing information such as the invoice number, purchase date, warranty expiration, and warranty contact information. This table should also include the brand and model number of the equipment. Finally, each asset should be classified into a predetermined group (e.g., printer, desktop, laptop, and calculator). Classifying purchased equipment into asset groups will allow the LMS to run queries to quickly answer questions, such as the serial number and warranty expiration date of all desktop computers in the library media center.

Whereas the previously discussed information (vendor name, vendor contact info, invoice number, purchase date, warranty expiration, warranty contact info, brand, model number, and asset type) represents columns or fields in a database, a record is one row in a database. Each record must have one field that is unique, called the primary key. This table should utilize an auto number (a number automatically generated by the database program) as the primary key so that each record is unique.

Room Assignment Table

If the equipment is stored in multiple rooms and primary responsibility falls to different staff members, the LMS should create a room assignments table. This table should contain a list of every room on campus and the responsible staff member. When room assignments or staff members change (as inevitably will happen), the LMS can easily make the changes on the room assignments table. Without this table, the LMS must modify each record individually. This table does not require an auto number as the room number serves as the primary key.

Equipment Table

This table should contain the serial number and cost of each item ordered. In addition, it should include the auto number from the purchase info table as well as the room number from the room assignments table. This effectively connects the data in all three tables. The LMS can add additional fields to this table as needed or desired; for example, a field for IP addresses or a notes field. The table should also note maintenance performed.

Using these tables will help the LMS create an effective database for tracking library media center equipment. Depending on the school site, additional information may need to be included. For instance, many schools and districts require schools to tag equipment with a unique asset tag. If this is the case, the asset number should also be included in the item table.

STAYING CURRENT

In June 1989, individuals could purchase a 20-megabyte (MB) hard drive for $899, a cost of $53 dollars per MB of storage. Ten years later (June 1999) individuals could purchase a 10.2 gigabyte (GB) hard drive for $299. One GB is equal to 1,000 MBs. Thus, in ten years the cost per MB of storage dropped from $53 to $.0321 (Smith, 2008). Today individuals can purchase 1 terabyte hard drives (which is 1,000 GB) for under $100 and 500GB hard drives for around $50. This represents a cost of $.0001 per MB of storage. Thus, in 20 years, from 1989 to 2009, the price per MB of hard drive storage capacity dropped from $53 per MB to $.0001 per MB.

The previous example demonstrates two points. First, computer technology rapidly evolves. Over time manufacturers have developed higher-capacity hard drives that were previously unavailable to consumers. Whereas a 1GB hard drive was once a luxury item, by today's standard a computer with a 1 GB hard drive has insufficient storage capacity. LMSs should learn from this history, understanding that today's "high-end" technology may well be average or even mediocre five years later. As computer technology and performance increases, software developers design more complicated software programs to take advantage of the new technology. Over time, older computers may lack the proper specifications to meet the demands of new software programs. Generally, more advanced computers (by today's standards) will last longer in terms of being able to meet the demands of future users.

Second, as a new technology becomes mass-produced and manufacturers become more efficient in production prices generally will decrease. Thus, LMSs should understand that today's technology will inevitably be cheaper in the future and that rapid price depreciation will occur. This is especially true with the latest and most advanced equipment. In the world of computing, generally the newer the technology is, the higher premium the purchaser must pay to obtain the best and latest technology. Thus, it is sometimes most cost-efficient to purchase a system that is good but not the best, even though the system may not last as long. To save on overall cost, the LMS can delay purchases of certain components, such as an advanced graphics card or a larger flat-screen monitor if users do not truly need that component. Later on, the LMS can upgrade the computer if needed. By postponing the purchase, often the LMS can achieve significant cost savings. In the previous example, if a new graphics card technology emerges, expect prices on the older graphics card model to decrease sharply. Ultimately, LMSs facing budget limitations must balance performance with price considerations.

Standards and Specifications

Keeping abreast of the latest and best computer specifications can be a daunting task. Many LMSs who are techies find joy in staying abreast of the latest news and trends. Wikipedia defines a techie as "a person who displays a great, sometimes even obsessive, interest in technology, high-tech devices, and particularly computers" (Wikipedia, 2009). Rather than trying to constantly stay abreast of the latest changes to computer specifications, an alternative to the "techie" strategy is to acquire a base knowledge of computer components. Then, whenever a new acquisition is necessary, the LMS can update his or her knowledge through product reviews and magazine and Web site articles. Magazines such as *Macworld* or *PC Magazine* can provide LMSs with reviews and technology news, as can Web sites such as Engadget (www.engadget.com) or CNET (www.cnet.com). The Resources list at the back of the book provides additional Web sites. In terms of base computer knowledge, anyone involved in computer acquisitions should be aware of the following parts of a computer.

Central Processing Unit (CPU)

The CPU might be considered the brain of the computer, as the CPU is responsible for the processing of data. Processor is another name for the CPU. More powerful CPUs can process data quicker. The two top CPU manufacturers are Intel and AMD, and each manufacturer offers a range of CPUs both in terms of price and performance. For instance, Intel currently markets for desktops the following processor families: Intel Core i7 Extreme Edition, Intel Core i7, Intel Core 2 Extreme, Intel Core 2 Quad, Intel Core 2 Duo, Intel Pentium, and Intel Celeron (Intel, 2009).

Before purchasing a new computer, LMSs should become aware of current CPU technology. Company Web sites can be a good source for initial understanding. Of course, companies will highlight the best features of their product, so LMSs should also conduct additional product research. Many Web sites offer product reviews. Often, these reviews include head-to-head tests and benchmarks. Benchmarks let users see how the different CPUs perform in real-life tasks. This can help the LMS determine if the additional performance gained by the more advanced processor is worth the additional cost.

Motherboard

The motherboard is the backbone of a computer. Some relate the motherboard to the central nervous system in humans. Motherboards contain slots, sockets, and ports to connect all of the computer's components together. Thus, the motherboard plays a large part in the quality, features, and upgradeability of a computer system. For instance, the CPU socket type on the motherboard determines the type of CPU the computer can have. Many motherboards come with integrated components such as sound or graphics cards. Motherboards will also have ports to connect additional devices. The number of ports will determine how many additional components a user can install in the computer.

Different types of ports exist off of the motherboard, including peripheral component interconnect (PCI), peripheral component interconnect express (PCI-e) and advanced graphics ports (AGPs).

Knowing the types of available ports on a motherboard is important, as different ports will transfer data at different bandwidths. For instance, the maximum bandwidth of a component connected to a PCI port is 132 megabytes per second (mbps). A component connected to an AGP 8X port can transfer at 2,100 mbps, and a component connected to a PCIe 16X port can transfer at a maximum bandwidth of 8,000 mbps (Penrod, 2008). Not only is it important to know the types of available ports, it is important to understand that manufacturers design components for a particular port type. For instance, users cannot install a PCIe graphics card into a PCI port. To meet the needs of end users, manufacturers may make several versions of the same component, with similar specifications expect for the port type. If presented a choice when selecting a component, choose the component that contains a port type compatible with your motherboard and that allows for the greatest bandwidth.

A motherboard will also have slots for RAM. A motherboard with four RAM slots will provide more upgrade flexibility than a motherboard with only two RAM slots. The motherboard specifications will indicate the type of RAM the LMS can install and the maximum capacity of installed RAM. In addition to slots for RAM, motherboards have a number of connectors. Some connectors will be for external devices, such as PS2 connectors for connecting a keyboard or mouse. There will also be USB 2.0 connectors, also for a mouse, keyboard, or other peripheral device such as a Webcam or USB flash drive. Finally, the motherboard has connectors for internal drives, such as hard drives and optical drives including DVD drives.

Random-Access Memory (RAM)

In simple terms, RAM is short-term memory. RAM is temporary data and thus disappears when an individual shuts down or restarts the computer. When a user runs a program such as Internet Explorer, the computer transfer data the CPU needs to run the program into RAM. The more RAM a computer has, the more tasks the computer can handle simultaneously. If the computer runs out of available RAM, the computer must store data in a paging file on the hard drive. This is problematic because to access data, the hard drive must spin, and the CPU can access data only in a certain order as the hard drive spins. However, the CPU can access data stored in RAM in any order (hence the term random-access memory). In addition, without sufficient RAM, the CPU may need to return data it is not currently processing in order to free up RAM for other data the CPU needs to process. This swapping of data can slow a computer down.

Keeping up on RAM technology can be difficult, as there are number of different types of RAM chips, including dynamic RAM (DRAM), synchronous DRAM (SDRAM), double-data rate SDRAM (DDR-SDRAM), and an improvement over DDR-SDRAM that provides double the speed (DDR2-SDRAM) RAM (Kioskea. net, 2008). Recently, even faster DDR3-SDRAM has become commercially available. RAM memory types are not compatible. For instance, a computer that uses DDR-SDRAM memory can not accept DDR2-SDRAM memory. In addition to the type of RAM, the LMS must also be aware of two additional items related to RAM: speed and capacity. In regard to capacity, RAM comes in different capacities or sizes (e.g., 512MB, 1GB, 2GB).

Hard Drive

The hard drive is the computer's long-term memory. Computer programs and data are stored on the hard drive for later retrieval. The larger the hard drive the greater the storage capacity. The faster the hard drive spins, the quicker the computer can write data to the hard drive or read from the hard drive. An emerging trend is solid state hard drives, which unlike current magnetic hard drives have no moving parts and thus transfer data faster than a spinning hard drive. In addition, no moving parts make them less susceptible to damage if the computer is accidently dropped while the drive is running, an issue especially with laptop hard drives. Currently solid state hard drives are cost prohibitive to the typical user. However, as prices decline the popularity and availability of solid state hard drives should increase.

Peripherals

This broad category comprises devices connected to the computer that are external to the central processing unit/motherboard. It is possible to have a peripheral device inside the case, for instance a video card attached to one of the ports on the motherboard. However, most individuals think of peripheral devices as outside, or peripheral to the computer case. Using this definition of a peripheral device, individuals have traditionally classified peripherals as input or output devices. An input device, such as a mouse, keyboard, microphone, scanner, or Webcam, is a peripheral that sends information to the computer. An output device, such as a monitor display, speaker, or printer, takes processed information from the computer. Over time, a new category of peripheral devices has emerged that includes USB flash drives and USB or Firewire disk drives. These peripheral devices do not fit the standard definition of peripherals as input and output devices. Instead, these peripherals fit into a new category of devices classified as peripheral storage devices.

As new technology emerges, definitions must be adapted to fit these changes. A good example is when users send an e-mail "CC." Originally, CC stood for "carbon copy," a process by which an individual could write something once and it would automatically copy onto a second piece of paper through pressure and the use of carbon paper. Thus, to CC someone was to provide them with a duplicate or carbon copy of the original. Over time, using CC became a standard business practice. When business users began to use e-mail over paper letters, the need to CC such letters to additional recipients still existed. Thus, software programs allowed users to CC an e-mail to additional recipients, even though technically through the process of sending an e-mail, users do not create a carbon copy. Now, some people refer to CC as "courtesy copy" in an attempt to redefine the definition to more closely match existing technology (4Teachers, 2006).

The same is true with peripherals, in that the simple definition of a peripheral as an input, output, or storage device has blurred. A good example is a USB flash drive on a computer running Microsoft Vista for its operating system. One feature new to the Vista operating system is Windows Ready Boost. In Vista, using a USB 2.0 Ready Boost compatible flash drive, users can choose to use the flash drive to expand short-term memory capacity, similar to RAM. As described earlier in the chapter, if the computer runs out of available RAM, the computer must store temporary data in a paging file on the hard drive. This is problematic because the hard drives spins, and the CPU can access data only in a certain order, whereas the CPU can access data stored in RAM in an order. Ready Boost increases short-term memory by allowing the CPU to store data to the USB 2.0 drive as needed. Thus, in this situation the USB flash drive is now more similar to a RAM chip (not considered a peripheral) than a data storage device. While installing additional RAM, if needed, is always the best choice for improving performance, Windows Ready Boost now provides a better second choice alternative, especially if all available RAM slots on the motherboard are occupied (Schmid, 2007).

Updates and Upgrades

Sometimes it can feel that as soon as a computer system is purchased it is immediately outdated. However, for most purposes, a computer system can support needed library functions for a few years, especially if components are changed and upgraded on compelling need, such as RAM cards. At this point, systems have become stabler, the main differences being size reduction, speed, and RAM/space.

Updates and upgrades are more likely to occur in software. Operating systems (OS) are probably the most crucial resources, although changing to a new version such as Vista or Snow Leopard requires careful thought and generally does not need to be done for a year when all the kinks are ironed out; for instance, Windows 7 came out relatively soon after the controversial Vista was launched. However, OS patches should be installed as they become available because they reflect bugs that undermine operations and enable the computer to keep functioning properly.

In addition, the model number of the computer can be useful if the LMS wants to upgrade the computer at a later date. For example, the LMS decides to improve computer performance by adding additional random access memory (RAM) to the computers. To determine the correct RAM to purchase, the LMS can open the computer case and inspect the existing RAM chip. This will tell the LMS the type, speed, and capacity of the existing RAM chips as well as the available open slots, if any, for additional RAM chips. However, it will not list the total amount of memory the computer can store or the maximum capacity for each slot. A better approach is to visit the support Web site of the manufacturer of the computer. Most of these Web sites provide a feature where the LMS can type in the model number or even serial number and quickly ascertain the type, speed, and capacity of RAM needed to upgrade that particular system.

In terms of needing to keep current with updates, probably the most sensitive application is word processing. Even though users can usually save documents in earlier versions, they tend to click "save" without considering in what version or format to save the file. The person receiving the document cannot open the file of a more current version, so he or she must ask the sender to resave the file. For this reason, much used applications such as Microsoft Office should be routinely updated once the programs have stabilized. Normally, the library is not alone in this decision; productivity software is usually a site or district decision, so the LMS just needs to be kept in the information loop and the library software updated along with the rest of the educational community.

The other program that needs to be considered seriously is the integrated library management systems (ILMS). Usually the service contract includes provisions for needed patches and updates. However, significant new upgrades might be offered that the library is not ready to embrace, particularly if the older version continues to be supported and the new version requires hardware upgrading. This situation reflects the library's status, not as a bleeding-edge program but indicative of solid practice. A good idea is to contact local LMSs with the same ILMS and ask them about their experiences and news about the company's plans. While staying with the present version is usually safe, LMSs should keep abreast of industry changes because software takeovers have become common these days.

As for other software upgrades, LMSs should make sure to submit software warranties, record those actions, and maintain contact with the software companies to make sure that they can be eligible for discounts on scheduled upgrades. Especially if a product is registered online, that company may well e-mail LMSs about forthcoming updates and offerings. Sometimes group discounts can also be used to cut down on upgrade costs, so LMSs should make sure to work with site and district technology coordinators to optimize purchases.

It should be noted when a system boots up, sometimes a pop-up screen appears to signal that an update is available for immediate installation. It is usually a good idea to jot down the message and *not* click on the automatic update, the reason being that sometimes malicious software is disguised as those notices, inviting itself to be installed into the computer. With that information in hand, the LMS should contact the network administrator to determine the legitimacy of that notice. As a preventative measure, the library computers can be configured to reject all such pop-ups with the intent that the network administrator will get that information and deal with it appropriately on a systemwide basis.

Refresh Cycles

Some LMSs purchase computers but give no consideration to how they will eventually replace those computers, even though this is an inevitable need. Waiting until the computer fails and can no longer be repaired is not an effective management plan, nor is waiting until the computer can no longer handle day to day tasks. Both situations will leave the LMS suddenly without needed resources. Thus, effective management of LMC equipment includes developing a plan to replace existing equipment, also know as a refresh plan. For LMC computers, the LMS should plan ahead, projecting future needs and establishing a clear date when the school will replace existing LMC computers. This plan needs to include the source of funding for the new acquisition and the LMS should communicate with and gain support from the appropriate stakeholders.

One strategy is to replace all computers in a library lab setting at the same time. New computers will come with different programs and specifications. Replacing all computers at once allows the LMS to maintain consistency. On a school or district level, replacing all computers at once is not feasible. Thus, a multiyear plan to refresh computers may be more appropriate. Davis Unified School District in Utah has a five-year plan to refresh computers. The district allocates to each school a set number of computers. Each year the school receives from the district new computers, representing 20 percent of their allotment. By year six, schools have reached their full allotment of computers. Thus, as the district provides new computers, the district salvages older computers, or, if the computers still meet minimum specifications for existing computers set by the district, those computers are put into a redistribution program for schools not yet at maximum allotment levels. This provides the district with a mechanism to ensure computers are up to date at all school sites. In addition, by replacing 20 percent of the computers at a time, the program allows for a more consistent computer expense by the district (Computer Refresh Committee, 2008).

WORKS CITED

4Teachers. 2006. "Technology Glossary." ALTEC. Available: www. 4teachers.org/techalong/glossary/ (accessed June 21, 2009).

Bailey, Gail C., and Jayne E. Moore. 2008. "Buying Power." *T.H.E. Journal* 35, no. 7 (July): 31.

Clark, Laura, and Denise Davis. 2009. "Findings from Site Visits." *Library Technology Reports* 45, no. 1 (January): 28–30.

Computer Refresh Committee. 2008. *Computer Refresh Program.* Farmington, UT: Davis School District. Available: www.davis.k12.ut.us/district/ets/sts/files/F4098BFBB691467885ED0E9EACF83CC3.pdf (accessed June 21, 2009).

Farb, S., and A. Riggio. 2004. "Medium or Message? A New Look at Standards, Structures and Schemata for Managing Electronic Resources." *Library Hi Tech* 22, no. 2 (February): 144–152.

Franklin, Pat, and Claire Gatrell Stephens. 2006. "Circulating Equipment: Keeping Track of Everything!" *School Library Media Activities Monthly* 22, no. 7 (June): 42–44.

Griffith, Eric. 2009. "Make the Most of Your New PC: Follow This Simple 12-Step Program to Guarantee Maximum Performance, Security, and Ease of Use. Plus, Decide How to Deal with All Your Old Stuff." *PC Magazine* (January). Available: www.pcmag.com/article2/0,2817,2337550,00.asp (accessed June 27, 2009).

Intel. 2009. "Intel Processors." Available: www.intel.com/consumer/learn/processors/ (accessed June 21, 2009).

International Digital Publishing Forum. "Wholesale E-book Sales Statistics." Available: www.idpf.org/doc_library/industrystats.htm (accessed March 30, 2009).

Kioskea.net. 2008. "Random Access Memory (RAM or PC Memory)." Kioskea.net, October 16. Available: http://en.kioskea.net/contents/pc/ram.php3 (accessed January 10, 2009).

Nadel, Brian. "Better than Buying." Scholastic. Available: http://content.scholastic.com/browse/article.jsp?id=11645 (accessed June 21, 2009).

Oliver, James. 1997. "10 'Must Ask' Questions When Developing a Technology Plan." American Association of School Administrators, April. Available: www.aasa.org/publications/saarticledetail.cfm?mn itemnumber=&tnitemnumber=&itemnumber=4797 (accessed June 21, 2009).

Penrod, Lee. 2008. "What Is PCI Express?" *Directron*, August 13. Available: www.directron.com/expressguide.html (accessed June 21, 2009).

Pinnacle Systems. "Pinnacle Studio." Pinnacle Systems Inc. Available: www.pinnaclesys.com (accessed June 28, 2009).

Schmid, Patrick. 2007. "Analysis: Vista's Ready Boost Is No Match for RAM." *Tom's Hardware*, February 8. Available: www.tomshardware.com/reviews/analysis-vista-ready-boost,1891.html (accessed June 21, 2009).

Smith, Ivan. 2008. "Cost of Hard Drive Storage Space," January 21. Available: www.alts.net/ns1625/winchest.html (accessed June 21, 2009).

Tortorice, Anthony. 2008. "IT Desktop Computer Maintenance and Support." Los Angeles Unified School District, May 30. Available: http://note-book.lausd.net/pls/ptl/docs/PAGE/CA_LAUSD/FLDR_ORGANIZATIONS/FLDR_INFOTECH/REF%201657%202%20IT%20COMPUTER%20AND%20PERIPHERAL%20MAINT%20AND%20SUPPORT%20V16.PDF (accessed June 21, 2009).

Wikipedia. 2009. s.v. "Techie." Available: http://en.wikipedia.org/wiki/Techie (accessed June 21, 2009).

Chapter 4

Technology Maintenance and Troubleshooting

Technology is an integral part of the library media center (LMC), both as a management and instructional tool. Library media specialists (LMSs) use technology in myriad ways to manage library media programs, such as integrated library management systems (ILMS) to control circulation library materials or security systems to protect library materials. LMSs choose to adopt new technologies for management when the benefits, be it increased productivity or enhanced features, outweigh the costs, be it in monetary costs or initial training costs.

As LMSs become more efficient through the effective use of technology, they can free up time to provide additional services. However, when that same technology fails, this situation can create a time crunch that reverberates throughout the library program. Preventing such failures through proper care and maintenance is the first step in effective management of library technology. Proactive maintenance allows LMSs to plan instead of react. Specifically, through maintenance LMSs control how and when to use technology instead of fixing technology in unplanned response.

Even with effective maintenance, technology will occasionally fail. Where some LMSs are lucky to have an on-site technician on demand, many LMSs find that in order to mitigate the impact of failed technology, it is necessary to self-diagnose and troubleshoot issues that arise. Thus, the second section of this chapter covers what to do when technology fails.

GENERAL MAINTENANCE PRACTICES

Effective use of technology requires ongoing vigilance from day one. By regularly monitoring the condition of the library's technology and dealing with issues before they become serious problems, library staff can keep technology in good working order for the lifetime of its usefulness.

Preventative Measures

The proverb "A stitch in time saves nine" applies to regular technology maintenance. Clean equipment and digital resources that are carefully handled last longer and cause fewer problems. The Southern Tier Library has a computer maintenance and security checklist that provides simple routines to ensure that library computers operate smoothly and reliably (www.stls.org/it/Computer%20 maintenance.htm). Scheduling weekly, monthly, and yearly tasks makes it easier to keep on top of maintenance and reduces the likelihood of repairs. The following Web sites provide practical tips and even repair guidelines. Some general Web sites are also listed in the Resources list at the end of the book.

- www.4teachers.org/techalong/glossary: A site geared to K–12 teachers offering simple, clear explanations of the basics.
- www.techterms.com: A free online dictionary of computer and technology terms that not just defines computer terms but explains them as well.
- www.zerocut.com/tech/c_terms.html: A no-nonsense basic list of terms.
- www.compinfo-center.com: A one-stop center for good computer information.
- www.wiredguide.com: A beginner's guide to computer help, Internet help, and general computing interest from chat to shareware.
- www.4teachers.org/profdev/index.php?profdevid=ttta: A professional development approach to computer maintenance.
- www.pla.org/Ala/mgrps/divs/pla/plapublications/platech-

notes/index.cfm: ALA's Public Library Association tech notes.

- managementhelp.org/infomgnt/tech_spt/tech_spt.htm: Basic technical support and maintenance of small computer systems targeted to nonprofit organizations.
- www.komando.com: A savvy techie woman's advice.
- www.commoncraft.com: Great videos on technology how-tos.
- www.wikihow.com/category:Hardware-Maintenance-and-Repair: Community-based how-to help.
- www.computercare.org/computerhowto/computerhowto. htm: A service company that provides tips for organizing technology, addressing e-mail and passwords, disaster recovery, and so on.
- www.tamingthebeast.net/training/ittraining.htm: A commercial spin on free Internet marketing resources, Web site development tutorials, ecommerce strategies, and software solutions.

Several technology companies provide online support. Here a few:

- www.microsoft.com
- http://pcsupport.about.com
- www.apple.com/support
- www.macfixit.com
- http://mobileoffice.about.com/lr/laptop_care/159520/4

Placement

Maintaining technology starts with proper placement. For instance, computer stations should be surrounded by air, not setting flush on the floor or pushed against the wall or encased in a small closed compartment. Air circulation is needed to keep the machine cool and to cut down on dust buildup. Similarly, cords and cables should have enough room so they can bend freely without being squished; the latter situation can lead to broken wires inside. It is also a good idea to label each line so that it will be easy to reattach it to the proper spot; black permanent marker on white bandage tape works well.

Portable equipment to be circulated should be stored in well-cushioned bags in order to absorb shocks from being bumped or dropped. Monitors should be strapped on a cart to prevent jostling. As with desktops, portable equipment cables and lines should be labeled for easy attachment; some newer systems color code the two ends, but older ones tend not to, so small code colored dots on both ends can serve the same purpose of aiding the user to attach parts together properly. A how-to reference sheet, a diagram of the equipment and parts, and a parts checklist should accompany the circulation equipment bag to cut down on crisis calls. Users should also be taught how to use any equipment before they borrow it. Equipment training cards can be created for each user, noting the training dates. In that way, library staff can check out equipment quickly and without worry. Of course, the equipment bag needs to be checked to make sure all components are present and in working order whenever it is checked out and checked in.

Cleanliness

Dust, dirt, and small debris will accumulate on equipment over time, especially in crevices such as between the keys on a keyboard, which can cause keys to stick or become inoperable. Dust built up inside a computer case, entering through holes such as the fan vent, impacts air circulation and can cause computer overheating. Therefore, regular cleaning of LMC equipment is a necessary task for keeping equipment operational. In addition to ensuring efficient operation of technology, cleaning provides other benefits. First, dirty equipment, just like dirty books, can reflect poorly on the LMC. Clean equipment tells patrons the equipment is valued. This unspoken message can impact how users interface with and treat your LMC equipment. Children and adults alike prefer using equipment they perceive to be new.

Clean equipment also sends the message to administration that the LMS effectively cares for and maintains equipment. Administrators are more likely to support spending additional money on future technology acquisitions for the library when they feel the equipment will be well cared for (Shade, 1996). The LMS should power off electronic equipment before cleaning. Physically unplugging the power cord is a best practice as a safeguard to ensure the device is not accidently turned on during the cleaning process.

Computer monitors need frequent cleaning. Monitors accumulate dust and fingerprints from users mistaking the monitor for a touch-screen. LCD (liquid crystal display) monitors are more difficult to clean than CRT (cathode-ray tube) monitors. CRT monitors have glass screens, which the LMS can clean with regular window cleaning products. On the other hand, the LMS can damage an LCD screen if too much force is applied or a rough cloth is used. In addition, certain cleaning products, especially those containing ammonia, may permanently damage an LCD computer screen. These products over time may cause smudges, fading, and yellowing of the screen. For LCD screens, it is important to obtain a soft, lint-free cotton cloth and gently wipe the screen without applying pressure. If necessary, office supply stores sell screen-cleaning fluid that can be used in conjunction with the lint-free cloth. Typically, LCD screen cleaning fluid is a mixture of water and isopropyl alcohol. When in doubt about safe cleaning products, consult the manual for the LCD display.

To clean a keyboard, computer consultant Gale Rhoades recommends that users turn off the computer, disconnect the keyboard, and then turn the keyboard upside down and shake it, which causes loose debris to fall out. The LMS can then use a compressed air can to blow away additional dust and debris. To clean inside the computer, the LMS needs to remove the computer's access panel, which may require removing a screw or two; the computer's manual can be consulted for directions. Once open, compressed air can gently blow away the dust, exercising care not to knock or touch the components. When cleaning dust, Rhoades recommends taking the computer outside, otherwise you may just be "shifting the dust and dirt bunnies back into your office" (Rhoades, 2007, p. 53).

Cable Care

Cables are sometimes overlooked when it comes to maintenance, but their longevity helps keep the rest of the equipment running smoothly. As noted, cables should be unplugged on both ends when equipment is being cleaned. The cables themselves can be cleaned, first with a dry cloth to get rid of dust and dirt and then with isopropyl alcohol solvent (applied to a soft clean cloth) if the cable sheath is smudged or yellowed. If the connector interfaces touch the solvent, they can short circuit and damage the equipment they connect to. Cables should be rolled up in their original direction, and power cords such as speaker wires or AC power cords should not be coiled at all.

Sometimes it can seem as if the back of the computer looks like spaghetti with various cables streaming in different directions. Not only does a mass of cables look messy, but the disarray can lead to accidental disconnects, dust buildup, and can be a fire hazard. Cables can be kept tidy in several ways: a side-slit tube, a cable caddy, cable hooks, Velcro straps, twist-ties and cable ties, a desk "trench," power distribution units, and raised flooring units. Sometimes a cable is too long, so a shorter version can be switched out to cut down on clutter. If cables have to go across a traffic area, it should be covered with a narrow rubber "runner" or equivalent; otherwise, people and carts may trip over the cables and dislodge either the equipment or the person.

When should a cable be replaced? If it is fraying, if the connector interface is loose, if is looks burned or melted. If the attached equipment starts to show flickering images or choppy sounds, and the problem persists when the cable is unplugged and replugged, it is a good idea to test the equipment with an equivalent cable. If the problem stops, replace the old cable.

Storage

When technology is not being used, it needs to be stored safely, securely, and be available for easy retrieval. Technology resources differ from print items in that the information container (such as videotape, microfiche, CD) requires a piece of equipment in order to access it. Furthermore, each format has specific storage requirements. No wonder that most LMSs store materials by format; they are easier to manage that way. Across the board, though, several storage environment factors need to be addressed: light, temperature, humidity, pollution, animals, and physical security. Different media prefer different conditions, but most LMCs do not have the luxury of customizing format-specific storage areas (Edmondson, 2004). The Library of Congress (2002) provides some general tips:

- Keep the area clean.
- Keep items standing up on edge, not flat.
- Although demagnetization usually is not a problem, keep

items away from loud speakers or operating machines such as vacuum cleaners.

- Keep items in a dark area, especially away from sunlight and unshielded phosphorescent light.
- Keep items in an area that is between 65 to 70° F and 45 to 50% relative humidity.
- Discs should the stored with full-height dividers spaced 4 to 6 inches apart. Do not place discs of different sizes together because it can cause warping.
- Plastic "sleeves" should be high-density polyethylene.
- Store valuable items in fireproof cabinets (avoid high temperatures).

Backups

Regardless of preventative measures taken, it is almost inevitable that a computer will crash and become inoperable eventually. At that point, reformatting the hard drive and re-installing software is often the solution. Formatting a hard drive is the process of preparing a hard drive for use by the operating system. Reformatting a hard drive wipes existing data from the hard drive. Often, reformatting the hard drive can be more time-efficient than attempting to diagnose unique problems caused by file corruption, viruses, or spyware. If the hard drive must be reformatted to resolve the problem, the LMS can attempt to utilize expensive data recovery services to access important data. In most instances this will be impractical and all data will likely be lost. Thus, the LMS must expect that computers will fail and include in their technology management a plan for backing up data.

Different levels of backup need to occur. First, when the computer arrives on campus it comes preloaded with an operating system (OS), software drivers and add-on software. Major computer companies, often as cost-cutting measures, have stopped providing installation discs automatically with the computer. Instead, computer vendors are saving the restore files to the hard drive, typically on a hidden partition. Some vendors provide restore discs for an extra cost. In addition, on the computer the vendors place a software program that allows the purchaser to create a set of restore CDs/

DVDs on their own. LMSs need to either purchase restore discs (if offered) or create restore discs when the computer arrives.

Without restore discs, the LMS must rely on the computer's restore partition to reload the OS. In day-to-day use it is possible for a hard drive to completely fail. If this happens, a hard-drive based restore partition installed on that hard drive is useless. Not having restore discs in this circumstance makes it impossible to restore the original image.

The manufacturer's restore disc reinstates the computer's software configuration to its delivery state. Many LMSs immediately install additional programs on the new computer when it arrives, such as software programs for which the school has site licenses. Configuring the computer to print is another typical setup task. In a few years, the computer will need a considerable number of software updates if it has to be restored back to its original state. Then having to install both software and released updates can be tedious. Therefore, the LMS needs a mechanism for having an updated backup that reflects the target configuration as opposed to the initial configuration. This practice saves the LMS valuable time.

Disk imaging, also known as ghosting, addresses this management need. According to Andrew Carheden, former project and technology editor for the magazine *WindowsITPro*, "Disk imaging is the process of making an exact data copy on a partition or hard disk and writing it to an image file or another hard disk. Using disk imaging to provision computers ensures that all your machines start out with identical and clean software configurations" (Carheden, 2005).

The Ultimate, Business, and Enterprise versions of Windows Vista includes Complete PC and Backup utility (www.microsoft. com/windows/windows-vista/features/backup.aspx), a program that allows users to create an image of the entire system and save it to external storage media such as CDs or DVDs. If the OS is not able to load, the Windows Vista installation CD allows the user to access an image saved externally. Windows XP users can use the provided backup utility (www.microsoft.com/windowsxp/using/security/learnmore/Backup.mspx) to back up the contents of the entire hard drive to an external USB hard drive. The latter is not a stand-alone solution in that the LMS must first reinstall the OS. The LMS would use the Windows XP backup utility in conjunction with the original restore disc to provide an effective solution in case of complete hard drive failure.

LMSs can back up files three ways on Mac systems: manually, using Snow Leopard's Time Machine, or using a third-party application. When no other activities are being done on the system, the Time Machine automatically asks the user to back up files and then opens its preference pane to the predetermined backup disk. When the backup disk is full, the oldest files are removed to make room for the newest files. The first time that the Time Machine is used, it backs up the entire hard drive; subsequently, it backs up files that have been added or modified since the first backup. The user can customize Time Machine, such as specifying how often backups should occur. Backup can also be done manually by copying individual files to a desired storage area, such as a writeable CD (remembering to "burn" the CD when ready). To save time, the LMS can save all files in a "documents" (or other named) folder so that just one copying process need be done. People often use their Home folder as their default space, in which case that folder is the one to be periodically backed up. Alternatively, a third-party commercial software can automatically back up indicated files daily at a predetermined time (such as at 2:13 a.m.). As with Time Machine, the first backup usually requires more time—and more space. Retrospect is one of the best backup commercial software programs, and it works with most operating systems.

Some computer vendors also provide free advanced restore tools with their computers. For instance, Lenovo provides ThinkVantage Rescue and Recovery (www.pc.ibm.com/us/think/thinkvantagetech/rescuerecovery.html) for its systems, and Mac's Snow Leopard uses Time Machine. The LMS can use these pre-installed programs to regularly back up a computer, with the backup saved to an external hard drive. Like Windows Vista Complete PC and Backup utility, the LMS can access ThinkVantage outside the operating system.

Typically, schools order multiple computers at a time. The previously mentioned software can assist the LMS in managing individual computers. However, when multiple computers need managing, the LMS may find other solutions more practical. For instance, the LMS might decide to replace all computers in the LMC. The new computers will have the same specifications and will require the same configuration. In this example, it makes most sense to set up one computer with the desired configuration and then use that configuration for all other computers. Many imaging software programs provide this feature, which saves time by allowing the LMS to install updates and software packages once instead of on each computer individually. After configuring the first computer, the LMS creates an image of the computer. Next, the LMS applies the image to the other computers, effectively installing updates and software programs on all of the computers.

To provide additional time savings and efficiencies, many imaging programs provide a central console where the LMS can create and deploy images. An Internet search for disk imaging brings up a number of products, including Acronis True Image Echo Workstation (www.acronis.com/enterprise/products/ATICW/) and Symantec Ghost Solution Suite (www.symantec.com/Business/ghost-solution-suite). For each managed computer, the LMS must purchase a license, but the benefits of centralized imaging in terms of additional program features and time savings can far outweigh licensing costs for the imaging software.

Another backup concern is the actual user files. At some schools, computers are part of a domain: a group of computer and network devices (e.g., printers) connected together. In a domain, rules and policies are managed centrally though a server, a special computer responsible for handling requests from the other computers known as clients. Servers run specialized software for servers, such as Mac OS X Server or Windows 2008 server. In a domain setup typically every student has a unique login as well as personal storage space on the server. As students move from computer to computer their profile (e.g., desktop settings, location of their files) roams with them. Thus, these profiles are called roaming profiles. Servers provide many functions, including storing files (file server) and controlling applications (application server). Server software typically uses redundant array of independent disks (RAID) to automatically back up user files on the server. With RAID technology, each file is replicated (hence the term redundant). Next, one or more additional hard disks connected to the server store the replicated file. Thus, at any given time each file is stored on two or more independent disks; if one disk fails, the data is not lost.

At schools without individual storage locations for each student and staff member, the LMS must decide where and how students will save their work. On LMC student computers, it is advisable to not allow students to save files directly onto the local computers because doing so creates additional management concerns. For instance, students may save inappropriate files onto the computer, so computers must be checked regularly, and inappropriate and outdated files need to be removed. When students save files to a specific computer, they become computer-dependent, needing to access that particular computer on subsequent visits. If that computer is in use, the student will need to wait for that one computer to become available. Overall, this creates unnecessary steps and work when students can use alternative means for saving their work, such as a USB flash drive.

If students need the ability to save files to the computer, instead of allowing students to save locally to the computer, the LMS can create a central network location for users to save files. In Windows, the LMS can redirect My Documents to a central network location, which allows students to continue to save to My Documents (a familiar procedure for them). Similarly, Mac OS servers includes a public folder. This solution simplifies maintenance, as all data files are in one central location and has instructional benefits. For example, the LMS can now efficiently collect student work electronically by directing students to save their work to this central location. With such setups, procedures for data purging must be determined, communicated with users, and implemented. A batch file can be written and then scheduled to run using Windows Task Scheduler or Apple's Workgroup Manager to automate this process.

For other LMC computers, the LMS must have a plan in place to regularly back up data. This includes computers at the circulation desk, the LMS's computer, or a server hosting the LMC circulation system files. ILMSs come packaged with software that has the ability to back up data. For other computers, operating system solutions as discussed earlier can address this need. For instance, the Complete PC and Backup utility is found on Windows Vista Business, Ultimate, and Enterprise editions; Mac OS has Apple Software Restore and Time Machine. In addition, the LMS can find a number of backup utility programs though an Internet search.

One free backup solution is SyncToy 2.0 from Microsoft (Bing, 2009), which allows users to pair folders between two storage devices. This can include the following:

- Local internal hard drive and a second internal hard drive
- Local internal hard drive and an external hard drive (e.g., USB, Firewire)
- Local internal hard drive and a flash drive
- Local internal hard drive and a mapped network drive (e.g., hard drive on a server).

Using SyncToy 2.0 the LMS can backup the contents of any folder, such as My Documents. The LMS can configure SyncToy 2.0 to "echo" changes made in one folder onto a second backup folder. For instance, if the LMS deleted a file from the source folder, SyncToy 2.0 would echo the change in the backup folder. If the LMS works on both a desktop and a laptop, the LMS can configure SyncToy 2.0 to "synchronize" thereby copying and deleting files in both directions, keeping only the last modified version of the copy. This action provides a backup (as all files are on both the desktop and laptop), ensuring that the LMS has access to important files whether using the laptop or desktop and allowing the LMS to create and modify files in both places without worrying about whether it is the latest version of the file (Bing, 2009). Mac's Snow Leopard's Time Machine, which is resident in the system, provides similar services.

Regardless of chosen method, the LMS will need to acquire a tape drive, external hard drive, or another storage device independent of the hard drive containing the original data. It is important for the data to be separate. Backing up the data to another portion of the hard drive does little good if the hard drive fails. The LMS must also plan for computer theft, fires, and other calamities. In many cases, the original data will be destroyed, so an effective backup plan must provide for off-site storage of backups. For example, the LMS can have two external hard drives: one off-campus and the other on-campus. Each week the LMS swaps the hard drives, ensuring that at the most the LMS will lose only one week's worth of data. Another solution is to purchase online storage and regularly upload a backup to the online storage site. Policies and procedures for prevention and responding to disasters are detailed in Chapter 7.

SECURITY

Patrons utilize school LMC computers for whole-class instruction, small group work, and independent access by students. This presents unique challenges for LMSs responsible for managing these resources. Chapter 5 discusses physical security of LMC equipment, such as the use of lockdown devices, which helps prevent computers and peripheral devices such as the keyboard from suddenly disappearing. However, physical security does not prevent changes to the operating system or installation of unauthorized programs. In such a scenario, the LMS must manage the security of computer configurations, which this section explores.

Consider a situation where the LMS planned a lesson that would require specific software, such as Audacity, for creating a podcast. After introducing students to the program they begin to access it. To the surprise of the LMS, a number of LMC computers no longer contain files required for the successful operation of the program. Thus, computers the LMS expected to be available for this lesson are no longer available, and diagnosing the issue wastes valuable instructional time. Such challenges can quickly impact the success of the lesson. Additionally, unexpected complications can discourage teachers from utilizing the LMC for instruction and especially LMC equipment, which ultimately impacts the success of the library media program.

Setting changes and program deletions are the tip of the management worries iceberg. Students may purposely or inadvertently download viruses, spyware, or malware to computers, which, in turn, can dramatically decrease performance or render computers unusable. Constantly fixing such issues wastes valuable time. Wouldn't it be great if there were a program that could just wipe away changes students made to shared computers or prevent students from accessing key system settings?

Computer security software addresses this management concern. Computer security software is software that protects a computer from unwanted tampering. Many different products fall within the category of computer security. Some focus on external threats such as firewall software or antivirus and antispyware software, whereas others focus on internal threats, such as a user who intentionally or unintentionally changes the computer settings. In addition, many computer security software products are multifaceted, providing several different levels and types of security. For instance, Bardon's Data Systems (www.bardon.com) Full Control blends access control, such as the ability to block downloads and installations, with intrusion control though spyware and malware protection features.

Software products frequently blend computer security features with lab management features. For example, software that allows the LMS to control print jobs and limit user sessions on LMC computers would be considered lab management software; however, if that same software contains features that wipe out user changes or restrict access to computer settings, this software would also be considered computer security software. In other words, many features found in computer security products could appropriately be described as lab management features, which are discussed in this chapter. The line between computer security products and lab management products is often blurred in part because many managers of computers prefer one-stop solutions to their computer management needs. For the purposes of this section of the book, the term *computer security software* refers to products aimed at protecting the computer's configuration from unwanted tampering by users.

Computer security software generally utilizes one of two approaches to computer security. The first approach is software that restricts user access to key settings of the computer. For instance, the LMS can set the security software to prevent access to the Internet Explorer control panel, preventing users from easily changing the Internet Explorer browser options. The second approach is software that does not restrict the user from making changes but instead erases modifications whenever the computer is restarted. Richard Wayne, a library technology consultant and systems group manager for the University of Texas Southwestern Medical library, recommends that LMS balance the need for security with the needs for functionality. As he writes, "[T]oo much security can restrict a patron from doing things that you both agree he or she should be able to do. Not enough security may put the computer and even the entire associated network at risk" (Wayne, 2005, p. 37).

One computer security tool is Windows SteadyState (www. microsoft.com/windows/products/winfamily/sharedaccess/default. mspx), which can be downloaded gratis for Windows XP and Vista operating systems. Microsoft describes Windows SteadyState as a "set it and forget it" approach to computer management (Windows, 2008). Using Windows SteadyState, the LMS can customize a slate of settings limiting user access to system settings. One of the most valuable features is the ability to wipe out any changes a user makes by simply restarting the computer; the software restores the original settings specified by the LMS. Using the previous example, the LMS could simply restart all computers prior to whole-class instruction to ensure all students begin instruction on a computer with the correct settings. Thus, Windows SteadyState combines restrictive elements with the wiping out of changes either through a manual restart or a scheduled restart. Mac OS X server has advanced features that function similarly. In general, Apple products tend to be more secure than Windows-based ones.

A number of other computer security software solutions are available. Some provide a central console, which the LMS can use to control all computers. One such program is the Enterprise version of Deep Freeze (www.faronics.com/html/Deepfreeze.asp) by Faronics. Deep Freeze works similarly to Windows SteadyState in that the program allows the LMS to "freeze" a computer. In frozen state, every time the computer restarts it reverts back to its original settings. To make changes to a computer, the LMS must first "thaw" it, which requires typing in a password and then rebooting the computer in a "thawed" state. The LMS can set the computers to automatically thaw each night, receive any Windows updates, freeze, and then shut down automatically. The LMS can install Deep Freeze's Enterprise version console on the LMC server (if applicable) or on the LMS's computer. With the click of one button, the console allows the LMS to send commands to multiple computers at once, including thaw, freeze, shut-down, and restart, which can save valuable time. Imagine the LMS who must walk around to physically turn off every computer each day when the LMC closes. Instead, the LMS can simply send one command through the central console. In addition, as the LMS acquires and updates software, the computer security program needs to be temporarily disabled for the software to be installed. Using Deep Freeze and its Enterprise console, the LMS can select specific computers or all computers and with one click thaw them to quickly and efficiently allow updates. Nevertheless, Deep Freeze and other security programs are the object of professional hackers who try to undo its actions, so LMSs still need to be vigilant in supervising computer systems.

As previously mentioned, Mac Workgroup Manager and Windows SteadyState help manage LMC computers running newer systems. LMSs charged with the task of managing multiple library media computers should also consider alternative solutions with advanced features such as a central console. When deciding to utilize computer security software, a number of management questions arise. Do the benefits of the software, in terms of time savings, availability, and functionality of LMC computers, outweigh acquisition and maintenance costs for the software? Is there a publicly known way to circumvent or otherwise defeat the software? If so, what other measures can the LMS utilize to address these concerns? Who will have access to any passwords used to disable the software (such as for computer upgrades and maintenance)?

With many computer security solutions, pricing may be calculated on a per installed computer basis, a set product cost or tiered pricing based on total users or total installations. LMSs considering the purchase of lab security software should investigate the possibility of volume pricing. For example, Deep Freeze provides volume pricing based on all schools in a single district with active licenses. Thus, large school districts with multiple school sites can achieve significant cost savings. Many computer security solutions require an annual licensing fee or provide optional maintenance packages. For example, when the LMS initially purchases Deep Freeze licenses, he or she must also purchase a maintenance package providing one year of technical support and product updates, which can be renewed annually.

This section of the book highlighted two computer security solutions to provide readers with examples of potential solutions. However, LMSs should be aware of the following vendors and their associated products:

- Bardon Data Systems (www.bardon.com): Full Control, Full Control Internet, and WinU
- Centurion Technologies (www.centuriontech.com/Library): Smart Shield
- Fortres Grand (www.fortresgrand.com): Clean Slate and Fortres 101

- Horizon DataSys (www.horizondatasys.com): Desktop Security Rx
- Hougton Mifflin Harcourt (www.hmlt.hmco.com/SUP-AS. php): FoolProof Security
- Intego Security (www.intego.com): VirusBarrier for Macs
- SecureMac (macscan.securemac.com): MacScan
- Userful Corporation (library.userful.com): Userful Desktop
- Visual Automation (www.visualautomation.com): Secure Desktop 7
- Winability Software (www.winability.com): Folder Guard

The features of each program vary, and most of these vendors offer free trials. This option is the best way to gauge the usefulness, effectiveness, and performance of a particular computer security program. LMSs should be aware that this list may not be exhaustive. As Richard Wayne writes, "[N]ew vendors enter the market and other vendors may merge or more in other directions" (Wayne, 2005, p. 45).

TROUBLESHOOTING

On paper, the job of an LMS is one of technologist rather than technician. A technologist is a knowledgeable user of technology. A technician is one who diagnoses and repairs technology. In an ideal situation, the LMS works hand in hand with the on-site technician to acquire, set up, and maintain technology in the LMC. However, sometimes the ideal does not match the reality. In many parts of the country, the LMS is both the technologist and by necessity the technician when it comes to LMC technology. As more technology is acquired and integrated into the LMC, the library media program benefits from new resources, improved features, and time-saving technologies. At the same time, such changes can also create dependence on the new technology.

Consider the old physical card catalog. Keeping cards organized was challenging, creating cards for each new item acquired time consuming, and many users struggled with the card catalog as an access point. Replacing the card catalog is a Web-based online public access catalog (OPAC) that is available anywhere (not just in the LMC), which contains helpful features like book pictures and provides more searching techniques such as allowing keyword searches. Vendor-provided MARC records can be quickly imported by the LMS, and even if the vendor does not provide MARC records, creating a MARC record is faster than creating a book card set, especially with tools such as MARC Magician (www.mitinet.com) and online resources such as the Library of Congress catalog (catalog. loc.gov), where the LMS can download MARC records to use as a base starting point. Finally, there may be visual searches, hyperlinked items, the ability to correct spelling errors, opportunities for users to contribute content such as book reviews, and much more.

No wonder few LMSs today maintain card catalogs. The benefits of the new technology clearly are vastly superior. That being said, the card catalog was available regardless of whether the Internet or Intranet was working, unlike its replacement, the Web-based OPAC. Thus, as LMSs have transitioned to newer technologies and abandoned older practices, they have also grown dependent on the technology. The OPAC is just one example of technology used in the LMC that has become an integral part of the library media program.

When technology works, everyone is happy. When is doesn't, then the frowns appear. Waiting for technical help can be frustrating as well as a real detriment to library service. Many problems can be solved quickly by the LMS with a bit of knowledge. Thus, this section explores ways to troubleshoot equipment. To provide an understanding of how this in done, a case study is provided, representing a typical issue LMSs may come across working in a LMC and how the LMS might go about troubleshooting the issue. Troubleshooting requires the LMS to know how the equipment works in addition to how the equipment is used.

Plenty of help is available to help the LMS troubleshoot technology, but not all of it is useful. Several additional factors need to be considered: timeliness, expertise, convenience, cost, and personal preference. Each source of assistance has its advantages and disadvantages. In any case, the LMS should send in warranty information and register products as well as keep a file for each resource in case servicing is needed. In the long run, though, one's own preferences may trump other sources; the person who hates manuals probably will not consult one, for instance.

LMSs can find many resources online that provide information on how certain equipment works. There are many free Web sites with troubleshooting tutorials and step-by-step directions for resolving common problems. Google is a great starting point for the LMS looking to troubleshoot an issue. If the problem includes a specific error code or phrase, this information should be included in the search terminology. Important phrases should be put in quotation marks, otherwise search engines will look for those key words individually instead of the exact phrase in Web documents.

In addition to online tutorials, numerous user forums are dedicated to resolving problems. Whenever an LMS has a computer issue, there is a good chance other users have also experienced the same issue and found a resolution. Searching these user forums, where one individual describes an issue and then others respond with solutions, is a great way to find solutions to technology problems the LMS may face. In addition to online sources, there are a number of books on troubleshooting and repairing computers and other equipment. The LMS may already have some of these books in the LMC and, if not, should consider purchasing some. Increasingly, computer repair titles are available as e-books because of their seemingly instant obsolescence. If not available in the LMC, the site or district technician may own such resources, and the local public library may own copies too.

Another often overlooked source of information is the equipment manual. Most manuals will have a help or common problems section, typically at the end of the manual. The manual may provide a link to the manufacturer's Web site, with more frequently asked questions and commons problems listed to supplement those found in the manual. Often, these issues and questions arise through use, well after initial publication of the user manual, which is why manufacturers often supplement the manual online. Many larger manufacturers provide knowledge databases. Through keyword searches, the LMS can access known issues and their solutions. In many cases, results from these databases, just like results from a subscription database, are not accessible through the typical search engine; they are part of what many refer to as the "invisible" Web. For this reason, it is important to access the manufacturer's Web site directly as one step in the troubleshooting process. In some cases, access is provided only if the product has been registered, which is another good reason to send in those warranties.

In addition to knowledge bases, many major computer and computer component manufacturers provide sophisticated tools for diagnosing problems. Some of these tools require the user to download and install a proprietary support program. Others are strictly Web-based tools. Features vary, but many of these tools can gather information about the computer or connected device needing support (e.g., the device's model, serial number, and error log) and test functionality to provide automated support. If the tool finds an issue with a known solution, often the tool will provide step-by-step directions for resolving the problem or, if able, even seek to automatically resolve the problem. In addition, if unable to resolve the issue, most tools can automatically pass the data to one of the manufacturer's customer support service specialists, which can save both the manufacturer and the LMS significant time.

For devices under warranty, the LMS may have access to free technical support. For out-of-warranty support, many manufacturers will offer similar support options. Most charge a flat fee per incidence. Support options can include telephone support, e-mail support, and Web-based chat. The latter can be useful in documenting the conversation, especially if the LMS is required to perform additional steps to further diagnose the issue or if multiple parties may be involved in resolving the issue. For instance, the LMS may have purchased a wireless access point to provide wireless access to the network. Faulty hardware could cause a wireless access point not to work. Inputting incorrect network settings could also be to blame. In diagnosing the issue, the wireless access point manufacturer may initially determine the problem to be incorrect network settings. At this point, the manufacturer will advise the LMS to contact the Internet service provider (ISP). However, what if through a call to the ISP, the settings are determined to indeed be correct? In this circumstance, the LMS will need to further troubleshoot with the wireless access point vendor. Having a written record of troubleshooting performed and conversations held will allow the LMS to more effectively communicate with the manufacturer and ultimately resolve the issue.

Some issues may require on-site repair. When the LMS is unable to self-diagnose and relies on outside assistance, the LMS should not be content with simply having the equipment repaired. Rather, the LMS should observe and learn from the technician, noting the steps the technician takes to diagnose the issue. If confused, the LMS should ask clarifying questions. Through observation and questioning, the LMS has a unique opportunity to learn from an expert and gain new knowledge. This will better prepare the LMS to diagnose and possibly self-repair the same or related issues in the future. Over time, through observation and questioning, the LMS will grow in technical expertise. In the end, a better understanding of how technology works is not only useful in supporting technology, it can also inform the LMS with regard to new uses and best practices for that technology.

Case Study: LMC Network Laser Printer No Longer Prints

There are many possible issues underlying the reasons that a network printer would not longer print:

- Printer is not powered on.
- Printer is out of paper.
- Cables are unplugged (e.g., Ethernet cable or power cable).
- Printer is out of toner or installed incorrectly (e.g., a user forgot to remove protective film when inserting new toner).
- Printer error occurs (e.g., paper jam).
- User printed to wrong printer.
- User selected wrong print settings (e.g., printed to wrong printer tray or printed using paper size not available).
- Printer settings were changed (e.g., IP address—discussed more in Chapter 5—is incorrect).
- Printer is not configured properly on computer (e.g., correct drivers not installed).
- Network is down.
- Ethernet cable failure occurs (either cable connecting printer to network or cable connecting computer to network).
- Network card failure occurs (either for computer or printer).
- Wall port failure occurs (either for computer or printer).
- Power cord on printer fails.
- Electrical outlet does not work.
- User accidentally paused printer in print queue.
- Printer needs servicing from professional repair shop (printer is dead and can't be revived locally).

When troubleshooting equipment, the LMS should start with simple actions and eliminate possible issues. For this and all scenarios, the LMS should begin by eliminating basic connection issues (all cords plugged in securely and printer turned on). Often the issue is simple, as would be the case if the printer were simply accidently turned off or a cord were accidently unplugged. Here are easy first steps.

1. Check the connection and make sure the switch is on.
2. If the printer won't turn on, test the electrical outlet by plugging something small into it, such as a pencil sharpener, to confirm that the outlet is actually working.
3. Replace the printer cord. If the printer still won't power on, the issue is internal, and a professional will need to service the printer.

Assuming the printer turns on, the LMS should check the front of the printer. The typical network printer will have an LCD interface, a series of lights, or both. The LCD interface may provide clues to the problem. For example, the LCD display might indicate "paper out," "wrong media type," or "load tray 3." These are all simple issues to address. With regard to the lights on the printer, an amber or red light may indicate a problem; whether the light is flashing or solid may also indicate a problem. If the light flashes, the LMS should note the pattern and speed of the flash as this may also be relevant. Next, the LMS can consult the printer manual, which gives explanations for the various light colors and patterns.

Network printers almost always have a Web-based interface that the LMS can access. As detailed in Chapter 5, each printer has a fixed IP address, which is assigned during initial setup. The LMS should record IP addresses in the equipment database discussed earlier in this chapter. Using this IP address the LMS can open a Web browser, type the IP address into the address bar, and access the printer's Web-based interface. This provides a convenient place to view the printer's status. The manual details how to print a printer configuration page if the IP address is unknown.

The LMS should use the LCD interface, the lights on the printer, and the Web-based interface to eliminate a number of potential issues, including paper jams, wrong paper sizes, wrong tray, toner issues, printer out of paper, or a printer error. With printer errors, some are resolved simply by restarting the printer. However, if the printer provides a specific error code, the manual can be used to further diagnose the issue. Manufacturers of the major printer brands also have detailed support pages on their respective Web pages. If the printer has an LCD display, the code will usually appear there. If not, the LMS can use the Web-based interface to access the printer log for error codes. Certain parts have a service life; it might be time to replace a part, such as the fuser. The code will assist in determining this.

In this step, let us assume the LMS is unable to access the Web-based interface. The LMS should confirm the IP address by printing a network configuration page. It is possible that someone reset the printer to its default settings, thus erasing the correct IP address. If the configuration settings are correct, the LMS can try accessing the Web-based interface from another computer. This eliminates the possibility that the computer is the culprit (e.g., bad wall port connected to computer, bad Ethernet cord, bad computer network card, etc.). For now, let us assume the printer's Web-based interface is not accessible from any computer. This indicates that (1) the printer is not on the network and (2) a problem with the network in general.

To eliminate a problem with the network in general, the LMS can try going onto any Internet site on the computer. If Internet is not available on the computer, the LMS should check other nearby computers to see if they can access Internet sites. If no computers have Internet access, a network switch (device that provides a network connection to multiple computers) may have failed. Or, the school's entire network may be down. Either way, this is an issue for the network administrator.

After eliminating general network issues, the focus now turns back to the printer. The LMS can swap the printer's Ethernet cable with a cable known to work. For instance, if a nearby computer has Internet access, that Ethernet cable can be unplugged and used to test the problem printer. If the printer now prints, the issue is the cable. Next, the LMS can check the Ethernet wall port. If there is a nearby wall port that is confirmed working, the Ethernet cable can be switched to the new wall port. If this resolves the issue, the wall port is the culprit. Damage to the actual wall plate may exist, the cable connecting the wall port to the network switch might have failed, or, if the switch is configurable, there may be a switch programming issue. These are all issues best addressed by a network engineer.

If there is no nearby wall port, the LMS can plug a laptop into the wall port in question. Again, if there is no Internet, the wall port is the culprit. If the network in general is working, the Ethernet cable is working, the Ethernet wall port is working, and the printer's configuration is correct, then the printer's network adapter has failed. If the printer has other connections such as a USB cable port, the LMS can purchase a USB network print server to bypass the printer's network adapter and restore connectivity.

Figure 4.1 (pp. 101–102) shows how the LMS can go through a series of steps to diagnose the problem and eliminate possibilities. In this example, certain discoveries led the LMS in a particular direction. For instance, not being able to access the Web-based interface led the LMS in the direction of a network communication issue that ultimately pointed to a failed network adapter. Without this piece of information, the LMS would have needed to diagnose additional issues, such as the computer itself. For example, the user could have changed the computer's default printer by accident and thus printed unknowingly to another location. The user could have accidently changed the printer's port on the computer. Or, the user could have accidently paused the printer in the print window and it simply needs to be resumed.

Another key moment in the troubleshooting process was when the LMS could not access the Web-based interface from any computer. If the Web-based interface was accessible from all computers except for the computer where the print job failed, this would have led the LMS in a totally different direction, because the problem now has to do with that computer's network connection. Just like the network card failed on the printer, the computer's network card also can fail. And, just like the LMS checked the printer's wall port and Ethernet cable, troubleshooting a computer's connection to the printer requires testing both the wall port and Ethernet cable as described earlier. As the troubleshooting progressed, the LMS would slowly eliminate possibilities. For instance, once the Ethernet cable and wall port successfully passed tests, the LMS would know the issue was with the actual computer. At this point, the LMS could check the network card to see if it is functioning properly. This action

Figure 4.1
Printer Problem Diagnostics

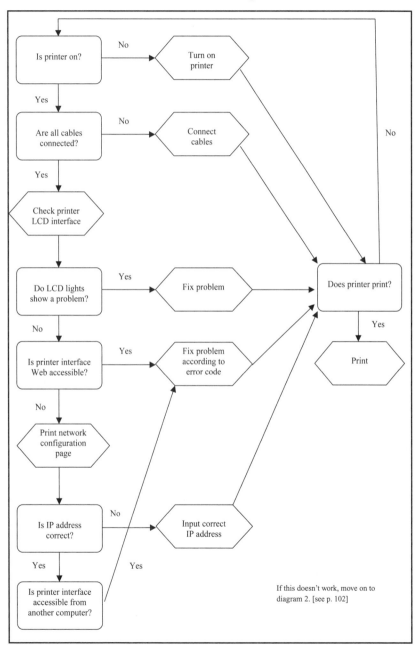

If this doesn't work, move on to diagram 2. [see p. 102]

**Figure 4.1 *(Continued)*
Printer Problem Diagnostics**

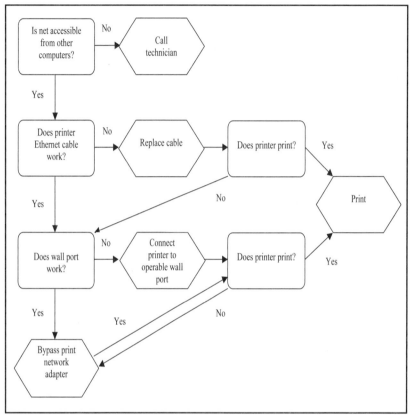

would include checking to see if the correct drivers are loaded (see Device Manager in Windows XP and Vista computers, or click on "About this Mac: More Info") and confirming the network card is not disabled (see Network Connections in Windows XP, Vista, and Mac computers).

Overall, the process of troubleshooting is a process of elimination. The LMS starts off with simple possibilities and eliminates these factors. Throughout the process, the LMS tries to find one fact that will eliminate an entire grouping of possibilities. This is more efficient than individually eliminating each factor. The LMS tests one possibility at a time and uses the results to determine the next step. Methodically the LMS eliminates possibilities until eventually the LMS discovers the issue or reaches a point where further troubleshooting is either outside his or her technical expertise or impossible given their access to that resource. For example, troubleshooting software configuration on a network switch would require both technical expertise as well as security access. If the LMS lacks either, further troubleshooting is not feasible.

COMMON MAINTENANCE ISSUES

One common complaint is a slow computer. A slow computer may indicate the need to upgrade components such as RAM (random-access memory) or the video card as discussed later in this chapter. Or, it may indicate the computer is nearing its natural life cycle. If the computer is newer and does not meet the this criteria, there is a good chance the computer needs maintenance.

Managing LMC computers requires a regular maintenance plan. At regular intervals, the LMS should check for unnecessary software programs because they take up hard drive space. As the hard drive fills, this limits the ability of the OS to use the hard drive as virtual RAM. In addition, the LMS should check for disk fragmentation. The hard drive spins as the computer reads or writes data to the hard drive. New files are written to the hard drive where there is empty space. On a fuller hard drive with little free space, files may need to be split and stored in many different locations. Also, over time through the process of installing and uninstalling programs your hard drive will have gaps of free spaces instead of contiguous blocks. The solution is to defragment the hard drive. Operating systems provide a tool to do this.

In addition to taking up hard drive space, extra programs may have components that are loaded into the computer's memory (RAM), even if those programs are not currently in use. This happens because certain components of the program may be set to load at start-up. If a sluggish computer has programs installed that indeed are not used and not necessary, uninstalling those programs can free up RAM, which will improve overall performance.

New computers arrive with many different programs; while some programs are needed by the LMS, others are simply trials or limited functionality versions of a program. The software vendor hopes that the user will decide to purchase or upgrade these programs, in which case the computer hardware vendor may receive a commission. In other cases, the computer hardware vendor may receive a fee upfront for including the software in their package to end users. Such marketing partnerships between computer hardware vendors and software companies ultimately lower the costs of computers by providing hardware vendors with an additional stream of revenue besides the actual profit on selling the computer. As an end user, the LMS should understand this relationship, and on receiving new computers, identify and uninstall programs users do not need that ultimately may hamper the performance of the computer. The freeware programs Revo Uninstaller (www.revouninstaller.com), PC Decrapifier (www.pcdecrapifier.com), AppCleaner (www.freemacsoft.net), and low-cost AppZapper for Macs (www.appzapper.com) can help LMSs in this process.

Malicious Hardware and Software

In servicing LMC computers, the LMS should ensure that malicious hardware and software is not installed on LMC computers. This section explores malicious hardware and software. Understanding how this software works can help ensure that computers remain operational and user privacy is protected.

Sniffers

A sniffer or network packet analyzer is software or hardware that runs on the network, seeking and intercepting network traffic. Many Web sites require users to enter usernames and passwords. In the process, the user sends this information over the network from his or her computer to the intended Web site. If the LMS types in data on a network where a cracker (a malicious hacker) is running sniffing software to intercept network traffic, this can lead to compromised passwords. This section is not meant to promote these tools but rather to inform the LMS of their existence.

Ace Password Sniffer by EffeTech Sniffer is a software program that can be used by a cracker to monitor network traffic, looking for usernames and passwords. Using a graphical user interface (GUI), the program listens for any potential usernames and passwords and displays them on the screen. The program captures usernames and passwords when users type them into a nonsecure Web site. A Web site accessed using hypertext transfer protocol (HTTP) is unsecure, whereas one accessed using hypertext transfer protocol over secure socket layer (HTTPS) is a secure site. Thus, the LMS should never enter sensitive information on a site that does not use HTTPS.

Ace Password Sniffer can also capture passwords when users use Outlook or a similar program to receive mail using the Post Office Protocol version 3 (POP3) or to send e-mail using the simple mail transfer protocol (SMTP). Therefore, the LMS should set up Outlook for use with Microsoft Exchange instead of through POP3 if given a choice. Finally, the program can capture passwords from file transfer protocol (FTP) sessions, so the LMS should always use secure FTP sessions.

Ace Password Sniffer is one of many programs that can detect passwords. A similar program, 1Passwd for Macs, keeps needed passwords. Others include dsniff, a collection of tools created for network auditing but that have the potential to be used maliciously to obtain usernames and passwords. In addition to programs that capture usernames and passwords, other sniffer programs such as AIM Sniffer or MSN Sniffer capture chat messages sent over the network. Mac users can download the following sniffer programs: EavesDrop, MacSniffer, and Ettercap.

Keystroke Loggers

Keystroke loggers, also known as key loggers, capture and record all keystrokes. Users can accomplish keystroke logging through hardware or software. Actual Spy is an example of a software keystroke logging program a user can install on LMC PC computers. Keylogger and Perfect Keylogger support Mac OS. Such programs capture keystrokes, Web sites visited, printing activity, and more. In addition, the installer can configure the program to send activity reports though e-mail as well as send reports to a specified site through FTP. Such programs can run in stealth mode; however they are detectable with Spyware program scans, such as Spybot-Search & Destroy (www.safer-networking.org/it/home/index.html).

Individuals install spyware software to gather information about the user, such as Web sites visited. Often users are unaware that spyware has been installed on their computers. When using a public computer, the LMS should understand the potential for keystroke logging software to be present and should avoid any activity that would provide the installer of the logging software sensitive data, such as a username or password. In addition, the LMS should install spyware detection software on LMC computers. This action will help ensure that no malicious software collects information from LMC users.

With hardware keystroke logging, a small device is usually inserted between the computer's PS/2 port where the keyboard is typically plugged in. Then the installer inserts the keyboard into the other end. The keystroke logger records user data. Any data the user types first passes through the keystroke logger before reaching the computer. The user of the computer is generally unaware that his or her keystrokes are being recorded because the typical user does not inspect the back of the computer for keystroke loggers before sitting down to use a computer.

In addition to keystroke loggers that plug into the PS/2 port between the computer and the keyboard, individuals can purchase keystroke loggers that are built directly into the keyboard. Some Web sites sell keystroke logging keyboards disguised as name-brand keyboards so the keyboard will not appear out of place. In the past, to access the data the installer of the keystroke logger needed to return to the computer and remove the keystroke logger. However, modern Bluetooth technology has lead to the invention of wireless Bluetooth keystroke loggers whose logs can be accessed remotely from a distance.

Viruses and Virus Definitions

To best protect computers from viruses, it is important to regularly update virus definitions. Microsoft defines computer viruses as "small software programs that are designed to spread from one computer to another and to interfere with computer operation" (Microsoft Security, 2008). LMC computers, like other public computers, are especially vulnerable to viruses due to the large number of users accessing the same computer. A computer can obtain a virus through e-mail messages and through files on Web sites. Malicious users can hide viruses in software installation programs. A common source of viruses is previously infected files brought to the computer from another computer. For example, patrons may inadvertently bring in viruses from infected home computers. With the large scale availability of USB flash drives, online storage, and networked computers, it is easy to transport files from one computer to another, facilitating the spread of viruses.

On essential library computers such as those used to circulate library materials, the LMS should consider preventative policies to limit potential exposure to viruses. For instance, since viruses are often passed through e-mail, especially through attachments, library staff might be required to use another computer to access their e-mail. As users visit Web sites on the Internet, they are actually downloading files to their computer, which is another way a virus can spread. Thus, essential computers should not be used for Internet surfing. Most important, install antivirus software on all LMC computers.

Antivirus programs detect viruses and attempt to delete or quarantine them to prevent further spread and harm to both the computer and other computers. Modern day antivirus programs use virus definition files as they actively scan open files to check for threats. A virus definition file is a listing of known viruses; antivirus software companies regularly discover new viruses and thus release new definition files. Outdated virus definition files put computers at risk, as the antivirus program cannot identify viruses it is unaware of. Thus, it is important to ensure not only that antivirus software is installed but that the computer is set to update its virus definitions regularly.

In addition to detection of viruses using definition files, more sophisticated antivirus programs use heuristics: a rule-based approach to detect new viruses. This approach works especially well with variants of already known viruses. Once a computer is infected, a common strategy of viruses is to prevent the computer from receiving additional updates, which helps protect the virus from being discovered by the user. If the system's virus definitions are out of date and will not update, but the virus definition subscription is up to date, this may be an indication that the computer has a virus. To troubleshoot, the antivirus software needs to be uninstalled and then reinstalled. The LMS should update the definitions and then run a complete scan of the computer to look for viruses.

Software Changes

As discussed earlier in the chapter, as computer hardware advances, software engineers develop more sophisticated programs that take advantage of these advances. The end effect is that programmers are able to provide new features and enhance user experiences. Operating systems release service packs, and manufacturers release updates to software. A good example is Web browsers, such as Internet Explorer. Each version of Internet Explorer has provided new features to the user. For example, one user enhancement in Internet Explorer 7 was the ability of users to open tabbed windows. In addition, each new version of Internet Explorer adds compatibility with more codes and commands that Web designers can use on their sites.

Some individuals upgrade software whenever one is available, especially in the case of free updates such as with Internet Explorer. Others upgrade when new features or compatibility issues provide compelling reasons to do so. More passive users adopt the newer software out of convenience. Cautious users may update only when the existing software does not support files from other users with new versions of the program; as more users adopt the newer version, it becomes accepted by the general public. As this happens, Web designers take advantage of new programming opportunities compatible with that browser version in order to improve the user's experience. In order to view the page properly, users may be required to download an update. This can further speed user acceptance of a new software version.

Over time, newer software and programming can challenge processing capacities of older computers. Users running newer software on older computers may find the computer feels sluggish. Most software programs list both minimum and recommend requirements. Eventually, older computers may become so outdated that users are not able to install the latest software because the computer no longer meets the minimum requirements for that software. At this point, the LMS must decide whether to upgrade or simply replace the computer. Even if minimum requirements are satisfied, installing software on a computer that does not meet the recommended requirements for that software can lead to a sluggish computer.

Based on the dynamics discussed earlier, it should a foregone conclusion that over time existing computers will no longer meet the needs of users. Large companies regularly replace computers every two to four years. For many schools, this is not a realistic timetable due to budgetary constraints. Thus, schools may stretch out replacement of computers for much longer periods of time, especially if the computer is used for simple tasks such as Web site browsing and word processing.

In such cases, upgrading the computers can improve performance and decrease user frustration. One of the most common upgrades is increasing memory. Adding more RAM is a quick upgrade many users can do on their own, and numerous Web sites and computer repair books provide guidance. If storage space is an issue, most desktops have room for a second hard drive, which the LMS can install. However, creating a shared drive on the network, discussed in Chapter 4, is probably a better solution to increasing storage space. Another easy installation is upgrading the graphics card. A new graphics card that has more memory can enable the computer to better handle video, animation, and graphics. It can also enable the LMS to upgrade to a better computer display with a higher resolution.

Updating Plug-Ins

One aspect of maintenance is the regular installation of computer updates. Microsoft and Apple regularly release updates for their current operating systems (OS). In addition to increased functionality, these updates often address security issues discovered after the initial release of the software. Besides the OS, other programs on the computer have available updates that the LMS should install. Adobe regularly releases updates to its widely used freeware program Adobe Reader. Java and Flash are two examples of plug-ins with regularly released software updates. A plug-in is software that is used in combination with another software program to increase functionality, such as plug-ins for Web browsers. If a Web site utilizes the latest in Flash technology and the Web browser has not been updated, this situation can impact how the Web site functions and appears within the Web browser.

Third-party vendors release updates to the drivers of components within the computer, such as the computer's network and graphics card. A driver is software that allows hardware to interface with the computer's operating system. Driver updates are software improvements that seek to improve how components of the computer function, whether the components are internal such as a graphics card or peripheral devices such as an external DVD drive.

Program Updates

In maintaining LMC computers, the LMS must decide if software features benefit the LMC program. The LMS should install software only if it addresses a need, resolves an issue, or provides a desired functionality. LMSs need to be careful not to inadvertently install programs or unnecessary features. When installing software, often there is a choice for an easy installation and an advanced installation. LMSs should select the advanced installation. This option provides the LMS with more choices with regard to what is installed, where it is installed, and how it is installed. Advanced installations may help the LMS discover components of the software that are unnecessary and that will only slow down the computer's operation. Thus, it is important for the LMS to read all prompts and understand what he or she is installing.

Software updates may attempt to install new software in addition to updating existing software. In such cases, the company may be using a popular and well-known program to promote successful distribution of another program. For example, Sun Microsystems, distributor of the Java Runtime Environment, struck a multiyear distribution deal with Google in 2005. As part of the new distribution partnership, users downloading Sun's Java Runtime program from Sun's Web site also received Google Toolbar, an add-in program for Web browsers. John Loiacono, who at the time of the deal was Sun's Executive Vice President of Software, was quoted as saying, "There is direct monetary value for us from being a distribution mechanism for the toolbar" (Shankland, 2005).

For such reasons, LMSs need to pay attention to installation prompts. Currently, the toolbar program is installed by default when installing Java, although users do have the option of unchecking the box. However, many LMSs are used to clicking through install prompts without much regard to the content (yes, I agree, yes, yes, etc.). In the previous example, the LMS would miss the opportunity to make an informed decision regarding the additive value of Google toolbar to the library media program. Not to say that the Google toolbar does not have additive value; rather, it is an example of a program that the typical LMS could unknowingly install on a LMC computer. It serves as a reminder to LMSs to read all installation prompts and make informed decisions when installing software.

SERVICING

Technology servicing can be done in-house (site or district) or outsourced; again, several factors must be taken into consideration in deciding how to proceed. In-house servicing is more physically convenient and the person knows the technology situation better, although the technician may be overworked or give the LMC a lower priority than other departments. The LMS needs to find out the technician's level of expertise for different types of products and services in order to have realistic expectations about the work to be done. Typically, no separate cost is attached to in-house work, although if done at the district level, the service may be billed to the site or the library. It should be noted that in-house technicians might not have the needed supply on hand and may have to order it, which can take time and a purchase order.

Many companies provide technical services, and their cost and expertise vary wildly. At the least, technicians should have appropriate credentials, such as Cisco Certified Network Associate. School districts may contract their technical service work out, usually based on bid. Agreements usually include a retainer fee that the company gets regardless of the amount of work as well as a per service fee. In some cases, a turnaround time is stipulated in order to avoid delays. If the company has several other clients, they might not provide speedy service. Hopefully, the outsourcing company works enough with the district and site that they can get to know the system and the people and feel a personal responsibility toward their client. One of the advantages of an outsourced company is that they are more likely to have the supplies and parts needed to take care of the problem.

Technicians can now service many computers remotely. For a computer to be accessed remotely it must be on the intranet or Internet. For instance, when off-site district technicians support LMC computers with a properly configured computer, these technicians can use remote access to take control of a computer, perform regular maintenance, and help resolve problems. In the business world, users sometimes use remote access when away from the office to access needed files off their computer. There are remote access applications for both Windows-based and Mac-based computers. For Apple, programs like Timbuktu Pro can be used to remotely connect to and control a Mac-based computer from another Mac-based computer. If the goal is to connect to a Windows-based computer from a Mac-based computer, the Remote Desktop Connection Client for Mac is offered for free and can be used.

On Windows-based computers, Remote Desktop Connection (RDC) is available by default with some versions of Windows, such as Windows XP Professional. Other versions may require a free download of the software. For remote access to work, the Remote Desktop Connection software must be installed on the computer that will be used to control other computers. In addition, on any computer the LMS or technician will control, the Remote Desktop client must be installed. Then, with the proper credentials (username and password for remote computer being accessed), users may control another Windows-based computer remotely. If outside of the network, border firewalls often will prevent remote desktop from working. Chapter 7 discusses border firewalls in more detail.

Regardless of the type of service used, the LMS should create and maintain a service log, noting on the log whenever LMC equipment receives servicing. The log should note the date the LMS reports the issue as well as the date the issue was resolved. It should also include the cost of repair, which would include shipping charges even if the item was under warranty. The log can help the LMS make effective management decisions. For instance, over the life cycle of the device, the LMS will collect the total service cost for that item. The LMS can then extrapolate that data and group by category. This will provide the LMS with the average service cost per type of equipment, be it a computer or television.

With this data, the LMS can make informed decisions about purchasing service contracts and warranties when acquiring new equipment for the LMC. If technology is supported locally through an on-site technician, the LMS can use this data to have accurate expectations for repair of existing equipment. In addition, the LMS can provide this data to stakeholders if the evidence points to the need for additional technical support. If the LMS notices trends with a particular model of equipment, the LMS can be proactive in planning.

For example, the LMS might be responsible for distributing laptop carts for classroom use, say, a total of five carts, each with a networked laser printer. For three of the carts, the LMS notices from the service log that the printer's network card suddenly failed. Considering this part already failed on a majority of the printers, the LMS can be proactive and order one additional network card as a spare. Then, if another network card fails (as expected) it can be replaced immediately, whereas if the LMS did not pre-order the component for the printer, then functionality would be unavailable until the part was acquired and replaced.

WORKS CITED

Bing. 2009. "SyncToy 2.0." Microsoft Corporation. Available: www.microsoft.com/DownLoads/details.aspx?familyid=C26EFA36-98E0-4EE9-A7C598D0592D8C52&displaylang=en (accessed January 17, 2009).

Carheden, Andrew. 2005. "Disk Imaging Tools: Install, Clone, Manage." Windows ITPro, May. Available: http://windowsitpro.com/article/articleid/45890/disk-imaging-tools-install-clone%20manage.html (accessed January 16, 2009).

Edmondson, Ray. 2004. *Audiovisual Archiving: Philosophy and Principles.* Paris: UNESCO.

Library of Congress. 2002. Preservation: Cylinder, Disc and Tape Care in a Nutshell. Washington, DC: Library of Congress. Available: www.loc.gov/preserv/Care/record.html#Storage (accessed July 7, 2009).

Microsoft Security. 2008. "What Is a Computer Virus?" Microsoft Corporation, November 18. Available: www.microsoft.com/protect/Computer/Basics/virus.mspx (accessed March 23, 2009).

Rhoades, Gale. 2007. "Tips for a Healthy PC." *Key Words* 15, no. 2 (April/June): 53–55.

Shade, Daniel D. 1996. "Care and Cleaning of Your Computer." *Computers and Young Children* 23, no. 1 (March): 165–168.

Shankland, Stephen. 2005. "Sun and Google Shake Hands." CBS Interactive, October 4. Available: http://news.cnet.com/Sun-and-Google-shake-hands/2100-1014_35888701.html?tag=mncol;txt (accessed January 10, 2009).

Wayne, Richard. 2005. "PC Management Software." *Computers in Libraries* 25, no. 2 (February): 37–45.
Windows. 2008. "What Is Windows SteadyState?" Microsoft Corporation. Available: www.microsoft.com/windows/products/winfamily/sharedaccess/whatis/default.mspx_(accessed January 9, 2009).

Chapter 5

Space Planning and Management for Technology

Space impacts teaching and learning, whether that space is explicitly considered or not. Indeed, educator John Dewey stated back in 1933 that "whether we permit chance environments to do the work or whether we design environments for the purpose makes a great difference" (p. 22), asserting that educational settings are better served by specificity rather than serendipity. With the advent of the Internet, and more specifically Web 2.0, education is impacted dramatically. Students engage daily in online social networking but may feel isolated physically from their peers. They may also feel disconnected from schools where mobile devices are banned and the learning environment resembles the nineteenth century more than the twenty-first. Library media centers (LMC) need to provide technology-rich learning spaces that bridge these different needs.

Yet rarely do library media specialists (LMSs) have the opportunity to build an LMC from the ground up. Even in cases of brand new LMCs, often the district dictates construction design, and deficiencies can exist in new facilities regardless of the contractor. As with most building construction projects, school architects design LMCs to meet existing needs at the time. When the LMS inherits LMC facilities built in the past, often the design can present challenges for supporting twenty-first century LMC technology.

This chapter begins by exploring the physical facilities needed to effectively manage LMC technology. This includes facilities for patrons to use technology as well as places to store LMC technology.

Because much of the technology managed by LMSs is expensive, desirable, and portable, this chapter also addresses security of space for technology. While nineteenth and twentieth century buildings can feel limiting in the twenty-first century, creative use of networking technologies can enhance how LMSs manage technology and allow the LMC to reach beyond its physical space. Thus, this chapter concludes with an exploration of how computer networks operate, and Chapter 7 discusses how to use computer networks to manage technologies for communications.

THE BIG PICTURE: LEARNING SPACES

Brown (2005) defines learning spaces as spaces that encompass the full range of places in which learning occurs, from real to virtual, from classroom to chat room. Contemporary design of learning spaces builds on an educational philosophy of active and social learning. This approach starts with the student learner, examines desired outcomes, and plans the physical conditions for an optimum learning environment. Keeping in mind instruction and learning style variances, learning spaces are designed to provide differentiated areas and grouping arrangements. In addition, items within these environments should support modification and customization to reflect users' interests and needs (Cannon, 1988).

Rather than seeing the library as a room with four walls, LMSs should think about the LMC as a flexible, open-ended physical and virtual learning environment that permeates not only the entire campus but providing space for lifelong learning anytime and anywhere. Scott-Webber (2004) identified five distinct types of environments to support knowledge sharing, which can be applied to library settings be they physical or virtual:

1. Environments for delivering knowledge (e.g., library instructional classrooms, library portals)
2. Environments for applying knowledge (e.g., library tutoring centers, library repositories)
3. Environments for creating knowledge (e.g., library production areas)
4. Environments for communicating knowledge (e.g., library presentation areas, library social networking venues)

5. Environments for decision making (e.g., library conference rooms, library surveys and wikis)

What might constitute an effective interactive e-learning space? Kaplan and Kaplan (1982) suggest four criteria for engaging physical spaces: coherence (cognitive organization), complexity (capacity to interest and stimulate activity), legibility (ease of use), and mystery/element of surprise (stimulate interest and interaction). These criteria also fit e-learning spaces: coherent content and "packaging," rich content and tools, ease of us, and novel features, particularly incorporating social networking.

In LMCs, technology plays a key role, both in terms of providing resources as well as integrating personal technology devices. Learning spaces also acknowledge the importance of virtual space and try to meld the virtual and the physical. Trends in incorporating technology into library learning spaces include ubiquitous wifi, technology tools for group work and collaboration, and discipline-specific technology tools (Oblinger, 2006).

It should be noted that although technology can enrich the library education experience, in itself it can distract from learning. With the instructor at the front of the class, students may well be tempted to play solitaire or check their e-mail on laptops. Students who are not tech-savvy may feel frustrated if they are required to use a sophisticated online application without teacher support. The issue is not physical space, per se, but rather an instructional concern. Nevertheless, LMSs need to pay attention to technology's presence in physical space as they design engaging learning experiences.

FACILITIES

While the LMC should extend beyond the four walls, it needs to start within them. Several facility factors affect technology use: room environment power, location, furniture, and storage. These elements need to be addressed even before the hardware arrives.

Utilities and Safety

The basic room itself and the associated utilities impact technology use. Carpeting minimizes sound, but it can also increase electric conductivity. Therefore, static control mats should be placed in high use areas such as the circulation desk. Adequate ventilation is needed to maintain temperature and minimize dust; computers should be placed away from windows and doors to avoid dust and dirt as well as light glare. The temperature should remain between 55 and 65° F, and the humidity should stay between 45 and 55 percent. Ambient light should be glare-free, and the LMS should be able to control its brightness locally. In preparation for emergencies, smoke detectors should be installed and tested regularly. Fire extinguishers for both chemical and paper fires should also be handy, and they should be checked yearly. LMSs should also learn how to use extinguishers, since quick action can save lives as well as facilities.

In addition, the location of power supplies and network ports can have a huge impact on how the LMC is organized, what technology the library can purchase, and where patrons will utilize LMC technology. For example, desktop computers, printers, and networkable copy machines need network ports in addition to electrical outlets, which constrains where the LMS can place these items.

The LMS needs to become acquainted with applicable safety codes and regulations. For example, regulations that require minimum clearance levels around doors or that require shelves and cabinets to be strapped to the wall, a common requirement in earthquake prone areas of the country. For equipment requiring electricity such as a copy machine, the device usually must be within reach of an existing outlet; utilizing an extension cord on a permanent basis is not permitted. Most school libraries were built before large-scale technology, so LMSs need to review the power supply in the library. Some obvious questions follow.

- Is there enough power for all of the technology in the library, and is the power reliable? Are additional outlets needed? Are there enough fuse boxes or circuit breakers?
- Do power supply and access meet OSHA (Occupational Safety and Health Administration) standards?
- Is voltage regulated at the building level?
- Is wiring accessible through conduits or other tracks?
- Are dedicated lines available for photocopiers and servers?
- Is there also a backup system for the site as well as smaller

power backup systems and surge protection within the library?

Someone on site is responsible for addressing these safety issues. It may be a school administrator, the school plant manager, or a teacher or coordinator designated as the safety coordinator. LMSs can work with this individual to ensure that the LMC is in compliance with all safety codes and regulations.

Standards

Many state school library associations have developed facility standards for school LMCs. Such standards can provide the LMS with positive ideas for managing facility space. They can also be an effective tool when advocating with stakeholders for new funding to support LMC technology, such as the purchase of furniture, or to support the enhancement of LMC infrastructure, such as electrical outlets and network ports.

The Massachusetts School Library Media Association (MSL-MA) facilities standards call for an electronic research area large enough to accommodate an entire class, with a ratio of one student per computer at the secondary level and two students per computer at the elementary level. The LMS should ensure that each computer has Internet connectivity and prints to a networked printer. The LMS should arrange all workstations to allow both the LMS and classroom teacher to supervise students as they work on the computers (Massachusetts School Library Media Association, 2003).

A modern goal for every LMC should be enough computers available to support at least one class of students. This area should also provide for instructional technology for the LMS and classroom teacher to use, such as an LCD projector and teacher computer workstation. Ideally, this area is set aside from other sections of the library, thus enabling whole-class instruction to occur in the lab while still providing quiet areas where students can work, study, and read. When arranging computers in an area designed for whole-class instruction, the LMS should ensure each computer is easily accessible so that the LMS can easily and quickly provide students with assistance on the computers as needed. Ideally, expensive equipment will be viewable from locations where the LMS spends considerable time, for instance the library office or circulation desk. Whenever possible, equipment should be arranged to meet this goal. Unfortunately, many facilities will not allow for such placement. In such cases, additional forms of security are essential, as discussed later in this chapter.

In many school districts, providing one computer per student at the secondary level can mean the LMS must acquire 40 or more computers to provide one computer per student in the typical secondary level classroom. Unfortunately, many LMCs do not have the physical space to support this. In such circumstances, the LMS should consider acquiring laptops to meet this goal, which in many ways is a minimum goal instead of the ideal. In addition to computers for whole-class use and student use during breaks and outside of the school day, the LMS may find it useful to have computers in a central area of the library, including a few limited-access computers reserved for functions such as searching the library OPAC (online public access catalog). As LMSs increasingly incorporate digital resources, each student in the class will need a separate computer, and larger LMC facilities that regularly book two or more classes simultaneously while still accommodating individual students should strongly consider the need for even more computers, if not now then in the near future.

Space Allocation

One of the reasons that technology is incorporated into the library is to save space. Many LMSs bemoan the lack of available shelving, to the point that to add another book to the collection the LMS must first weed another book from the collection. In some cases, the LMS may lack space to add more shelving. This can be problematic, especially if the current library collection is not sufficient to meet school, district, or state goals in terms of books per student. In such circumstances, the LMS should focus on managing technology to create a virtual library, offering library resources to patrons outside the walls of the physical library through a virtual or digital library on the Web. Increasingly, LMCs provide online subscription periodicals and reference databases as well as e-books rather than take up valuable space with print versions that quickly become outdated or stolen. Chapter 6 discusses how LMSs can create an LMC Web site to organize resources and communicate with LMC patrons.

It should be noted, though, that technology is not guilt-free in terms of space allocation. Unlike books, which need only a shelf for storage, physical digital resources not only need shelving space but the equipment necessary to use them, which takes up space as well. Desktop stations in particular can be space hogs because they require a table or desk and a working surface large enough to handle the monitor and keyboard as well as the student learning tools, be they paper or mobile devices. Even laptops, which may seem like a smart space solution, require space for their storage when not in use. Complicating the issue is that different technology formats may need unique equipment, such as audiocassette players or microfiche readers. With digital resources, fortunately, such issues are becoming obsolete as digital equipment is able to converge into single systems.

Interior Organization

Location of technology shapes use and ultimately learning. Centralizing hardware may facilitate supervision, but it can also segregate research by format. How do traffic patterns facilitate or impede use? Ideally, the LMC should dedicate different spaces of the facility to different kinds of learning activities and their associated technology. A production area could include several multimedia computers with relevant peripherals (e.g., scanner, printer, or camcorder or digital camera). A conference area might have a video "drop" and recording equipment. A lecture or presentation area would have a multimedia station with Internet connectivity as well as a projection system. Within each area, hardware needs to be considered in terms of supportive furniture, access, and security. For example, some general principles apply to all computer setups:

- Students should look down to the screen, not up.
- Feet should touch the floor.
- Monitors should not have glare on them.

The desktop surface should be at the right height to foster good posture and a 90-degree typing angle. Furthermore, different tasks require different lighting; for example, video viewing requires low lighting, but detailed video editing may require more intense lighting. Overhead projectors need lower light than data projectors.

The circulation desk itself requires special attention. Cords should be out of student reach but accessible to staff for troubleshooting. Desensitizing equipment should also be out of sight. The circulation monitor screen might be useful for students to see, so an angled approach or swinging "arm" may be necessary so that the staff and students can see the screen in turn. At the least, the monitor should be able to swivel to some degree. A good quality power strip, secured to the furniture, enables peripherals and other equipment to be plugged in. Because equipment changes may occur, having modular circulation desk components is handy. The circulation staff should be able to look ahead or down on the monitor, so either the equipment needs to be lower or the staff needs a high, comfortable chair on wheels. At least one OPAC should be located near the circulation desk and near reference. A 42" height enables the user to access the station while standing up. Of course, one station needs to be about 34" high for wheelchair access. Staff should be able to get out from behind easily; they'll appreciate a central swing door in a long counter.

A computer station and a telephone should be located at the reference desk to facilitate quick fact retrieval as well as library catalog guidance. A photocopier in the reference area facilitates in-house use of restricted materials. Other terminals should be available to users in the reference area to support the idea of information access across media. Of course, each piece of equipment needs adequate space, lighting, electrical power, and security.

Terminals used for studying need to be placed alongside open work space. Because of radiation emissions, the backs of monitors should not be close to students. Placing the backs of monitors against the wall is the best solution. Additionally, stations should not impede traffic flow nor block other resources or access to shelving. Terminals should be accessible by all users, so younger students may need lower surfaces, and at least one station should be at a desk that can accommodate wheelchairs.

While technology has the potential to level the educational playing field for all students, it can do so only if facilities are made accessible to all students. The obvious start is traffic flow:

- Can students with physical challenges, particularly wheelchairs, get to the desired equipment?
- Is aisle space at least 36" wide, with 32" between furniture?
- Are technology work areas at least 34" high, with 27" knee clearance?
- Are station tables at least 30" wide and 19" deep?
- Are cables and outlets protected and safely out of the way?
- Are permanent signs about technology between .625" and 2", and do they include braille format?

If possible, LMSs should talk with building managers and technology experts before installing technology. LMSs can network with their peers, comparing notes about successes and failures in terms of facilities accommodating technology. Professional organizations sometimes have workshops on facilities issues run by experts in the field. It is much easier to think about, identify, and deal with these issues ahead of time than to try to solve problems after the technology is in the door. The following sources provide valuable insights into technology requirements with respect to facilities:

- Sannwald, W. 2008. *Checklist of Library Building Design Considerations*, 5th ed. Chicago: American Library Association.
- National Clearinghouse for Educational Facilities, www.edfacilities.org/rl/libraries.cfm.
- American Library Association's Library Technology Reports.

PHYSICAL SECURITY

Chapter 4 focused on supervision and security from the perspective of technology maintenance; for example, the use of lab security software to prevent unauthorized changes or lab management software to supervise proper use. This section focuses on physical security of technology, discussing strategies that LMSs can employ to deter loss. The National Center for Education Statistics defines physical security as "the protection of building sites and equipment (and all information and software contained therein) from theft, vandalism, natural disaster, manmade catastrophes, and accidental damage (e.g., from electrical surges, extreme temperatures, and spilled coffee)" (National Center for Education Statistics, accessed 2009).

Much thought goes into the acquisition of computers: what brand, what specifications, how many, what vendor, what type, what funds, and where to set up and store them. Physical security of equipment deserves similar consideration. However, often LMSs do not give it the same consideration. As the Federal Trade Commission (FTC) writes, nobody "thinks their laptop will be stolen—at least not until they find the trunk of their car broken into, notice that their laptop isn't waiting at the other side of airport security, or get a refill at the local java joint only to turn around and find their laptop gone" (Federal Trade Commission, 2007).

The first consideration in security is the physical security of the building itself. An intrusion alarm system that provides an audible alarm can scare off burglars. In addition, a monitoring service can receive the alarm notification and dispatch police. If the room contains outside facing windows, the LMS should consider having bars installed on the windows. Some LMC facilities may include separate rooms, including a library workroom, equipment storage room, main library area, conference rooms, and a separate computer lab. All external doors should have locks, and the LMS should ensure that access is limited. The equipment storage room and the room housing the computers (if applicable) should have separate locks, and again access should be limited.

Video monitoring systems are a popular approach to prevent theft and vandalism. Closed circuit television (CCTV) monitoring systems include one or more video cameras connected to a monitor. The monitor allows for remote monitoring of key areas of the LMC such as the exit. With the addition of a security videocassette recorder the LMS has the ability to record surveillance. A security videocassette recorder is a specialized cassette recorder that automatically rewinds at the end of the cassette and then begins recording again, providing a video recording solution with little maintenance. Even better, a digital video recorder (DVR) security system provides the ability to record content in a digital format, which can result in a better quality recording. In addition, digital storage devices can increase total recording time capacity over the recording capacity of a videocassette while taking up less physical space. Digital storage devices also provide the benefit of being able to increase the storage capacity as needed through the acquisition of additional hard drives or by replacing the existing hard drive with a higher capacity hard drive.

DVR security systems with a network card and appropriate software can automatically forward recordings to a remote location. This functionality provides remote access and also ensures that if the DVR security system is stolen, backup recordings forwarded to the remote location will still be available. Wired or wireless network security cameras in conjunction with a computer and software can also provide remote monitoring and recording. For example, D-Link's D-ViewCam 2.0 (www.dlink.com/products/d-viewcam20/) is included with D-link network cameras. Using this software, the LMS can manage up to 32 network cameras at once.

Many school districts have established policies regarding the use of video monitoring equipment. LMSs should ensure that planned expenditures for such monitoring equipment comply with such policies. Often, the threat of video surveillance is enough to deter theft and vandalism. Thus, LMSs may want to consider investing in fake security cameras. A number of vendors sell fake cameras, which will often include features meant to further convince observers the camera is real, such as a motion sensor feature that causes the camera to move.

In addition to monitoring and recording devices, the LMS can purchase security hardware to anchor desktop computers to desks, tables, or walls. Typical security hardware includes a cable, lock, and metal anchors or brackets. Anchoring methods vary, but most require the LMS to attach an anchor to the computer using a strong adhesive that resists tampering. The cable routes through the anchor. The computer case is the most expensive piece to replace as it contains all internal components of the computer, including the motherboard, central processing unit (CPU), hard drive(s), optical drive(s), and random access memory (RAM). While using a cable to attach the computer case to a wall or heavy piece of furniture makes it harder to remove, a determined thief, given enough time, can usually find a solution. Like a house alarm, a cable is not a guarantee against theft. That said, hopefully the security hardware provides enough of a deterrence that the thief will look elsewhere.

Ideally, the security cable will contain a bracket to secure all peripheral cables such as the keyboard and mouse. Peripheral devices are much smaller and thus easier to conceal in a bag or backpack. Thus, while not as expensive as the computer case, the likelihood of someone stealing a peripheral device is much higher. For this reason the LMS should purchase security cables with a design that also secures peripheral devices. In addition, the LMS must secure the cover to the computer case. To deter theft, the LMS can replace Phillips and Slotted screws with Allen, Torx, or another less common screw type.

Ever more difficult to secure are laptops, which present unique management challenges when it comes to security. Laptops are small and built to be portable. Users can easily hide a laptop in a backpack. Every modern-day laptop comes with a special Kensington security slot. Using a compatible lock, users wrap the cable around a fixed object and then lock the cable into the laptop, which makes it more difficult for someone to pick up and walk out with it. Many LMCs have long rectangular tables. Usually, the only place to wrap the cord on such tables is the around one of the four table legs. However, this is not a very good solution as someone can simply lift a table leg to remove the cord from the table. Thus, the lock will not prevent theft, only deter.

Laptops run on batteries so they constantly require charging. The LMS needs a place where the laptops can securely charge. A locking laptop cart is essential for this purpose, as it provides a secure location to lock the laptops while at the same time allowing them to recharge. Each laptop should be numbered and have a reserved place in the laptop cart. This will assist the LMS in quickly identifying which laptop is missing.

Even if the LMS institutes a number of theft-deterrent measures, it is still possible that a thief may steal an LMC computer, either during school hours or when the LMC is closed. Adeona (adeona.cs.washington.edu) is a free program that the LMS can install on computers. Adeona tracks computer locations so it can be used to locate a stolen computer. During the Adeona installation process, the LMS picks a password. At the end of the installation process, the program creates a file containing the selected password in an encrypted format. The LMS saves this file to another computer. After installation, the computer will secretly contact the Adeona server to regularly provide location updates. One drawback is that the computer uses the Internet to communicate location updates to Adeona, so the program works only if the user connects to the Internet. In the case of theft, the LMS uses the file created during the installation process to locate the computer and provide this information to local authorities. According to the Web site, the program was "designed to protect against the common thief—for example, a thief that opportunistically decides to swipe your laptop from a coffee shop or your dorm room and then wants to use it or perhaps sell it on online" (Adeona, accessed 2009). Note that reformatting the hard drive erases Adeona, which is one way to defeat the program's purpose.

For a more comprehensive solution, Absolute Software Corporation, the leading commercial provider of theft recovery software, sells Computrace Complete (www.absolute.com/computracecomplete/laptop-tracking.asp). Computrace Complete works by installing a small software agent on the hard drive. Once a day, provided the computer is on the Internet, the software agent secretly contacts Absolute Software's Monitoring Center. According to the company, the computer "reports location, user, hardware and software information" and the administrator can "track and manage your computer assets, including remote/mobile computers, using reports, alerts and administration functions from the secure Customer Center website" (Absolute Software, 2010).

Even better, Absolute Software Corporation has partnered with a number of computer manufacturers who ship computers with a special feature in the computer's basic input/output system (BIOS). When activated as part of the install process for the Computrace Complete software, the Computrace BIOS module rebuilds the Computrace software agent on the hard drive if it is accidently or intentionally deleted. Thus, even if the user reformats the hard drive, the security is not defeated. As with other programs, the user still needs to connect to the Internet, otherwise the program cannot communicate location updates. If the user is aware of the specific security tool in use and has the necessary technical expertise, Internet searches can lead to sites providing removal instructions that claim to eliminate or defeat the security tool.

Many LMSs install book theft detection systems in the LMC. Most work with radio frequency (RF) or electromagnetic (EM) technology. LMSs often use these book theft detection systems to secure mobile technology as well. For instance, fake bar codes containing a RF tag are available for purchase and can be adhered to portable technology. If a user tries to remove a laptop from the LMC the RF tag will trigger an alarm. While nothing prevents a user from removing the tag, using such techniques can complement other security approaches, providing redundancy when one method fails.

Often the LMS wants technology to be visible in order to help promote it. For instance, DVDs generate more use if out on display rather than being stored away for security purposes. When a piece of technology is too small for a security tag or placing a tag on the device is not a viable option, security cases can help. These cases contain a locking mechanism that requires a special key or detacher to unlock. Without the special key or detacher, the user is not able to open the case, rendering the DVD or other piece of technology unusable. Thus, it deters theft as the potential thief gains no economic benefit from stealing the item. For extra security, a security tag can be placed on the inside of the case. To prevent users from discovering the tag, the LMS can purchase labels to apply over the tag. Avery makes a number of label shapes and sizes that the LMS can use to create custom labels.

Some items may require storage behind the circulation desk or in an equipment or work room. This is true especially with equipment that is both expensive and portable. For example, the LMS needs a secure place to charge camcorder batteries. The LMS may store equipment that is small and fairly sturdy in ziplock bags: for example, one freezer size ziplock bag to store each microphone the LMC owns. As discussed in Chapter 3, the LMS should number the bags, along with the microphones, so at any time the LMS can look at the empty bags and determine how many and which microphones are circulating. This practice is easier than looking at bar codes or, even worse, serial numbers. All of the bagged microphones can then be stored in tubs.

If a ziplock bag is not practical due to size, the LMS can purchase storage containers, which come in various sizes. The LMS should pick the container just large enough for the piece of equipment in order to maximize overall storage space. Containers with lids help ensure that parts do not accidently fall out and allow the LMS to stack containers. Many LMSs prefer clear containers as this allows for easy viewing of the container's contents. Once in containers, the items store nicely on shelves or in cupboards. To ensure security, wherever these containers are stored, the LMS needs to limit access. For example, it would not be a good idea to simply place the container of microphones on shelves in the library stacks. If there are no shelves in a lockable workroom or equipment room, the LMS can purchase lockable storage carts to provide a secure storage location.

For fragile equipment that users will take outside the LMC, the LMS should provide special carrying cases and bags designed specifically for the item. Sample items include laptops, digital projectors, cameras, and camcorders. For large or heavy equipment such as projectors and televisions being used on campus, the LMS should provide a rolling cart. The LMS should securely affix the device to the cart to prevent the item from falling off and becoming damaged, or, even worse, injuring the user. This practice also ensures the equipment remains with the cart. Special straps and cables are available for this purpose. In addition, zip ties can prevent cords from disappearing. For example, on a television/VCR rolling cart, a zip tie can connect the television power cord, VCR power cord, and any audio and video cords to one another as well as to the rolling cart. This procedure makes it impossible to take a cord without first cutting the zip tie and can discourage casual theft.

SUPERVISION

Supervision of students as they utilize computer resources can be problematic in many LMCs. As discussed at the beginning of the chapter, facilities built prior to the widespread use of computers or without proper planning for layout of computers present management challenges for the LMS. Availability of power outlets may limit where the LMS can install new computers. Positioning desktop screens so that all are facing outward, facilitating access and monitoring, may not be feasible given the available facilities.

One common need is the ability to reserve computers and lock out unauthorized users. Using computer management software, a centralized staff member at the circulation or reference desk can grant patron access to a particular computer. In addition, with many computer management programs users can self-authenticate using their library ID card. PC Reservation by Envisionware (www.

envisionware.com), SAM Professional by Comprise Technologies, (www.comprisetechnologies.com), cross-platform RMIAdmin (www.topshareware.com/RMIAdmin-%5BMAC-OS-X%5D-download-39889.htm), and Apple Remote Desktop (www.apple.com/remotedesktop) exemplify this type of computer management software.

Another management issue is controlling usage of consumables, such as printer ink and paper. A software program can be used to track and release print jobs. While this process usually requires a dedicated printer computer, the cost-benefits can be worth it. Increasingly, schools are using prepaid cards or other payment mechanisms to decrease printing costs and make the user responsible for printouts. Of course, if the network permits users to e-mail or download files, then printing can be further reduced.

Schools demand that students are on-task during school hours. Computers in this regard are like a double-edged sword. Computers provide definite benefits in allowing students to access resources previously unavailable and presenting information in more engaging and accessible formats to students. At the same time, computers link students to online games and a myriad of engaging Web sites not related to the task at hand. Even Microsoft Paint can provide hours of diversion to students wanting to avoid school-related work. Students who lack academic motivation, students with learning disabilities, students with language and other access barriers, and students with a history of failure within the school system may practice avoidance by using technology in nonacademic ways.

Therefore, for the LMC to have a positive impact on student achievement, the LMS must work with classroom teachers to ensure that technology promotes student achievement rather than distracts students from working. Monitoring student displays assists the LMS in identifying students that need more assistance or that may be off-task. In addition, the school district will have an acceptable use policy (AUP) in place that all computer users are required to follow. Administrators expect that all staff regularly supervise student use of computers to ensure compliance with the AUP.

Students may not always follow AUPs when utilizing library media program computers. They may use Web proxies to bypass content filters or access Web content that the school or district has determined inappropriate within a school environment. In other cases, the school or district may simply block certain Web resources such as the video-sharing Web site YouTube (www.youtube.com) or other resources because the bandwidth utilized by multiple students accessing such resources simultaneously can challenge and slow down computer networks lacking high capacities. Chapter 7 discusses Web proxies and content filters in more detail. Detecting students who bypass content filters can be important, especially if such usage negatively impacts overall network performance or places the student in danger. However, supervision may be difficult if the LMS cannot easily view student displays.

For these reasons, many LMSs utilize computer management software to monitor and control LMC computers. Computer management software, also known as lab management or classroom management software, is a program that allows for control of computers or printers through a central interface. Typically, the LMS installs a small client program on student computers and then installs the teacher module on the computer used to supervise student computers. These programs enable the LMS to view student displays remotely if physical access to such displays is impractical or inconvenient. Effective use of classroom management software by the LMS may increase student on-task time, thus supporting student achievement. For example, during whole-class instruction, the LMS can lock student computers (prevent them from being used). This process can include blanking the screen or displaying a default message in addition to preventing the keyboard and mouse from functioning. Because students enjoy computers so much, they often get engaged in the computer and can miss class instruction or directions. In blanking screens, content on the computer is not accessible so it does not divert student attention from the lesson.

Computer management software program features vary but most have the ability to lock student computers and broadcast a demonstration to all computer screens. Even a student computer can be used to broadcast information to all computers, which can be used to share positive student work. In addition, typical management software allows the LMS to send files to student computers, collect files from students, log on and off computers, and shut down computers. With lab management software, the LMS can observe all content displayed on student computers. The LMS can view all computers simultaneously in small windows or can pull up a specific computer to view it in full screen. The LMS can take screenshots of the content for later use such as documenting student violations of the AUP. The ability of lab management software programs to remotely monitor and control student displays can be controversial; LMSs must balance ethical issues, such as student privacy, with legal issues and student safety concerns. For instance, students might access Web sites that potentially put them at risk of identity theft or worse. Chapter 7 discusses these issues in greater detail. On the positive side, students may need assistance with using a computer at the same time that the LMS may be unable to leave the circulation desk. Consider the situation where a student is having difficulty printing double-sided, a requirement of their project. The LMS can log in to the computer remotely and take control without leaving the circulation desk.

Lab management software assists the LMS in managing student computers within the context of the instructional program. However, lab management software can also support computer organization and maintenance. For example, through lab management software the LMS can select and log in to multiple computers simultaneously. Performing regular maintenance on LMC computers requires the LMS to log in to each computer using a username and password with administrative rights. Depending on the total number of computers in the LMC, logging in to each computer can take considerable time.

Take for instance a LMC with 45 computers where logging into every computer takes 20 seconds, a reasonable assumption provided the LMS has to move from computer to computer and type in the password. Logging into every computer alone would take 15 minutes. Since computers need to be regularly updated at regular intervals, over the life span of this equipment the LMS could easily spend hours just logging in. Lab management software accomplishes in less than one minute a process that could take much longer.

When utilizing lab management software, a number of management questions arise. Will the LMS notify students and parents about the lab management software? If so, how will the LMS do so? What expectations will there be regarding frequency of monitoring? Will the LMS monitor computers consistently or sporadically? Who will monitor student computers? What is the purpose of the monitoring software (what exactly is monitored)? Who determines the definition of inappropriate content or uses of LMC computers? How will LMC staff address inappropriate content or use of library media computers if discovered?

When budgeting and planning for lab management software, the LMS must determine which computers to utilize when monitoring student computers. For continual monitoring, LMSs might consider utilizing dual computer screens with one computer. By extending the desktop onto the second screen, the computer will be able to display two full-sized windows simultaneously. The circulation program (or whatever normally runs on the computer) can appear on the first screen and the lab management software on the second. The mouse can traverse between the two screens as if they were one larger screen. This functionality permits continuous monitoring while avoiding the need to purchase a second computer to provide that function. If the existing computer is not capable of supporting dual displays, replacing the computer's graphic card might be a good solution since video cards with dual video out are readily available.

The features of each lab management program vary, but most these vendors offer free trials or demos. Trial testing allows the LMS to download, install, and test a wide range of lab management products in real life applications before making an informed purchasing decision. Some products (student computers) are priced based on the total number of clients controlled. Other products base pricing on the total number of teacher modules (such as computers used as control devices). Listed here are representative vendors and their lab management programs that can remotely control computers:

- AB Consulting (www.abconsulting.com): AB Tutor
- Apple (www.apple.com/remotedesktop): Apple Remote Desktop
- Computers by Design (www.cybraryn.com): CybraryN
- GenevaLogic (www.genevalogic.com): Vision
- Hi Resolution Systems (www.hi-resolution.com/productpages/ma4/products_admin_overview.html): MacAdministrator
- Horizon DataSys (www.horizondatasys.com): NetControl2
- JAMF Software (www.jamfsoftware.com/products/casper-suite): Casper Suite

- NetSupport School (www.netsupportschool.com): NetSupport School
- SMART Solutions Technologies (www.smarterguys.com): SychronEyes
- Softpedia (mac.softpedia.com/get/Math-Scientific/LabRep.shtml): LabRep

NETWORKING

Increasingly, decisions LMSs make in managing library technology require them to understand how computer networks work. Unfortunately, how computers communicate with one another is a gray area for many individuals. However, a basic understanding of computer networking benefits the LMS and can help inform decisions. Here are some practical examples:

- The LMS wants to purchase additional computers for the LMC. However, there are not enough wall ports to provide network access for every computer. Understanding the network setup, the LMS purchases a network switch that will allow multiple computers to share one wall port.
- The LMS purchases a new subscription database. The database comes with a username and password that allows LMC patrons to access the database on or off campus. However, to facilitate easy access to the database on campus, the LMS obtains the range of public IP addresses assigned to the school. The LMS provides this range to the company providing the subscription database, which in turn automatically logs in any computer accessing the database within that IP range (a process called IP authentication).
- The LMS purchased a network printer but was never able to get it to work with all computers, so the LMS has it connected to only one computer. Knowing the difference between a fixed and dynamic IP address helps the LMS to properly configure all computers.
- The LMS considers purchasing a video streaming subscription. However, the LMS learns that the bandwidth capacity between the school's intranet and the Internet is not sufficient for multiple users to stream videos. Streaming video over the

Internet would impact Internet access for all users. However, the school's internal network or intranet is sufficient for this. Thus, the LMS purchases a video on demand server to stream videos over the intranet to students and staff.

- The LMS runs the LMC circulation program off the LMC server. Students who are on campus are able to access the Web-based OPAC, but students who are off-campus cannot. The LMS realizes this is because the LMC server is on the private local area network. The LMS works with district officials to allow an exception to the firewall so the LMC server can be accessed off-campus.
- The LMS currently has an LMC printer but it is in a location that makes it difficult to manage and oversee. Knowing how the network is set up, the LMS moves the printer to a better location, solving the management issue.

Each example required the LMS to have a working knowledge of how network devices communicate. If terms in these examples, including bandwidth, LAN, intranet, firewall, IP authentication, fixed and dynamic IP addresses, switches, and ports cause confusion, this next section of the book should be of interest.

Most people know that the Internet works but do not necessarily understand *how* it works. In order for computers to communicate with one another they must be in a network. A network is a group of two or more devices, such as computers and printers, connected together and able to communicate with one another. Understanding how networks work can positively enhance the LMS's ability to manage technology resources, so it is worth taking some time to explain network communications in more detail.

At the basic level, two devices linked together form a network. The LMS can physically link devices with an RJ-45 Ethernet crossover cable or a bidirectional USB cable, such as Belkin's Easy Transfer Cable for Widows Vista and XP. A wireless access point (WAP) creates a wireless network between two or more computers. Finally, an Ethernet hub or switch connects two or more computers, printers, or other network devices on a wired network (Mitchell, accessed 2009). Each of these is an example of a local area network (LAN). To further illustrate, the network for one school site within a district is an example of a LAN. Another name for a LAN is an intranet, an internal network (so named by combining the prefix "intra," meaning internal, and the word network).

Typically, resources on an intranet are private, accessible only to users within that network. Thus, many schools use a central server on the LAN as a file server where staff may store and share files. LMSs can use the intranet to provide private documents to their users. For example, passwords for electronic databases can be stored in a document on a LAN server. The LMS can link the document to the LMC Web site, noting that the link is available on campus only. Library media program users can then access the password document on campus. However, if external users from outside the network try to access the document, it will not be available to them.

Two or more LANS connected together form a wide area network (WAN). It is typical in a school district for the LAN of each school site to connect together forming a WAN. The WAN connects school sites with central district resources such as student information systems or even central LMC automation systems. A WAN can provide school sites access to central resources within a private network. Some refer to LANs connected together in close proximity to one another as a metropolitan area network (MAN) instead of a WAN. Because the basic definition of WAN is two or more connected networks, the Internet can technically be an example of a WAN. However, when most people speak of a WAN they are referring to a private network of LANs as opposed to the Internet, which is a public WAN.

The term "surfing the Net" is a term used to describe accessing Web sites on the Internet. When using the Internet, users are accessing network resources outside the internal network. Thus, the Internet is a global network consisting of numerous interconnected computer networks. The Internet spans the globe, and it includes trustworthy sites along with malicious Web sites that attempt to download viruses, spyware, and steal personal information.

Computers connect to the Internet through an Internet service provider (ISP). At home, most users obtain high-speed Internet connections through a cable or telephone line. According to the Pew Internet & American Life Project, over one half of all American households now have high-speed Internet access. Speeds can vary depending on the type of service and package purchased, with some households purchasing premium packages that promise higher connection speeds (Horrigan, 2008). If the high-speed connection is through the cable line, users normally connect a cable modem between their cable line and their computer. If the high-speed connection is through their telephone line, users normally connect a (digital subscriber line) DSL modem between their telephone line and their computer.

Many households now have multiple computers. A network router allows multiple computers to connect to the Internet. The modem (cable or DSL) connects to the router, and the router typically has four or more ports to physically connect computers. The installer typically uses an RJ-45 Ethernet cable to connect the router and the computer. RJ-45 is the type of connector at the end of the cable.

The actual cable used is Category 5 (CAT-5), Category 5 enhanced (CAT-5e), or Category 6 (CAT-6). CAT-5 is capable of transmission speeds of 100 megabits per second (mbps), and CAT-5e and CAT-6 are capable of transmission speeds of 1,000 megabits per second (mbps), which can also be referred to as 1 gigabit per second (gbps). While these cables are capable of the listed transmission speeds, most home users do not have connections from their ISPs capable of transmitting at these speeds. Therefore, for home users, the real advantage of CAT-6 over CAT-5 cable is for intranet traffic, assuming the router is also able to transit at the higher speed. Many households now have laptops and want to connect wirelessly to the Internet. A wireless router provides the additional function of serving as a WAP in addition to providing wired ports for connections. This type of network enables users to work with their computers freely around the house.

At schools, a wall port is typically used to plug in network devices. These ports usually run to a group of network switches known as an intermediate distribution frame (IDF). Each IDF then runs to a main distribution frame (MDF). The MDF represents the end of the LAN. From the MDF, network connections often route to a WAN. For example, in the Los Angeles Unified School District (LAUSD) each school's LAN connects to one of four geographical nodes. A node is a connecting point where several lines come together.

In the LAUSD, each school connects to the node through a T1 or better connection. T1 stands for T-carrier 1 and is a dedicated connection. A T1 connection is also known as a digital signal 1 (DS1) connection. The data transmission capacity, or bandwidth, of a T1 line is 1.544 megabits per second (mbps) of data transmission capacity, and multiple T1 lines can be bonded together to increase bandwidth. A T1 connection can use copper or fiber-optic wiring. While many people think of T1 as a fast connection, especially in comparison to residential connections, fiber optic connections have increased the speeds well beyond 1.544 Mbps. These connections includes DS3 or Digital Signal 3 connections at 44.736 mbps, Optical Carrier 3 (OC-3) connections capable of 155.52 mbps, and Optical Ethernet Metropolitan Area Network (OPT-E-MAN) service with transmission speeds up to 1 gigabit per second (Los Angeles Unified School District, 2006).

From the end user standpoint, several factors impact how fast the user can upload and download files from the Internet: the quality and capacity of the intranet (school network or LAN), the speed of the connection from the school to the district (WAN), the speed of the connection from the district to the ISP, and even the speed of the network card. The latter is more of a concern with antiquated computers containing older network cards (Henke, 2007).

The physical connection of computers, whether in a LAN or WAN, in itself is not sufficient to effectuate communication. In order for communication to occur, norms, rules, and procedures that will guide the processes by which the communication will unfold must be in place. Such norms are called protocols. Internet protocol (IP) is the language used by computers and other network devices to communicate over the Internet.

For a network device to communicate with other network devices over the Internet using the IP, it must have a unique numeric public IP address. The Internet Assigned Numbers Authority (IANA) coordinates globally the assignment of public IP addresses. IANA distributes large blocks of IP addresses to regional Internet registrars (RIRs). RIRs in turn distribute blocks to ISPs, which in turn distribute them to specific clients (Internet Corporation for Assigned Names and Numbers, 2005). Clients can then assign an ISP address to a specific network device.

An IP address in the Internet world is akin to a house address in the physical world. If schools did not have a physical mailing address that was unique, individuals would not be able to send mail to the school. If telephone numbers were not unique, individuals would not be able to call one another. The same is true with a server hosting a Web site; if that server does not have a unique address, other computers across the world will not be able to visit that Web site. Continuing the example, if someone moves to a new house their address will change, just like if a Web site moves to a new Web hosting company it will have a new IP address.

To access a specific Web site the LMS must know the IP address of the server hosting that Web site. For example, 134.139.1.60 is the IP address for www.csulb.edu, the Web site home page of California State University, Long Beach. The IP address for www.neal-schuman. com, the Web site home page for the publishers of this textbook, is 74.54.55.252. Note these IP addresses are accurate as of the date of publication. However, at any time the individual, company, or institution that hosts a particular Web site could elect to switch to a new ISP. In doing so, the new ISP would provide a different range of IP addresses, and the individual, company, or institution would then need to assign the server hosting the Web site a new IP address from within the newly provided range of IP addresses.

The typical user is not even aware of a Web site's IP address. Rather, it is common for users to use domain names, such as www. csulb.edu or www.neal-schuman.com. The domain name system (DNS) associates numeric IP addresses with a specific domain name. DNS makes the Internet more user-friendly. Instead of remembering and typing in long strings of IP addresses to visit sites, with DNS individuals can instead remember and type in more meaningful domain names. DNS is like having a permanent mailing address. If the IP address of a server hosting a Web site changes, the Webmaster simply notifies the DNS of the server's new IP address. Thus, users can simply remember the domain name and not worry about changes to the IP address.

A DNS server keeps track of which IP address is associated with which domain name. Each time a user types a new Web address into their browser using a domain name, the browser contacts a DNS server in the background. The DNS server then reports back the IP address to the browser. Continuing this example, if the user types in the domain name www.csulb.edu, the Web browser contacts the DNS server. The DNS server then reports back to the browser with the IP address 134.139.1.60. The browser then uses this IP address to access the requested Web page.

An IP address consists of four sets of whole numbers, with a period separating each number. With Internet protocol revision 4 (IPv4), the numbers range from 0 through 255. However, the world is slowly running out of available addresses, so networks are utilizing Internet protocol revision 6 (IPv6), selected as the replacement protocol to IPv4. The new protocol increases the total number of possible IP addresses from approximately 4.3 billion IPv4 addresses (4,294,967,296 to be exact) to over 340 undecillion IPv6 addresses. To give an idea of how many that really is, here is the number printed in its long format: 340,282,366,920,938,463,463,374,607,431,7 68,211,456 (St. Sauver, 2001).

At any given time, two devices on the network, whether printers, Internet-enabled PDAs, computers, or servers cannot share the same IP address. Such a possibility would cause confusion as to the intended target of network traffic. Two basic methods exist for assigning IP addresses: static or dynamic. A static IP address, also known as a fixed address, does not change. A dynamic IP address does change. The dynamic host configuration protocol (DHCP) server temporarily assigns an IP address to a network device.

Network devices configured to receive a dynamic IP address contact the DHCP server when turned on. The DHCP server has a range of IP addresses it can assign. The DHCP server gives a unique IP address to that network device and removes that IP address from the pool of available IP addresses it has to offer. DHCP servers issue dynamic IP addresses for a set period of time, referred to as a lease. Prior to lease expiration the computer or network device automatically renews the lease. The network device releases the IP address when turned off. At this point the IP address goes back into the pool of assignable IP addresses. Next time that network device it turned on, it will contact the DHCP server to receive a new IP address.

Network devices accessed by other devices over the Internet or intranet, such as a network printer, need a static IP address. For example, to set LMC computers to print to a network printer, the LMS must know the IP address of the network printer. The IP address tells the computers the location of the printer on the network. A printer's IP address can be determined by printing out a printer configuration page, which is normally done when the printer is first unpacked and plugged into the network. The LMS prints a network configuration page and uses the provided software driver to configure the relevant computers to the printer.

A case study shows the importance of IP addresses. Say that the LMS has success printing to the aforementioned new printer over the network. At the end of the day the LMS turns off the printer. The next day the LMS turns the printer on, but printing no longer occurs. Network printers generally receive a dynamic IP address by default. Thus, in this example the IP address of the printer changed when it was turned on the second day. Printing failed because the computers no longer know the correct IP address or network location of the printer. The only solution is to reconfigure every computer. This can be time-consuming and repetitive over time. Providing the network printer with a static IP address resolves this problem. Thus, any device accessed by other devices over the Internet or intranet needs a static IP address. However, for other devices, DHCP is the preferred method to avoid the time and labor of manually configuring each device with a static address as well as keep a written log of all used IP addresses to ensure two devices are not given the same address.

MANAGING SPACE FOR E-LEARNING

The chief educational function that has embraced the concept of intentional, redesigned learning space is the LMC, which is increasingly labeled an "information commons" or "learning commons." Because LMCs cross curricular lines and promote student-directed learning, these spaces serve as models for needs-based, flexible learning spaces that support e-learning. Some of the salient features include the following:

- Differentiated spaces for individual and group work, some with presentation/projection capabilities; some classrooms may also be available
- Mix of office- and leisure-style furniture (including bean bags and diner booths), much of which may be moved
- Pervasive technology, including multiple computers with a variety of software programs, wifi capability, large-screen

dynamic display/signage, multimedia consumption, and production areas where students can be relatively messy
- Service centers: reference, technology, writing, thesis/research assistance, instructional design, faculty development
- Supply areas
- Recreation/entertainment areas

Some of the properties that apply to virtual e-learning spaces for K–12 education, which can apply to LMCs, include the following:

- Customizable group areas to facilitate privacy while inviting interaction
- Multiple e-group meeting areas
- Differentiated e-spaces for reflection and "play"/exploration
- Dedicated e-spaces for projects such as wikis
- Presentation and public e-spaces for large-group events
- Stimulating visual and sound objects
- Personal e-learning spaces such as customizable RSS feed aggregators
- Fun tools: gaming, virtual toolkits, online polling
- E-service centers: reference, technology, writing, thesis/research assistance, instructional design, faculty development

LMSs may be involved in several different aspects of e-learning, which impacts management issues.

- **Digital resource management**: providing access to digital resources. This function may be implemented as simply as developing a library portal with hyperlinks to online resources to coordinating an online integrated learning system (ILS). In either case, the LMS serves a valuable role in selecting, organizing, and facilitating the equitable retrieval of relevant digital resources.
- **E-learning synchronous facilitation**: providing real-time intellectual access to e-learning environments and resources. This task can be accomplished at a surface level by incorporating e-mail as part of library information services. Students prefer instant messaging (IM) and texting, which can be

accomplished by embedding SMS (short message service) applications such as the open source program Meebo on the library portal. It should be cautioned, though, that IMers expect a quick response, so LMSs may feel tied to their electronic devices. A possible solution consists of providing a district- or consortium-based SMS so that LMSs can take turns answering user online questions. Another simple solution is to place a link from the library portal to a digital reference service such as QuestionPoint; users can get help anytime, although the virtual librarian probably will not know the curriculum or the school site so is likely to give more generalized assistance.

- **E-learning asynchronous facilitation:** LMSs can provide just-in-time e-learning instruction by locating (or developing) Web-based documents and tutorials that support e-learning. Representative examples include subject-specific Webliographies, Web site evaluation rubrics, research process tutorials, technology tool reference pages, and FAQs (frequently asked questions). The main work is in finding developmentally appropriate Web sites and organizing them for easy access.
- **E-learning collaboration:** LMSs can work with classroom teachers to provide appropriate e-learning resources and the technical skills with which to manipulate those resources. This function works well when the teacher has a Web page in which the LMS can be embedded. If the school or district uses online ILMSs, then usually the LMS e-learning component can easily link to several teachers or departments from one area. Both static documents and interactive chat can be provided. Another form of collaboration consists of serving as the virtual librarian (or cybrarian) for distance education courses. For example, students from across the state may take an online course with a virtual teacher; the LMS can serve the same librarianship role virtually as physically. Sometimes virtual schools designate an LMS as the program's cybrarian, serving all of the students across the curriculum, which can be an exciting job.
- **E-learning coordination:** Increasingly, LMSs are called on to coordinate some aspect of e-learning, be it distance learning courses or e-textbooks. This function calls on the LMS's

management skills of scheduling and supervision. Sometimes the job requires circulating supporting equipment.

Because the library media program serves several distinct functions, the following should be considered when designing virtual e-learning spaces:

- **Virtual entrances**: establish the sense of the library and engage the learner via displays of student work, FAQs, and immediate service links.
- **Teaching e-spaces**: support a range of purposes and offer group clusters with virtual social spaces.
- **E-learning centers**: this space is self-regulating in terms of activity/behavior (e.g., personalized learning venues such as blogs).
- **Social spaces**: increase student motivation and participation by providing chat areas, common virtual areas for both students and faculty (Joint Information Systems Committee Development Group, 2006).

The underlying message should be that learning is inviting, interactive, and personally meaningful.

Technology plays a central role in design and specification requirements. Regardless if the e-learning space is physical or virtual, technical requirements must be addressed: terminal/workstation requirements, system platform configurations, network hardware, Internet connectivity issues, and administrative software. With the incorporation of social networking, another layer of considerations are required: cross-device sharing, parallel awareness, group archiving, and groupware in general. Additional security and privacy measures (including issues of remote access) also need to be taken with Web 2.0 incorporation. Online 24/7 technology support needs to be calculated as part of planning and implementation endeavors.

It should be noted that virtual interaction (e.g., Second Life) does not replace face-to-face interaction because the former is an artificial environment; therefore, it is important to consider blending physical and digital worlds. For example, LMCs can embed technological systems for interaction, and students can bring their personal digital devices to hook up to the central system and participate actively together (Milne, 2007). LMCs often bridge physical and virtual space through 24/7 digital reference service, Web tutorials, online repositories of learning objects, and links to coursework. Further findings about library commons may be found in Henning's (2005) report about information commons.

WORKS CITED

Absolute Software. 2010. "CompuTrace Cosamplete." Absolute Software Corporation. Available: www.absolute.com/ products/computrace-complete (accessed January 4, 2010).

Adeona. "Frequently Asked Questions." University of Washington. Available: adeona.cs.washington.edu/faq.html (accessed January 17, 2009).

Brown, M. 2005. "Learning Spaces." In *Educating the Net Gen,* edited by D. Oblinger and J. Oblinger, 12.1–12.22. Boulder, CO: Educause.

Cannon, R. 1988. "Learning Environment." In *Encyclopedia of Educational Media Communications and Technology,* edited by D. Unwin and R. McAlees, 342–358. New York: Greenwood Press.

Dewey, John. 1933. *How We Think.* New York: D. C. Heath.

Federal Trade Commission. 2007. *FTC Factors for Consumers.* Washington, DC: Federal Trade Commission. Available: www.ftc.gov/bcp/edu/pubs/consumer/tech/tec03.pdf (accessed February 3, 2010).

Henke, Karen Greenwood. 2007. "How Fast Is Fast Enough? The Question of Adequate Bandwidth Is Increasingly the Issue of the Day." *Technology & Learning* 28, no. 3 (October): 16–20.

Henning, J. 2005. "Final Report." Available: jhenning.law.uvic.ca/final_report.html (accessed August 16, 2009).

Horrigan, John B. 2008. "Home Broadband Adoption 2008." Pew Internet & American Life Project, July. Available: www.pewInternet.org/pdfs/PIP_Broadband_2008.pdf (accessed January 8, 2009).

Internet Corporation for Assigned Names and Numbers. "Abuse Issues and IP Addresses." IANA, October 17, 2005. Available: www.iana.org/abuse/faq.html (accessed January 16, 2009).

Joint Information Systems Committee Development Group. 2006. *Designing Spaces for Effective Learning.* Bristol, England: University of Bristol. Available: www.jisc.ac.uk/media/documents/publications/learningspaces.pdf (accessed June 11, 2009).

Kaplan, S., and R. Kaplan. 1982. *Cognition and Environment: Functioning in an Uncertain World.* New York: Praeger.

Los Angeles Unified School District. 2006. "Educational Technology

Plan." Los Angeles Unified School District, July 1. Available: http://notebook.lausd.net/pls/ptl/ptl_apps.elib_item.show_item?p_item_id=259499 (accessed January 15, 2009).

Massachusetts School Library Media Association. 2003. "Facilities Standard." Massachusetts School Library Media Association, April. Available: www.mslma.org/MediaForum/Apr2003/Facilities.html (accessed March 28, 2009).

Milne, A. 2007. "Entering the Interactive Age." *Educause* (January): 13–31.

Mitchell, Bradley. "Connect Two Home Computers for File Sharing." About.com. Available: http://compnetworking.about.com/od/homenetworking/a/connecttwocomp.htm (accessed January 9, 2009).

National Center for Education Statistics. "Safeguarding Your Technology: Practical Guidelines for Electronic Education Information Security." U.S. Department of Education. Available: http://nces.ed.gov/pubs98/safetech/ (accessed January 25, 2009).

Oblinger, D. 2006. *Learning Spaces*. Boulder, CO: Educause.

Scott-Webber, L. 2004. *In Sync: Environmental Behavior Research and the Design of Learning Spaces*. Ann Arbor, MI: Society for College and University Planning.

St. Sauver, Joe. 2001. "What's IPv6 . . . and Why Is It Gaining Ground?" *University of Oregon Computing News* 16, no. 3 (Spring): 14–16.

Chapter 6

Managing Technology Resources for Communications

For many students the library media center (LMC) can be an intimidating place. In order for them to learn the library lingo, library media program procedures, structure and organization of the LMC, and to discover its myriad of resources, the library media specialist (LMS) must be able to effectively manage technology resources for communication. Publicizing and promoting is essential in creating an effective school library media program. Technology provides cost-effective, innovative, and efficient methods to promote the library media program.

Web 2.0 tools in particular provide LMSs much needed tools to inform and engage patrons. Karen A. Coombs, head of libraries' Web services at the University of Houston Libraries, contends that "Web 2.0 is transforming the Web into a space that allows anyone to create and share information online—a space for collaboration, conversation, and interaction; a space that is highly dynamic, flexible, and adaptable" (Coombs, 2007, p. 17). Michael Stephens, assistant professor at the Dominican University Graduate School of Library and Information Science writes, "Web 2.0 tools won't solve all your problems, but you may find some solutions that will make your work life easier. You might also find more time to engage with your users than ever before" (Stephens, 2007, p. 67). At the same time, he reminds LMSs not to implement technology for technology's sake. Rather, utilize Web 2.0 tools to serve users, replace outdated processes, and improve efficiency.

PURPOSES FOR COMMUNICATING

The library media program has little impact if no one knows about it. LMSs need to articulate the library program's mission and their vision with the rest of the school community and beyond. Likewise, the school community also needs to share information about the school's charge, their role within the school's program, and their accomplishments. Furthermore, communication is one element of information literacy for which students need to demonstrate competency. The LMC offers a cross-curricular venue for sharing and exchanging information effectively.

It should be noted that communication is both a one-way and two-way endeavor, but altogether the school community should be sharing information in order to improve the school as a whole and each person in particular: a learning community. In the process, new information can be generated; information is not just transferred between people in a closed loop but is open to new possibilities. Such creative efforts constitute part of twenty-first century learning skills, which can occur and be applied in LMCs.

In educational terms, communication is the vehicle by which teaching and learning occurs. Information is externalized and articulated to be communicated to the learner, who responds to this information in one of several ways: ignore it, reject it, internalize it, apply it, build on it. If the information recipient changes attitude or behavior as a result of that information, then learning has occurred. The LMC is filled with information in a variety of formats, and the LMS sets up the conditions so that the information can be communicated and acted on.

In any case, for communication to be effective, the message must be conveyed clearly, accurately, and usually succinctly. The communication needs to consider the target audience—student, parent, administrator—in order to customize the message to facilitate understanding. The communication channel also needs to be chosen carefully to align the content/message with the audience and the intent. For instance, posters serve as quick reminders and learning stations while reports can offer in-depth analysis.

The objectives of communication can be facilitated with the incorporation of technology for several reasons: variety of format possibilities, potential speed of communication transmission, relative freedom from the constraints of synchronous communication in the same physical space, and the ability to transform the communication for different purposes or audiences. The possible choices are impressive: desktop publishing, databases, spreadsheets, presentation programs, telecommunications, Internet, digitized images, audio, video, and mixed media. With the advent of Web 2.0 and the concept of interactive technology, another dimension is added as messages are co-constructed and continue to evolve, thanks to technology. As a result, communication is as much a process as a product. As "Information Central," the LMC should offer the means to communicate using these different technologies: providing the equipment, the software, production space, and instruction.

Managing these communication tools can be challenging because of their variety of format and application. Each piece of equipment has been associated with a different media, such as a camera for still images. However, this picture is changing as technology devices can be used for several kinds of communication, such as the "smartphone." Nevertheless, LMSs must know the possible communication purposes and features for each kind of equipment as well as know how each operates. Furthermore, LMSs must make sure the communication technologies are well maintained and accessible for the user.

PUSH-AND-PULL TECHNOLOGY

"Push technology" refers to communication (the default mechanism being the Internet) that can be "pushed" to a specific audience automatically whenever an event occurs or at regular intervals. The recipient activates push technology's process, unlike much of spam e-mail; in this respect, the user is initiating the "pulling" of information. In the earlier print environment, this kind of service was called "selective dissemination of information (SDI)," whereby the clientele indicated to the LMS an area of interest, such as research on year-round schools. Whenever the LMS saw a relevant document, he or she sent it to the interested party. SDI and its technological counterpart push technology provide timely relevant information to the user and demonstrate the power of accumulated information that is shared. Once the user identifies the type of information desired, he does not have to pull the information from the Internet or other content provider; rather, the information is pushed to the user.

Using the criteria for technology acceptance laid out in the introduction, the advantages of a new technology need to outweigh other alternatives, be it in terms of saving time, saving money, or providing new or enhanced services or products in order for it to be successful. In addition, enough people need to use it in order for others to develop products or applications supported by the new technology. Content users appreciate the convenience of having new content pulled from Web sites and delivered to them immediately once it becomes available without needing to constantly navigate those sites to locate the same information. On the other hand, digital content publishers appreciate the ability to push content directly to their subscribers rather than waiting for users to visit their site to discover new content (or worse, never finding it at all). RSS is one such "push" technology.

RSS stands for Really Simple Syndication or Rich Site Summary. RSS allows users to subscribe to many sources on the Web. It is similar to subscribing to a print newspaper or magazine, but for the Web. Just like someone might subscribe to a print magazine to be delivered to their house, a user can subscribe to an RSS feed for many Web-based resources. With this subscription, the user receives new information whenever the Webmaster publishes new content. Extending the example of subscribing to a print publication such as a magazine, the user needs a destination for delivery of subscriptions. For a print magazine, it is generally the postal mailbox. To receive RSS feeds, the user needs a feed reader, also known as a feed aggregator or news aggregator.

One such feed aggregator is Bloglines (www.bloglines.com). The introduction of Bloglines in 2003 provided one of the first practical and user-friendly applications of RSS feeds. Availability of online content via RSS subsequently exploded. On August 12, 2004, Bloglines issued a press release announcing that "more than 100 million live, dynamic articles are now indexed and tracked by the service. These articles come from hundreds of thousands of unique news sources and blogs, representing the freshest and most diverse voices on the Internet today" (Bloglines, 2004). In 2004, *Time* magazine named Bloglines one of *Time* magazine's 50 Coolest Web Sites. Today it continues to be a popular and heavily utilized

Web site (Buechner, 2004). Most major Web sites, especially commercial sites, now offer feeds for their users to subscribe to using a feed aggregator such as Google Reader. Many Web 2.0 tools have integrated feeds into their services, including blog services like Blogger (www.blogger.com) and social bookmarking sites such as Delicious (www.delicious.com).

Another popular format for syndicating content from Web pages is Atom, developed as an alternative to the RSS format. From a user standpoint, both technologies are similar in that they provide a feed to syndicate Web page content. From a technical standpoint minor differences exist. Unlike the VCR versus Betamax format wars in the 1970s and 1980s where consumers generally had to choose one technology over the other, the good news is most feed aggregators, including Google Reader, can aggregate both RSS and Atom feeds. Overall, feeds provide a mechanism for content publishers from the Live Web to easily share content. The Live Web is a term coined by blogger Allen Searls in 2003 to describe Web 2.0 content created by average people that is fluid, dynamic, and interactive, unlike the traditional Web site that tends to be static (Searls, 2008). Sites such as Blogger fall under the definition of the Live Web.

The initial creation of a Web site can be time-intensive as any LMS who has worked with Web authoring software knows. However, the end result can be a wonderful resource for the library media program. Using RSS feeds on a Web site, the LMS can better manage this content by providing a mechanism to ensure that users will know when the LMS publishes new content. This promotes more effective communication and ultimately increases use of the site. Most LMSs put so much effort into the creation of a LMC Web site that it makes sense to incorporate feeds to maximize its effectiveness.

More specifically, LMSs can use feeds to communicate library media program updates to patrons. For instance, the Multnomah County Library in Oregon provides various RSS feeds for its online public access catalog (OPAC), breaking the feeds into categories including Teen Fiction, Children's Fiction, Graphic Novels, and Picture books/easy readers (Multnomah County Library, 2008). Patrons no longer have to periodically search the OPAC to discover new titles as they arrive. Rather, patrons simply subscribe to the category feeds they are interested in, and when new books arrive, the RSS feed notifies the patron. In addition to highlighting new resources, LMSs are using feeds to inform patrons of services and upcoming programs and events. For example, the Nicholas Senn High School Library in Chicago has an LMC blog regularly updated with announcements (Nicholas Senn High School Library, accessed 2009).

In terms of feed management, it is easiest to start with the existing content on the LMC Web site. Determine how many feeds will be available to users. Each feed or channel should represent a certain type of content: for instance, book reviews versus library media program news. From a management perspective, it may make sense to start with one feed with the knowledge that the LMS can add additional feeds at a later date. This allows the LMS a chance to start slowly, getting used to managing the feed. To create a feed file, place the content in an extensible markup language (XML) file. LMSs with technical expertise in Web design utilizing hypertext markup language (HTML) will find this as a viable option.

As mentioned earlier, LMSs without technical expertise in Web design utilizing hypertext markup language (HTML) may not find the manual creation of feeds a viable option. Thus, a somewhat easier option is to create a blog (described in more detail later in this chapter). Blogs, such as those offered by Blogger (www.blogger.com), are free, and they provide an automatic feed that the LMS can use to add content to their Web site. Here is a quick overview:

1. Take the feed address to a free Web site like RSS-to-JavaS-cript (www.rss-to-javascript.com). Follow the prompts.
2. This site will provide JavaScript code the LMS can copy and paste into his or her Web page. Whenever the blog is updated, the RSS feed likewise will be updated.

Since the JavaScript pasted into the Web page uses the RSS feed to display content, the end result is that whenever the LMS updates the blog, the RSS feed through the JavaScript will update Web site with the same content. Users will be able to use the same RSS feed coming from the blog to subscribe to the content.

A key management consideration with RSS feeds involves patron use. Providing RSS feeds has no benefit if users are not familiar with this technology. Thus, effectively managing RSS feeds

---

TECH MOMENT: ADDING A FEED TO A WEB SITE

Several online tutorials provide guidance in adding a feed to a Web site. Here is a quick overview.

1. First, format the content per RSS specifications, save as an .xml file, and then upload it to the LMC Web site.
2. Once the RSS feed is uploaded, confirm it is formatted correctly by using Feed Validator (www.feedvalidator.org) or another free feed validator service to inspect feeds for any errors.
3. Next, run the feed address through a free service like FeedBurner (www.feedburner.com). This service provides statistics on the usage of the feed such as the number of users subscribing to the feed. Without this, the LMS won't have access to valuable statistical information on the feed's usage, which from a management perspective can help inform future decisions about needs to promote the feed, training needs, and ultimately the viability of long-term upkeep of the feed.
4. The final step is creating a link to the feed file on the homepage of the LMC Web site and any other places where it would make sense for users to look for such feeds. When creating a link to the feed, use the standard orange feed icon to notify users of the availability of feeds. Mozilla Foundation (www.mozilla.org) created this icon, which is free on their Web site. Note that if the site has multiple feeds, it makes sense for the orange icon to lead to a feeds page that lists and provides a direct link to all available feeds on the LMC Web site.

---

includes providing staff and student training. For staff, this might include workshops and other forms of professional development to introduce them to this emerging technology. Chapter 8 discusses the use of RSS as a tool for ongoing professional development.

For students, one promising use of RSS is in conjunction with long-term research projects. Using the RSS search tool available through Yahoo! News (news.yahoo.com/rss) and some online subscription databases, students researching a particular topic over an extended period can create their own RSS news feeds using specific key words relevant to their research.

Incorporating RSS training into classroom-based lessons is a great way to address the management need of developing educational opportunities for students. In addition, instructions posted on the LMC Web site for patron use, either written or in the form of a broadcast such as a screencast, podcast, or vodcast (discussed in the next section of this chapter) are all potential training strategies, as is the use of brochures, handouts, and incorporation of RSS training into LMC orientations. Regardless of the approach taken, training is a necessary component in effectively managing this technology.

TECH MOMENT: GETTING STARTED WITH RSS USING GOOGLE READER

Here is how you get started using Google Reader:

1. Create a free Google Account if you have not already. Go to Google and look for the sign-in button near the top right of the screen. Follow the prompts to create your account.
2. Log in to your Google Account.
3. Under "Try something new," find Google Reader.
4. Once you are in Google Reader, you should watch the video introduction from Chris, a Google engineer (press the play button), and take the tour. One you are in the tour, the first slides discuss getting started. Notice that on the left of your screen there are more links, including Common Questions, Finding Feeds, etc. You should review these links also.
5. Try some library and tech-related searches by using the Add Subscription link inside Google Reader. For instance, the keywords "school library" will result in "*School Library Journal* Breaking News" among other things.
6. Next, try some searches outside of Google Reader. Just open up a new window and go to http://blogsearch.google.com. Type in your desired keywords and search for blogs. If you find one that appeals to you, copy then paste the feed URL into your Google Reader.
7. Enjoy! Remember, the worst thing that can happen is you won't like the content and will need to go to Manage Subscriptions to unsubscribe.

BROADCASTING TOOLS

LMSs can disseminate information in schools via several broadcast formats. Some schools have closed-network channels that allow them to broadcast video throughout the school via cable lines.

Other schools utilize public address (PA) systems to broadcast announcements via speakers located throughout the school. The Walter Reed Middle School Library in Southern California has a video on demand (VOD) server, which allows the LMS to broadcast videos over the Web and be accessed by students and staff via their Internet browser (Bobrosky, 2007). To reach parents in emergencies, many schools have tools in place that can broadcast messages via traditional phone lines as well as through e-mail and text messaging. Staff use e-mail distribution lists to send messages to multiple recipients simultaneously. Some modern integrated library management systems (ILMS) can automatically broadcast overdue notices to patrons by e-mail or text message.

These are all examples of broadcast tools. The basic function of a broadcast tool is to send out a message from a source directly to, or accessible by, multiple recipients in multiple locations at the same time. The broadcast can be targeted to a specific group of individuals, such as an e-mail distribution list, or it can be open to anyone within range of the broadcast, such as a radio signal. To access the broadcast, users must have the appropriate hardware or software for that type of broadcast. For example, an RSS feed is useless without an RSS aggregator, just as a television signal is useless without the appropriate television tuner and display on which to watch the signal.

Within the realm of school libraries, there are a number of broadcast tools, such as VOD servers, ILMS, and e-mail distribution lists as noted. A strong case could even be made that a Web site is a broadcast tool in that when the content provider is sending out information it then becomes accessible to multiple users in multiple locations at the same time. If RSS technology is incorporated into the Web site, undoubtedly it becomes a broadcast tool, with the RSS continually syndicating the content to feed aggregators. Due to the immense number of tools used in libraries that could fall under the definition of a broadcast tool, this chapter explores just a few key emerging Web-based broadcast tools.

To be clear, the act of broadcasting differs from archiving a broadcast, just as airing a television show differs from TIVOing it; in the former situation, the content provider is disseminating information, and in the latter, the viewer is storing it. In some cases, the content provider might store the broadcast so that it can be "played" or broadcast on request (as in iTunes). In the original broadcast situation, the viewer must be available and accessible, but the onus of effort is on the broadcaster. When a content provider makes a broadcast available more or less permanently (recorded), the central issues are storage and viewer initiative. In this respect, a book resembles a recorded and available broadcast, although it differs significantly in that originally it is not broadcast to multiple users simultaneously (unless it is an e-book broadcast or podcast). The importantance of this distinction emphasizes the fact that libraries can broadcast information for timely reception, and can also record, archive, and make available the same broadcast for later consumption.

'Casting Communication

'Casts have become a "hot" communication tool set for LMSs. 'Casts leverage the popularity of mobile devices and signal the LMS's "cool" factor to tech-savvy teens. The section discusses their communication benefits and explains how to manage these tools.

Podcasts

A podcast is an audio production published to the Web. At the simplest level, this is a recording of one or more people speaking. More sophisticated podcasts may include sound effects interspersed throughout the podcast as well as opening music that fades away as the speaker begins to speak. The word "podcast" was originally derived from the two words "iPod" and "broadcasting." Users typi-cally publish podcasts on a regular basis (e.g., weekly, monthly, etc.). Audiences follow the podcast series, subscribing to the podcast via a feed. Sites like Podomatic (www.podomatic.com) allow LMSs to upload content onto the Web and provide an RSS feed that allows users to subscribe to it.

To date, the most prevalent use of podcasts in libraries as a broadcast tool has focused on creating booktalks. The use of podcasts enhances the traditional booktalk by allowing for mul-tiple "takes" until the recording is perfected, unlike the traditional booktalk, which is performed in front of a live audience (although a podcast could possibly be a recording of the live performance). Additionally, the LMS can integrate music and sound effects to increase student appeal. While booktalk audio files have existed for years, linking a finished podcast on LMC Web sites and making it available via an RSS feed provides users with 24/7 access to this content to a degree that was impossible before. For example, LMS Naomi Bates at Northwest High School in Texas has an LMC Web site containing multiple booktalk podcasts that users can subscribe to through the available RSS feed (Bates, accessed 2009). LMS Seanean Shanahan at William Clinton Middle School in California creates booktalk podcasts, posting them to her site "The Library Lady" on Podomatic (Shanahan, accessed 2009). As a built-in feature of Podomatic, users can subscribe to her podcasts through an RSS feed, so she does not need to create her own site feed.

LMSs should consider the benefits of working with a classroom teacher, enhancing the traditional written book report by having students create their own booktalk podcasts. Over time, the LMS could grow quite a collection of resources that would help promote reading at the school. This practice provides two added benefits. Operationally, the LMS will spend less time making podcasts, which will free time to manage the newly created student resources, including posting the podcasts to the Web. Additionally, there is an instructional benefit in having booktalks performed by students, as other students may be more apt to relate to another student's podcast and thus decide to read the book. In essence, students promoting books through podcasts is a marketer's dream come true, as peers often relate best to their peers.

Identifying classes to create booktalk podcasts means collaborating with teachers. Such teachers may be unaware or unfamiliar with this technology and thus leery about implementing it in their classroom. When trying to sell a new technology, Michael Stephens, assistant professor at the Dominican University Graduate School of Library and Information Science, recommends developing a prototype in order to demonstrate the benefits of the new technology. In addition, he reminds LMSs that they should implement social tools only if those tools support the mission and vision of the school library media program, such as supporting student academic achievement (Stephens, 2007). The Florida Center for Instructional Technology provides strategies in the article "Ideas for Podcasting in the Classroom," which is available on the Web (Florida Center for Instructional Technology, accessed 2009). For podcast samples for LMSs to use as they get started, Nancy Keane's site "Booktalks Quick and Simple" has a daily booktalk/podcast feed (Keane, accessed 2009).

TECH MOMENT: CREATING PODCASTS

To create a podcast you need a mechanism for recording sound in a digital format; any basic microphone should work. You can use a stand-alone microphone or find a microphone connected to a headphone. The most important feature is the ability to cleanly record your voice. You may also need to purchase a 1/4" to 3.55 mm adapter if your microphone comes with a 1/4" (standard) plug (as many microphones do), because the "mic in" on computers will accept only 3.5 mm (mini) plugs.

When selecting a microphone, you will probably want a unidirectional microphone rather than an Omni directional microphone. Unidirectional microphones pick up sound in one direction, so they are ideal for doing podcasts in noisier environments because they don't pick up background sound. Omni directional microphones pick up sound from virtually any direction, so they are ideal for recording more than one person (for example, an interview where the microphone sits between the two people). In lieu of a microphone, you can use a digital recorder with a built-in microphone. With a digital recorder, you can record anywhere; you are not confined to a microphone attached to your computer. The recorder then connects to your computer, usually with a USB cable, so you can transfer the recordings to your computer (similarly to how a digital camera connects to your computer).

Once you have captured the digital audio recordings, it is time to edit them and transform them into podcasts. An open source software program called Audacity makes this an easy task when combined with another piece of free software: the LAME MP3 recorder. The latter program is needed to export your file as an .mp3 format. If you do not have any experience with Audacity, many good resources on the Internet are available to teach you how to use this program (as.how-to-podcast-tutorial.com/17-audacity-tutorial.htm). Many tutorials include video clips or screenshots.

Part of the fun in making podcasts is incorporating sounds and music. Through Creative Commons, there are many free sound and music resources on the Internet, such as CCmixter (www.ccmixter.org) and the Freesound Project (www.freesound.org).

When finished with editing, export your finished product as a MPEG audio layer 3 (mp3) file and upload to the podcast hosting site of your choice.

Vodcasts

A vodcast is a video production published to the Web. When first introduced, vodcasts were video enhancements to podcasts so they were termed "video podcasts," which was ultimately shortened to vodcast. As with podcasts, users typically publish vodcasts on a regular basis, and audiences follow the vodcast series, subscribing via a feed. YouTube is the most popular place for publishing and viewing vodcasts. If district or school officials have blocked YouTube on school computers by district Internet filters (as is the case in many school districts), LMSs can consider alternative video sharing Web sites such as BlipTV (www.blip.tv), TeacherTube (www.teachertube.com), or NextVista (www.NextVista.org).

As with booktalk podcasts, utilizing video to create booktalk vodcasts is a great way to enhance the traditional booktalk. Many educators who have created or have had their students create vodcasts have focused on video book trailers. The concept is similar to trailers shown prior to the viewing of the scheduled feature film in a movie theater. Just as a movie trailer entices the viewer to watch a movie, the ultimate goal of a vodcast booktalk is convincing students to read the book. The Web site Digital Booktalk (digitalbooktalk.com), hosted by the University of Central Florida (UCF), provides a number of examples of this medium. UCF students and K–12 students across the country created these booktalks. The site also includes the downloadable UB-the-Director curriculum program to assist educators in implementing digital booktalks into their curriculum. Themed video booktalks are another common use of vodcasts. The Web site Bookwink (www.bookwink.com) contains many examples of video booktalks geared for students in grades 3 through 8. Many of the videos contain multiple books connected by a similar theme, such as love, witches, popularity, volcanoes, and sharks (Bookwink, 2007).

TECH MOMENT: CREATING VODCASTS

To create a vodcast, you need access to a device that can record image and sound. Digital camcorders, Webcams, and many cell phones can capture digital video, albeit with varying degrees of quality.

A Webcam is generally the cheapest alternative if a basic recording device is all that is needed. A Webcam connects to your computer and records using software on your computer, such as Windows Movie Maker or iMovie. Often the Webcam itself comes packaged with recording software. Webcam features vary greatly; check for degree of resolution, frames per second rate, focus options, and presence of a built-in microphone.

If using a camcorder, it is important that the camcorder records in a digital format (rather than in analog format). Camcorder features vary greatly; check for optical and digital zoom, image stabilization, focus options, recording modes, video resolution, built-in microphone and audio recording quality, storage options (such as flash memory, internal hard drives, DVD discs, etc.), and availability of ports for connecting devices such as an external microphone.

What matters the most, though, is that you are able to get whatever you record easily transferred onto your computer, either through a USB cable, firewire cable, or removable media. For creating vodcasts, camcorders that store video on flash memory or a hard drive have a clear advantage over tape-based camcorders. With a tape-based camcorder, one hour of footage will take one hour to transfer to the computer. The user presses play on the camcorder, and the video then is transferred in real time. However, flash and hard drive based models transfer the entire file in considerably less time.

Once you have captured your video, Apple's iMovie can import your work. Similarly, Windows Movie Maker is a free program included with Windows XP and Windows Vista. Microsoft provides a short slightly comical video that will serve to introduce you to the program (www.microsoft.com/windowsxp/wmx/AWE/awe_dayinlife_genxp_300.asx). Microsoft also provides a number of tutorials and tips for using the program (www.microsoft.com/windowsxp/using/moviemaker/default.mspx).

If using a high definition (HD) camcorder, know that two HD formats exist: AVCHD (advanced video codec high definition) and HDV. As of early 2009, Windows Movie Maker is still not able to edit AVCHD format videos. Thus, alternative commercial programs such as Adobe Premier Pro CS4 (www.adobe.com/products/premiere/) or Sony Vegas Pro 8 (www.sonycreativesoftware.com/vegaspro) need to be used instead.

Regardless of platform, the first step is to import clips. Windows Movie Maker and iMovie make it easy to edit video and to add clips onto the storyboard: the default view for viewing and organizing video clips in your movie. Once clips are organized, you can add transitions between clips as well as video effects, a title screen, and credits. Afterward, create or edit music and sound in a program like Audacity and import it into Windows Movie Maker using the timeline to line your sound and music up with the video clips. With Macs, you can incorporate Garage Band for sound productions and move the results easily into iMovie. Export your final project as a Windows Media video (.wmv), iMoive (.mov), or as a cross-platform format such as QuickTime, to then upload it to the video hosting site of your choice.

Screencasts

A screencast is the video recording of a computer screen. Using encoding software such as Windows Media Encoder (a free download for Windows XP and Vista users) or Adobe's free Media Encoder for Macs (www.adobe.com/support/downloads/product.jsp?platfo rm=Macintosh&product=160) LMSs can capture whatever is displayed on the screen including mouse movements and clicks, input text, and so on. LMSs can provide voice narration while recording a screencast or add it later when editing the video using software such as Windows Movie Maker or iMovie. The end result is content that captures visual elements, which might be suitable for a series of vodcasts providing instructions on using particular electronic databases or using the LMC OPAC.

Management Issues

Podcasts, vodcasts, and screencasts provide modern media for LMSs to use in broadcasting relevant information about library media programs: advertising new and existing library media program resources, promoting special events, or providing services. The possibilities are endless. As discussed, these tools provide a great way for students to contribute to library media program resources. However, a number of management issues arise when implementing these technologies, particularly with students.

First, creating a podcast, vodcast, or screencast requires the necessary equipment. Depending on the task, production equipment can include Webcams, microphones, camcorders, digital recorders and, of course, computers with editing software such as Audacity or Garage Band for podcasts, and iMovie or Windows Movie Maker for vodcasts. As groups create the products, the LMS must address questions regarding how they will reserve and access the equipment. Take, for instance, a class set of 40 microphones. Will the LMS check out the entire class set to the teacher, or will students individually check out the microphones? If a student is absent or not able to finish recording during class time, are there extended LMC hours to allow the student the opportunity to finish? If not, will the equipment be available for checkout? If so, what happens if the student does not return the equipment in a timely manner and the LMS or a classroom teacher has reserved this equipment for use by another class? Chapter 7 explores in greater detail management issues regarding the circulation of LMC equipment.

Another management consideration is power. Microphones plug directly into the computer and typically do not need power. Webcams typically plug into a USB port that, in turn, powers the device. Camcorders typically have a rechargeable battery. Adequate space and electrical outlets need to be present to charge these batteries as needed. The LMS should purchase additional batteries if demand for the equipment by users will be intense during the year or during certain periods of the school year. This will allow the LMS to swap out batteries with fully charged batteries whenever existing batteries need to be charged. Otherwise, the LMS may find LMC equipment is regularly unavailable due to charging needs. The LMS will also need a secure location to charge the batteries. Chapter 5 explores the management of facilities for technology.

Digital recorders tend to have AA or AAA alkaline batteries that are not rechargeable, and over time the LMS will need to replace the batteries. Management of digital recorders includes developing procedures for checking batteries to ensure they have enough charge for the intended purpose and for supplying adequate replacement batteries whenever users check out the equipment. This brings up additional management questions regarding the process—and funding—for obtaining replacement batteries. The LMS should consider purchasing rechargeable batteries along with appropriate battery chargers for equipment students or staff will utilize often or if the school supports a green philosophy. This can provide significant cost savings in the long run and is more environmentally friendly than traditional batteries. Of course, LMC staff and users have to then remember not to toss out these batteries since they cost significantly more than nonchargeable ones.

In the editing process of creating podcasts, vodcasts, and screencasts, students need access to computers. Multiple management issues surround the use of computers, including ensuring that the appropriate software is loaded onto the computers, the school obtained appropriate software licenses as needed, and the computers are kept operational. Chapters 3 and 4 discuss these management concerns in greater detail. In addition, students are likely to incorporate music and sound into their podcasts, vodcasts, and screencasts. Posting podcasts to the Web is an act of publishing. Thus, if students use copyrighted materials the LMS will need to obtain permission for such use. Creating original works or using works licensed under Creative Commons simplifies this management task. Thus, Chapter 7 discusses ethical and legal issues, including copyright law, fair use, and Creative Commons. Finally, if the LMS will post the final product onto the Web, the LMS must address additional management concerns such as privacy and confidentiality needs. Chapter 7 addresses these issues.

WEB 2.0 COMMUNICATION TOOLS

Probably the most recent influential change in teaching with technology within K–12 education has been the introduction and increasing acceptance of interactive Web 2.0. Knowledge is collaboratively built and shared. Whereas earlier decades focused more on instructor-produced content, which could involve high-level technical expertise, Web 2.0 tools are often easy to use so that content can regain intellectual focus. Web 2.0 tools facilitate group communication and collaboration. Adding this broad based authoring set of tools to the educational concept of constructivism results in student-centered curriculum. This "democratization" of knowledge generation can also bring management headaches as responsibility and accountability are dispersed.

Blogs and Wikis

Blogs and wikis are two Web 2.0 tools that are being rapidly adopted by the public at large and increasingly by schools and LMSs. The term blog comes from the phrase Web **log**. The early uses of mainstream blogging focused on creating online journals. Later, blogs began to incorporate reader comments in blog entries. While a simple blog can still be set up and be "live" within minutes, many of today's blogs resemble full-fledged Web pages, with areas for static and live content, professional looking templates, and the ability to customize virtually all aspects of the blog through modifying the source code. Here are typical features and things to know about blogs:

- Blogs have entries—each entry tends to cover a particular topic.
- Entries are arranged chronologically.
- Blogs can have one or more authors/contributors; however, most don't.
- By default users can comment on entries. However, comment on entries can be enabled, disabled, or require moderation.
- Authors can publish entries via e-mail.
- Blogs are often personal in nature.
- RSS feed is available to push out new entries to subscribers.

A wiki is a Web page or Web site (collection of Web pages) intended to be built collaboratively and quickly using the graphical user interface (GUI). The name "wiki" comes from the name of a shuttle bus operating at the Honolulu Airport called the *Wiki Wiki.* "Wiki" is Hawaiian for "quick," thus the use of the term "wiki" for this Web 2.0 technology was selected to stress the speed at which Web pages and entire Web sites can be created (Cunningham, 2003). Wiki pages have an edit button, used to switch the wiki page to edit mode. The creator can then make desired changes and press save, at which point the changes are live. Here are typical features and things to know about wikis:

- Wikis have pages—each page tends to cover a particular theme or subject.

- Wikis tend to be group-oriented and often have multiple authors.
- Wikis can be open access (all readers can modify page content) or closed access (user authentication via username/ password login required).
- Wikis provide a history of changes.
- Tracking changes allow users to revert a page back to any previous state.
- A discussion page for each wiki page provides a forum for discussing and agreeing on proposed page edits. This is especially useful for a topic where wiki contributors have not reached consensus on content.

Overall, blogs and wikis provide easy-to-use methods for broadcasting LMC information and for providing students with a voice. Blogs and wikis can also promote LMC participation and increase two-way communication. For instance, some LMSs use book recommendation blogs and wikis to garner student input. Enabling students to directly contribute to LMC resources is one of the most powerful aspects of wikis and blogs. To encourage student participation in newly implemented social tools such as a booktalk blog, Topeka Shawnee Library Virtual Branch manager David Lee King recommends the use of passive and active invitations. Examples of passive invitations include offering RSS feeds, allowing commenting, and providing hyperlinks to more information. Examples of active invitations include asking users to "fill out an online poll or survey, ask opinions and or otherwise direct participation" (King, 2007).

Student participation also brings up multiple management issues. What happens if an LMC sponsors a blog connected to the LMC Web site, either directly through RSS-to-JavaScript technology or through a link to the blog from the LMC Web site. The blog might contain student-contributed book recommendation entries. The first management question to address is how students will post their entries. Will students have direct access to the blog, or will students submit their work for the LMC staff to input and post? One suggestion is to create a free e-mail account that students can use to submit entries to the LMC, which at least saves LMC staff time in retyping the entries.

Once the LMS determines how students will submit entries, the next step is to determine which students will post book recommendations. For example, if the LMS decides to permit students to have direct access to posting, the LMS will need to list any student contributors as blog authors. If using Blogger, this means students will need to have a Google username and password (Blogger is owned by Google). For example, some LMSs utilize LMC volunteers or service students to contribute to the blog.

Utilizing students to post entries also brings up student privacy and confidentiality concerns. A good management strategy for this tool when utilizing student entries is to develop a contract that establishes guidelines for use for the parent and student to sign. Note that this contract is in addition to any other forms required by the school district when publishing student work online, as discussed in Chapter 7. In lieu of identifying specific students ahead of time, the LMS can provide students with a generic username and password and disseminate it across campus. However, this strategy takes away the LMS's ability to effectively manage and control the blog, because when students begin posting, the LMS will not be able to determine who actually posted a specific entry. Thus, this practice should be avoided.

In managing the blog, the LMS needs to decide who will have permission to post comments on entries and whether comments need to be monitored. For posting comments, the LMS could decide to limit comments to authors only; that is, one student who is an approved author could post a comment on another student's entry. At the other extreme, the LMS could allow anyone to post comments, including anonymous users. As a compromise, the LMS could require users to be registered users, meaning they have signed up for a Blogger account. On one hand, requiring users to be registered provides the LMS with more control over the blog as the LMS will be able to determine the specific number of individuals participating in the blog by posting comments. This practice can be useful for analyzing the success of a blog. On the other hand, requiring users to register before posting will likely serve as a deterrent for many students and may decrease the overall use of the blog. Thus, if the primary goal is to increase two-way communication, then the LMS should strongly consider enabling anonymous comments.

Finally, the LMS must decide whether to moderate comments;

that is, user comments will not appear publicly on the blog until an authorized LMC staff member approves the comment. If through a management plan the LMS decides to enable comment moderation, the LMS must also determine who will moderate comments and allocate appropriate time to this task. As a book blog grows and becomes more popular, moderating comments could take up more and more time.

When utilizing Web 2.0 technology such as blogs or wikis, LMSs should develop communication policies that dictate proper use of the technology and ensure that it is alignment with the district's acceptable use policy (AUP). Once established, effective management must include ensuring that users follow the communication policy, otherwise over time users will ignore it. With wikis, reference Librarian Nicole Martin points out that "because wikis include 'histories' of the corrections and revisions, inappropriate or inaccurate information can be traced back to the creator or modifier" (Martin, 2007). This feature simplifies management.

Online Groups

Ineffective communication among staff is an issue for many schools. As the information hub, one role the library media program can serve is to facilitate open communication among staff. As the information specialist on campus, the LMS is often the individual most aware and best suited to support the school community in utilizing new and existing communication broadcasting tools. Online groups are one such tool the LMS can implement at a school site to support effective communication.

Online groups are specialized Web sites for users who share a common interest. Users create and maintain these online groups. For example, individuals have created online group sites for specific schools and universities, sports team, occupations and specific interests such as cooking. Individuals participate in the group by joining the group and becoming a member through a registration process. Typical features of an online group include the following:

1. Shared group Web site
2. Threaded discussion forum (that is, a running commentary of messages between people)

SAMPLE

TO: Library Blog Contributor

FROM: _____

SUBJECT: Library

Thank you for serving as a Library Blog Contributor.

By signing this form and receiving the Library Blog password, you agree to the following:

- **Not share the blog password with anyone.** You need to take steps to make sure the password is not lost or stolen. A compromised password should immediately be reported to _____ in the LMC.

- **Post only appropriate material.** Content on pages must not be offensive and must promote a culture of high community and educational standards. Use proper spelling.

- **Maintain privacy at all cost.** Do not post pictures that identify students on campus. Also, never use your full name, or anyone else's, when posting.

- **Follow copyright laws.** Do not post any picture or item for which you do not have permission to post. If not stated, always assume a picture **is** copyrighted. Do not plagiarize.

By signing this form and receiving author access to the Library Blog, you understand the following:

- **Collective good overrides individual desires.** Whenever you post something, it should be for the benefit of our school as an organization rather than your personal motives. Blogs rely on the contributors (you) to maintain a blog site that reflects on the group in a positive way. If you see something objectionable, it is your duty as an appointed blog contributor to immediately modify the blog, removing the objectionable content.

- **Posting rights are a privilege.** The school may terminate posting privileges at any time. If your blog password gets out and rampant posting occurs, please note that this could lead to the discontinuation of the Library Blog page.

- If you have any concerns related to the Library Blog, notify _____ in the LMC.

Library Blog Contributor Agreement

Parent: My student has permission to be a contributor to the Library Blog located at _____.blogspot.com.

Student: I agree to be a Library Blog Contributor and follow the guidelines established above.

_____	_____
Student Name:	Student E-mail Address
_____ _____	_____
Student Signature Date	Parent Signature

3. Place for posting files
4. Member profiles (each member can post basic information about himself or herself such as the member's name, geographic location and picture, building a sense of community within the group)
5. Electronic mailing list
6. Electronic bulletin board

Like other Web 2.0 technologies, there are a number of Web sites that provide free hosting of online groups, including the underlying software to provide group features such as threaded discussion forums and electronic mailing lists. Three of the most popular free online groups are Google Groups (groups.google.com), Yahoo! Groups (groups.yahoo.com), and MySpace Groups (groups. myspace.com).

At Northridge Academy High School (NAHS) in California, LMS and book co-author Marc McPhee utilizes Google Groups to facilitate communication among school staff. Like other online group sites, Google Groups provides a free online Web site for every group created. However, the primary reason NAHS implemented Google groups was to provide its staff members with a quick and easy method to e-mail other staff at the school. For each Google Group created, Google provides a unique e-mail address for that group. When a member of that group sends an e-mail to the group e-mail address, Google forwards that message to all group members. Thus, Google Groups functions as an e-mail distribution list.

At NAHS, the LMS has created multiple Google Groups for its staff. For instance, the NAHS_AMC Google Group membership is comprised of staff in the Arts, Media, and Communication (AMC) Academy, whereas the membership of the NAHS_Teachers Google Group is more inclusive, including all certificated staff at NAHS. As mentioned earlier each Google Group has a unique e-mail address. Thus, the creation of multiple Google Groups by the LMS allows NAHS staff to effectively target e-mails to the most appropriate audience. This helps to minimize extraneous e-mails, for instance teachers sending e-mails about AMC activities use the NAHS_AMC Google Group e-mail address instead of the NAHS_Teachers Google Group e-mail address.

Prior to using Google Groups, the LMS used an e-mail service with distribution lists. Not only was it difficult to explain to staff how to set up the lists, but maintaining and managing current e-mail addresses was problematic. Whenever a staffing change occurred or a staff member decided to change his or her e-mail address the LMS needed to send an updated list to staff. Subsequently, all staff then needed to update their distribution lists. Unfortunately, not all staff members were proactive about updating their distribution lists. Over the course of multiple years, it became apparent that some staff members were utilizing outdated distribution lists, sending e-mails to old staff members no longer at NAHS while at the same time leaving newer staff members out of the loop. Management of the tool was becoming problematic, thus the LMS began looking for a solution that would provide a more central approach to managing and maintaining the e-mail list.

When the LMS established Google Groups at NAHS, initial training consisted of written directions with screen shots e-mailed to staff and placed in mailboxes. Follow-up training during the first semester consisted of a screencast as well as some one-on-one assistance. Within six months of the online group inception, 177 threaded topics and a total of 221 messages were sent to the group "NAHS_Teachers," and nearly half of the certificated staff started at least one discussion thread. At this point, Google Groups has permeated the school culture, shaping how staff discourse and interact. Now when information is requested, whether at a staff, departmental, or academy meeting, the reply is generally something to the effect of "I'll send that to everyone through Google Groups."

In terms of LMC communication, Google Groups provides the NAHS LMS an easy way to communicate library media program information with school staff, such as special events and new resources. Initial setup of a Google Group involves collecting e-mail addresses, signing up for a Google account, and creating a Google Group. When setting up the group, the LMS can invite staff members to join or the LMS can add staff members directly to the group. The latter is easiest as staff do not need to take any action to begin receiving or sending e-mails. Make sure to notify staff in advance of setting up the group, otherwise they may mistake the initial welcome e-mail and subsequent e-mails as unwanted spam.

Under Group settings, two changes in the default configuration are recommended at setup. First, under E-mail Delivery, change the replies setting so that "Replies are sent to the author of the message." The default setting will send all messages back to the group, regardless of whether the users click "reply" or "reply all" in their e-mail program. This changes the configuration to send replies to the message author, with users still having the option to e-mail the entire group by selecting reply all. This makes the tool conform to staff experiences in sending e-mails and helps prevent staff members from accidentally sending a personal reply to the entire group. A second recommended change, also under E-mail Delivery, involves the subject prefix. To help users more readily identify messages as coming from the Google groups, consider adding a group name in the subject prefix box settings enclosed by either square brackets [ ] or curly braces { }. Every message sent to the group in turn will have this prefix in the subject line. This will help group members easily identify group messages.

When using Google Groups, members can send e-mails to the group using the assigned group e-mail address or they may log into the group's Web site and send a message directly from the Group Web site. Whereas the former method requires access to e-mail service, the latter does not. As mentioned earlier, whenever one user sends a message to the group everyone in the group receives it. Additionally, messages sent become part of a threaded discussion forum on the group's Web site. Thus, members have two access points for reading group e-mails: their individual e-mail as well as the discussion forum on the group's Web site.

Some users will rely solely on e-mail to participate in the discussions. This is okay and fulfills the initial purpose of the tool, which is to provide all staff members, especially the LMS, a quick and efficient method to broadcast e-mail messages to the rest of the staff. When implementing new technology with staff, best practice is to start simple by providing staff with the basics needed to get started. Over time as staff members realize the benefits of the new technology, the LMS can introduce advanced features. In the meantime, provide early adopters with the information they need to self-explore and fully maximize the resource. These users will serve as resources for additional staff training when the time comes. Specifically for this technology, advanced users will want to create a free Google account and log into the Google group. Here they will be able to access additional group features, including the posting of files, archives of discussion threads, adding a self-picture, options to configure their membership settings, and more.

Unlike the maintenance of distribution lists, which required every staff member on campus to update their records whenever a change was made (e.g. new staff member, new e-mail address), the benefit of Google groups is that the change needs to be made online only by one person. Collectively this is a huge time saver. For the most part, the group is self-managing. Members can update their e-mail addresses on their own. If a member wants to subscribe to the group with an additional e-mail address (some staff prefer receiving group mail at both home and school e-mail addresses), this can also be accomplished online by the user, with the group moderator needing to approve the request only in the case of private groups such as the ones utilized by NAHS.

Unlike listserv resources discussed in Chapter 8, where individuals can join and leave the listserv as desired and information generally supplements knowledge, a Google group used as described is effective only if all staff members are group members. The LMS can send important messages only if there is a high probability that users will receive the message. Otherwise, the LMS should broadcast the information through another medium, for instance a letter or flyer placed in staff mailboxes. Yet such methods are more costly in terms of copying and paper costs. These methods are also more time intensive, in terms of the time required to make the copies and place them in the mailboxes.

Ensuring all staff members remain comfortable belonging to the group means the LMS must monitor the use of the group. This is the largest management piece. For example, the LMS can create new subgroups for even more targeted e-mails. This will help ensure group members will not receive e-mails not applicable them. Additionally, LMS should consider group norms. For instance, what restrictions if any will there be on the types of e-mails members can send?

Consider the following scenario. A staff member uses the group to disseminate personal messages regarding a charity he is involved with and candy his child is selling for a fund-raiser. Anticipating such usages and establishing appropriate policies at the school site ahead of time allows the LMS to be proactive instead of reactive. Using this example, it could be policy that group members may not use the listserv for personal messages unless previously approved by the Technology Committee, Library Leadership Team, or another appropriate governance group at the school site. Once policies are established, a plan needs to be in place to inform users of the policies. One option is to append group norms to the bottom of every e-mail sent. The LMS can create message footers by accessing group settings. The LMS can then append the footer to every message sent to the group. Such policies will help alleviate concerns users may have about being inundated with excess e-mails. Of course, the policy needs to be acted on and enforced when abuse occurs; otherwise, it will be ignored.

REAL-TIME INTERACTION

In learning with others, hardly anything beats face-to-face communication in real time. People pick up valuable visual and oral clues and get immediate information and feedback. Nevertheless, telecommunications can provide useful means to interact in real time across spaces. The telephone is a classic example, but new technologies provide additional or different formats for instant connections.

Text-Based Interaction

The term "chat" typically refers to typewritten communication (i.e., text chat) that occurs in real time; as the keystrokes are typed, they are relayed to the other party. Chat rooms were popular in the 1980s and predated instant text messaging (IM). While two people can chat with each other, chat can accommodate small groups of people (beyond ten people, it becomes hard to keep track of conversation "threads" unless the structure of the chat focuses on presentation rather than lively interaction). Real-time online chat (e.g., www.tappedin.org) offers a way to provide guided group discussion; the chat is recorded and archived, and virtual offices store group documents. Tapped In also enables users to see Web sites in real time. Because chat can be supported by low-end computers, it is a useful "gateway" for real-time technology-based communication. Chat requires just an Internet-connected computer, a chat "location" (usually a Website), and a specified time.

Particularly for one-on-one communication, IMing is the favored form of text chatting. At this point in time, IMing is more popular than e-mail for Millennials. Either on the computer or on mobile devices, IMing provides quick and easy short communication that can be synchronous or asynchronous (such as leaving a message). Increasingly, libraries are incorporating IMing into their portals as a way for users to quickly and conveniently contact the librarian at point of need. One tool is Meebo (www.meebo.com). Meebo is a free Web-based instant messaging (IM) service. Unlike many other IM services that require the user to have an IM account, users of Meebo can participate in chats and enter Meebo rooms (group rooms) without an existing IM account. Users do not even have to have a Meebo account, as they can participate in chats as guests. Using Meebo, users can create their own Meebo room. In addition, the LMS can embed the room on a Web site, blog, or wiki.

The newest trend in IM service is short messaging service (SMS) that employs microtexting: typing fewer than 200 characters. Made popular in text-supported cell phones, microtexting enables one to send a short message, and anyone who "follows" the messager instantly gets that message. Technically, SMS is not interactive in that it is basically just broadcasting a little bit of text, but receivers may well respond in kind. The most known SMS application is Twitter, which is currently free. Its main usefulness for libraries lies in announcing events to people who follow the library's Twitter.

Voice-Over IP

For people who prefer talking to texting/typing, voice-over IP (VOIP) is an attractive option for easy real-time conversation. VOIP might be considered as a computer-based telephone; the user clicks (rather than dials) the intended VOIP number and then speaks using a microphone to the person on the other end of the computer line. VOIP is particularly useful for longer international calls because the cost is absorbed in the Internet service provider fee rather than as a separate and sometimes expensive bill. The disadvantage of VOIP is that the party on the other end either has to keep their VOIP application open constantly or they need to know ahead of time when the "call" will commence so that they can open the VOIP program in time.

The most popular VOIP program is Skype, which is free (and

can be upgraded to a more sophisticated program for a fee). Skype not only supports VOIP, but also includes chat and video. Users can instant message other Skype members, which facilitates scheduling the conversation. Skype also permits users to phone land lines and mobile phones, for a fee. Users can search for other people who have Skype accounts, and can create personal contact lists for quicker connecting. Skype also links to MySpace.

Virtual Realities

Virtual realities (VR) resemble real environments but are digitally developed and hosted. Currently, most VR environments display three-dimensional simulated spaces. Multi-user virtual environments (MUVE), such as Second Life, enable participants to synchronously chat, speak, and "move" using avatars to represent themselves in visually rich computer-generated environments. Documents may be stored in these environments.

Increasingly, libraries are incorporating VRs and MUVEs into their programs. If their schools or districts have VR "property," sometimes their libraries also have a virtual presence. The LMS might mount the ILMS, provide links to digital libraries, conduct virtual reference service, instruct students about twenty-first century literacies, or facilitate virtual literature circles and other types of discussions. As a beginning action, LMSs can participate in the Second Life Library 2.0 Project in order to experience library-related VR and then can volunteer to help with virtual library functions such as information services, which they can publicize to the school community.

LMSs should venture into VRs cautiously because several management issues are involved. The most obvious issue is the technology itself, which needs to be capable of supporting such programs. Systems need to have adequate RAM and speed so the avatars can move successfully, for instance. Moreover, every time a new version of a virtual environment is mounted, the participating computer stations have to be reimaged (Czarnecki and Gullett, 2007). Even with adequate technology, many schools block VRs as inappropriate, even though, as with many other online environments, participants must register and be authenticated. Sites that are used by all ages, such as Second Life, are very difficult to control, and predators can hide behind their avatar appearance. LMSs have to get written permission to mount resources online. Because they could be used for malicious reasons, XML scripts may be disabled (Swanson, 2007). Teen Second Life is less likely to have inappropriate participants (for instance, only authorized adults who have their backgrounds checked may access the virtual site), but restrictions also make it more difficult to construct a virtual presence, and libraries must pay for such constructions as they would in Second Life (Czarnecki and Gullett, 2007). Even in this safer environment, teens may need some training time; most adults experience a steep learning curve in these VR venues. Nevertheless, virtual environments hold some promise as a novel communications venue.

Webcasts

Webcasting is a more general name for Web-based broadcasts. Essentially, the Internet is used to transmit an audio or video broadcast, similar to a television or radio broadcast. The Webcast happens in real time and can be recorded and archived for later viewing. The term "streaming" refers to "live" transmission, whereby the signals are sent on an ongoing "feed." Once the Webcast is recorded and stored, it can be downloaded as a complete file (although some Webcasts can be accessed only as a stream because the producer does not want the user to download the product for later use). While the biggest Webcasters are commercial mass media, independent companies and nonprofit organizations have embraced Webcasts as a cost-effective way to transmit and share information across distances.

The Webcast format can vary greatly: from streaming audio to an interactive Web page that supports desktop sharing and group discussion. Real-time, interactive, enhanced Webcasts generally include the following features: chat, VOIP, some kind of "whiteboard" or shared space where the moderator—and sometimes participants—can share presentations, Web sites, or other types of files. Most Webcast applications enable participants to communicate via polls or surveys, and many Webcasts also enable the moderator—and sometimes participants—to communicate via video. In any case, the broadcaster and the audience need to have the same basic program to transmit and receive the Webcast. The more sophisticated the product, the more likely that the user has to download plug-ins (i.e., tiny applications) such as Java. High-end products may also require training for participants and presenters.

Webcast software licenses can also be expensive if used by many sites, such as a school district; however, free open source applications are available, at least for smaller groups. Representative products include Adobe Acrobat Connect Pro, Elluminate, ePresence, GoToWebinar, PointCast, and Webex. DoWire has developed useful guidelines (dowire.org/wiki/Enhanced_Webcasting_Specification) on selecting Webcast products; the organization focuses on the public sector.

Videoconferencing

Videoconferencing (VC) as a collaborative tool for communities of practice provides a way to address some of the limitations of virtual communities. Using cameras, microphones, network connection, and supporting hardware (e.g., a videoconferencing terminal that includes a codec, "compressor/decompressor," and a user interface), two or more parties can see and hear one another in real time. Current technologies make it possible for people to conference from their computer workstations for free with very little technical setup. The Video Network Initiative gives good technical guidelines (www.vide.net/cookbook).

Videoconferencing has several benefits for facilitating communities of practice:

- Participants feel included because they can experience everyone, including body language. Current technology provides high-resolution images with little if any time delay for voice synchronization so that subtle expressions can be decoded accurately.
- Groups can access and consult with outside experts easily through this virtual medium.
- The live atmosphere is more relaxing than an audio or text-only setting, and it encourages more conversation and better problem solving.
- Live demonstrations can simplify instructions, and questions can be handled immediately.
- Documents and realia can be shared more easily.

- Multiple sites can be supported, a task that is much easier to do now than in the past.
- External resources—computer, document stand, whiteboard, telephone link, dataconferencing link—can be incorporated.

In their research on virtual communication, Wainfan and Davis (2004) found that videoconferencing has greater impact when participants know one another and are committed to a sustained professional relationship. Participants will work harder and accomplish more. Both group dynamics and goals need to be positive and worthwhile. Videoconferencing groups should get to know one another ahead of time, ideally face-to-face, but even a telephone conversation can frontload acquaintanceships. Additionally, videoconferencing group roles and expectations need to be more explicit than for face-to-face groups. Nor should videoconferencing constitute the sole means of interaction; ongoing communication to group members and ongoing work toward achieving goals, be it process or product, is required. Particularly since most videoconferencing sessions have time limits, continuous communication, be it traditional or digital, can lower stress and frustration.

On the whole, VCs offer a more personal, relational online learning environment for meaningful group interaction than other computer-mediated or audio medium. This form of communication also paves the way for LMSs to work with their site teachers and administrators to organize VC collaboration opportunities with grade levels and departments outside of their district or state. Typically, videoconferencing has been used by librarians within large school districts, library consortia, and professional organizations. East Carolina University's Teaching Resources Center planned and implemented a Librarian to Librarian Networking Summit video conference. The INFOhio Instructional Development Task Force has used video conferencing since 2004 to provide statewide professional development and timely updates about Ohio's virtual library. This method allows local experts to give consistent and efficient, high-quality training from their site to the rest of the state as needs arise. LMSs have leveraged California's new K–12 high-speed network (K–12HSN), which offered free hardware and connectivity to offer a stable virtual video conference environment. The state's Department of Education library services uses video conferencing to overcome travel restrictions; Orange County Department of Education's library services provides professional development for LMSs, sometimes in partnership with classroom teachers; and the Computer Using Educators Library Media Educator special interest group established a teacher librarian video conferencing network (teacherlibrarians.ning.com) that involves not only its members but school districts around the United States and other professional organization affiliates. Web 2.0 and other interactive tools complement the video conferences to archive ongoing efforts.

Managing videoconferencing communication requires thorough planning, especially if technology support is not handy. Time checks with participants and video hosting services need to be established and confirmed. Equipment needs to be checked to make sure it is in good operating order and that connectivity is clear. If groups are conferencing, the room needs to be set up ahead of time to make sure that seating is comfortable and good eye contact can be maintained. Microphones may need to be placed strategically throughout the room to pick up voices. During the videoconference, group dynamics need to be monitored, and ideas should be summarized frequently (Ertl, Fischer, and Mandl, 2006; Wainfan and Davis, 2004).

LIBRARY WEB SITES

Web sites can be one of the most powerful resources the library media program offers. By making the LMC computers and/or school computers default to the LMC Web site when the user opens a Web browser, the LMS now has an easy way to communicate with students and staff. A Web site serves as a way for the LMS to inform, publicize, and organize. It can also become a vital part of the LMS's daily instruction to students.

An LMC Web site helps bring the library to students in a setting most youth find extremely comfortable to navigate and use. As Annette Lamb and Larry Johnson point out, "Many young people live on the Internet. Use their interest in online communication as a bridge to your physical library resources and services. Advertise services, post programs, seek volunteers, poll students, and get involved with engaging online activities" (Lamb and Johnson, 2008, p. 71).

Portals

A Web page is a single document on the Internet that users can access via a unique URL. A Web site is a set of interconnected Web pages including a homepage. A Web portal is a Web site or page that functions as an access point to information, especially external resources. In creating a Web site, LMSs should ascertain whether their goal is to create a Web presence or to physically bring their services online. With the former, the focus of the Web site is on static content such as library policies. However, in the Web 2.0 world in which we live, an effective LMC Web presence not only includes static content, it allows the user to interact and connect virtually with patrons. The LMS can utilize tools such as Meebo (www.meebo.com) so that Web users can interact with, ask questions of, and even receive handouts and other files from LMC staff. The LMS can integrate reading blogs, and students can be encouraged to contribute to its content.

The primary benefit of a LMC Web site is greater promotion, awareness, and use of library media program resources and services. Some LMSs are reluctant to create Web sites because of the time needed to both create and maintain them. Indeed, management of an LMC Web site is an ongoing endeavor for which the LMS must allocate time. As Marshall Breeding, Director of Innovative Technologies and Research for the John and Alexander Heard Library, writes, "A site that a library might have commissioned from a consultant or volunteer 5 years ago may look a little stale by today's standards. A Web site's content, design, and appearance require constant updating" (Breeding, 2006, p. 31).

While both the creation and maintenance of quality LMC Web sites is time intensive, time savings afforded can offset this, to the point where many Web sites are either time neutral or add back time into the LMS's schedule. For example, if the LMS posts engaging and useful booktalks on the Web site and students are aware of the resource, students will access and use them. This means fewer students each day may need book guidance from the LMS, allowing more focus on students who need extra attention. Many LMSs spend weeks at the start of each school year providing orientations for students. Instead, the LMS can post much of the orientation content online. Students can still visit the library for an orientation, but rather than the LMS utilizing a whole class approach, the LMS can direct students to Web resources. A follow-up assessment can gauge whether or not students learned.

The LMS can post screencasts demonstrating step-by-step instructions for using commonly used tools like the library OPAC to the Web as well as for videos introducing the library and its organization. Annette Lamb and Larry Johnson recommend that LMSs examine the frequently asked questions they receive throughout the day. In doing so, LMSs will notice trends. When multiple users repeatedly ask the same or similar questions, the LMS can create a brief handout, how-to tip sheet, or even a podcast, vodcast, or screencast and then post it on the LMC Web site. This in turn allows users to answer frequently asked questions on their own and will save the LMS considerable time (Lamb and Johnson, 2008).

POTENTIAL LMC WEB CONTENT AND MANAGEMENT IMPACT

The following is a listing of content that could appear on a LMC Web site. The content is organized by how time-intensive the items are to maintain.

Relatively Little Time Required
  Book recommendation site links (e.g., YALSA Quick Picks)
  Citation help links
  Electronic database links
  Library media program guidelines and policies
  Library media program procedures
  Local public library links
  Online public access catalog link
  Webmaster information/last updated notice

Moderately Time-Intensive
  Faculty and staff information
  Internet safety sites
  Orientations
  Reading lists
  Teacher tools
  Tutorials
  Useful links

Time-Intensive
  New Books
  Pathfinders
  Book reviews
  Calendars
  Contests
  Upcoming library media program events

TECH MOMENT: CREATING A SCHOOL LMC WEB SITE

To create a school LMC Web site, follow these steps:

1. **Why.** The first step in creating a quality school LMC Web site is to identify your purpose in creating the Web site. This is the "why" step. In this step, you do the following:

   a. **Brainstorm.** Make a list of the kinds of services you want to provide to patrons via the LMC Web site and what functions you want your LMC Web site to perform. This could include easy access to specific resources, such as your OPAC or electronic databases. Also common is information on library media program policies and available services.

   b. **Research.** Visit other school LMC Web sites. One good source for locating school LMC Web sites is CoreCollections.net (www. school-libraries.net). Get an idea of the content these LMC Web sites provide and how information and resources are organized. What do you like? This may also help you identify the why.

   c. **Think.** For any potential Web content, what are the implications in terms of maintenance? If I create a page of "research links," will I have the time to maintain this page, or will the links become outdated and broken over time?

   At the end of this step, you should have a clear idea of *why* you want to create a school LMC Web site. You should also have a list of the content you want to include on your Web site. Content should be divided into information that you would like to add to the Web site during the creation process (short term) as well as information that will be added after the Web site is up and running (long term). Start small; you can always grow content.

2. **Plan.** In this step, take your list of content and organize it.

   a. Identify general categories for the content you will include on your LMC Web site. For example, hours of operation and circulation policies might both fall under the category of "Info" or "About the Library."

   b. Organize your categories into a graphic organizer. Start with the homepage and identify subpages.

   c. Consider whether your Web site design allows for expansion and growth over time. You don't want to have to redesign your Web site two years down the road to fit in new content.

3. **Learn.** In this step, you will decide how to create your Web site. There is an abundance of Web design programs that offer WYSI-WYG design. WYSIWYG stands for "what you see is what you get." Using a WYSIWYG design tool requires little to no knowledge of

Web authoring skills. For instance, you can create a document in Microsoft Word and save it as a Web page. Ten years ago, it was essential to know HTML (hypertext markup language). Today such knowledge is no longer essential; however, it can be helpful. While tools such as Microsoft Word are great and enable the fast creation of Web pages, providing such simplicity for the user can lead to frustration when something doesn't display exactly like you want it to. In such circumstances, the LMS needs to know how to "look under the hood," looking at the HTML code directly.

For this reason, LMSs who embark upon a Web site project are strongly encouraged to take some time to learn the basics of HTML. The Web site W3Schools (www.w3schools.com/html/html_intro. asp) is one of many Internet sites that can help grasp the basics of html. Here are some basics to get you started:

a. Commands are enclosed in angle brackets < >, for instance <b>. This is called a tag.

HTML is symmetrical (there is a start tag and an end tag). For example <b>**bold text**</b> or <i>*italicized text*</i>. Notice the slash (/) is used to indicate the end of a command.

b. The code for creating a hyperlink is <a href="url">text to be displayed</a>.

At the end of this step, you should understand the basics of HTML.

4. **Choose** a Web authoring program and explore the program to learn how it works. If you are unsure what program to use, seek recommendations from colleagues or use a search engine to locate Web authoring programs. The former is preferred, as having someone who is already familiar with the program you select will be beneficial if you have questions or run into unexpected problems. Many programs offer free trials. Your best bet is to use a program that specializes in developing Web sites such as Adobe Dreamweaver (www.adobe.com/products/dreamweaver) or Microsoft FrontPage (www.microsoft.com/frontpage).

With a program like Dreamweaver or FrontPage you will have more control over the aesthetics of your LMC Web site. On the other hand, numerous Web 2.0 tools allow you to create suitable Web sites using simple online interfaces. Even a blog or a wiki can contain typical LMC Web site content in a less formal structure. While not a Web site by definition, many LMSs use blogs and wikis to provide similar communication benefits. Thus, if you find learning new technologies on your own to be difficult, the time you will need to invest to master a program like Dreamweaver or FrontPage probably is not worth the added benefit obtained by a more aesthetic and streamlined Web site.

In this step, you will want to consult with the Webmaster for your school or district. Some schools and districts have detailed style guidelines for Web sites that must be adhered to in order for the finished product to be published. In addition, some school sites use a particular Web hosting provider and require that all pages are created using established templates that are accessed through a specialized site for which the school pays an annual maintenance fee.

5. **Create.** Start with your homepage. The homepage is the most important page, as it is the first point of contact for your Web patrons. To begin creating your homepage, you should start by drawing out how you want it to look on paper (e.g., where you will have menu items, text items, pictures, etc). When designing your school LMC homepage, you should ask the following questions:

   a. Does your Web page make a good first impression with your target audience? Consider colorful graphics and text.
   b. Is your homepage is easy to navigate?
   c. Is a clear menu of choices available?
   d. Does the homepage fit on a standard 1024 x 768 pixel screen, or does the user need to scroll left or down to access all of the content on the homepage?
   e. How does the homepage look using higher screen resolutions and using different Web browsers?

6. **Add Content.** Link pages to the homepage. Be sure to create a unifying theme. Be sure each subpage links back to the Web site homepage and other main pages. As you add content, make sure to adhere to accessibility guidelines. The article "Principles of Accessible Design" from WebAIM (www.webaim.org/intro/#principles) provides good guidelines.

7. **Publish.** The final step is publishing your school library Web site to the Internet. To publish a Web site you must upload it to a Web server. If your school already has a Webmaster, have her or him publish your LMC Web site to your school's site. If the school does not have a Webmaster, you may have found yet another way to make yourself indispensible. Consider becoming the Webmaster for your school.

Integrated Library Management Systems

ILMSs serve as powerful communication tools, enabling the school community to know what resources can be accessed via the library. Nevertheless, LMSs often overlook the communication "channel" itself, thus missing a great opportunity to be responsive to user needs and pro-active in promoting the LMC. By managing the communication interface of ILMSs, LMSs can optimize resource retrieval and user participation. Each of the following features can be accessed through the administrative module and are typically configured on initial installation.

The most obvious communications aspect of ILMSs is the opening search screen. Search options should be developmentally appropriate; usually a basic search bar is used in elementary schools. Icon-based browsing also typifies elementary school ILMSs. Any screen text should also be at the reading level of most users. Some ILMSs have different thematic layouts or "skins" that can reflect the LMC's intended atmosphere: academic, lighthearted, energetic.

The result screen also conveys a variety of information, which the LMS can customize. The public view of the source's record can display just the bare information or all of the fields. Increasingly, the result screen resembles a search engine "hit" page, giving just enough information to locate the item and enabling the user to click for more information. Visually, the book's cover can be displayed, tag or subject "clouds" can be shown, and second-step research assistance can be provided (sometimes called "faceted navigation") (see Figure 6.1).

The newest communication tool for ILMSs is a catalog "shell" that acts like a portal, enabling the ILMS to incorporate additional functions. This outer interface does not change the ILMSs itself, but it does activate interactive features such as patron postings of book recommendations. With this added layer, the OPAC can look and function like a simple Google search screen with a single point of entry, linking the user to relevant sources from the library catalog, subscription databases, and in-house repositories; searching can be federated. The interface also supports "fuzzy" spelling ("Did you mean . . . ?"), RSS feed, links to other libraries' catalogs, online reference service, and MyLibrary folders for each user to personalize (including personal tags for books, comments on reading, and

Figure 6.1
Catalog Screen Page from California State University Long Beach Library

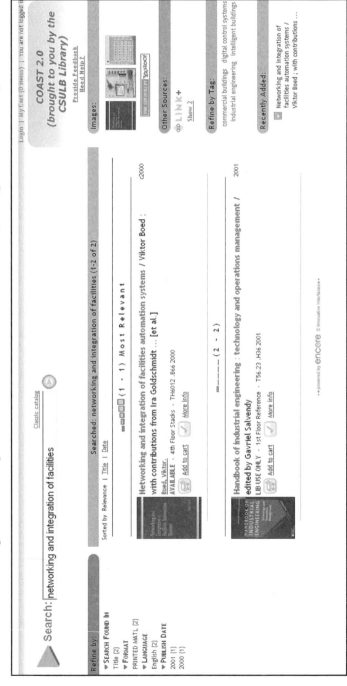

personal bibliographies that can be shared if the user so desires). The major brands of this next generation interface include AquaBrowser (Medialab Solutions), Encore (Innovative Interfaces), Primo (Ex Libris), WorldCatLocal (OCLC), Polaris (Polaris Library Systems), and open-source products Evergreen and Koha (Breeding, 2007).

While such participatory communication aspects of this next-generation ILMS appeals to users, their management and incorporation into the library's digital collection system can involve sophisticated technical support, which is usually *not* inexpensive. The National Initiative for a Networked Cultural Heritage (2002) mentions several issues. Communication customizations need to be well documented and maintained. In addition, complying with intellectual property regulations is very difficult; digital rights management technologies are being employed to control content use. While automated systems conveniently take care of authentication issues and facilitate fair royalties compensation, they may jeopardize privacy rights and leak into discriminatory profiling practices. Who said talk was cheap?

WORKS CITED

Bates, Naomi. "Booktalk Podcast." Northwest High School. Available: www.nisdtx.org/120820731141528687/podcasts/browse.asp?A=39 9&BMDRN=2000&BCOB=0&C=70101 (accessed July 3, 2009).

Bloglines. 2004. "Bloglines Marks Search Milestone of 100 Million Blog and News Feed Articles." IAC Search & Media, August 12. Available: www.bloglines.com/about/pr_08122004 (accessed July 1, 2009).

Bobrosky, Mark. 2007. *Walter Reed Middle School Faculty Services Handbook.* Los Angeles: Los Angeles Unified School District. Available: www.reedmstech.com/library/images/PDF/fac_hndbk.pdf (accessed January 5, 2009).

Bookwink. 2007. "Video Booktalk Archives." Bookwink.com. Available: www.bookwink.com/archives.html (accessed June 30, 2009).

Breeding, Marshall. 2006. "Web 2.0? Let's Get to Web 1.0 First." *The Systems Librarian* 26, no. 5 (May): 30–33.

Breeding, Marshall. 2007. "Introduction." *Library Technology Reports* 43, no. 4 (July/August): 5–14.

Buechner, Maryanne Murray. 2004. "50 Coolest Websites." *Time.* Available: www.time.com/time/techtime/200406/ (accessed January 1, 2009).

Coombs, Karen A. 2007. "Building a Library Web Site on the Pillars of Web 2.0." *Computers in Libraries* 27, no. 1 (January): 16–20.

CoreCollections.net. "SchoolLibraries.net: Web Pages Created by School Librarians." H.W. Wilson. Available: www.school-libraries.net (accessed July 1, 2009).

Cunningham, Ward. 2003. "Correspondence on the Etymology of Wiki." Available: http://c2.com/doc/etymology.html (accessed July 1, 2009).

Czarnecki, Kelly, and Matt Gullett. 2007. "Meet the New You." *School Library Journal* 53, no. 1: 36–39.

Ertl, Bernard, Franz Fischer, and Heinz Mandl. 2006. "Conceptual and Socio-Cognitive Support for Collaborative Learning in Videoconferencing Environments." *Computers & Education* 47, no. 3 (November): 298–315.

Florida Center for Instructional Technology. "Ideas for Podcasting in the Classroom: Book Talks." Available: http://fcit.usf.edu/podcasts/book_talks.html (accessed January 3, 2009).

Keane, Nancy. "Booktalks Quick and Simple." Available: www.nancykeane.com/booktalks/ (accessed July 1, 2009).

King, David Lee. 2007. "Inviting Participation, Part 4: Specific Tools—Blogs," January 17. Available: www.davidleeking.com/2007/01/17/inviting-participation-part-4-specific-tools-blogs/ (accessed July 1, 2009).

Lamb, Annette, and Larry Johnson. 2008. "The Virtual Teacher-Librarian." *Teacher Librarian* 35, no. 4 (April): 69–71.

Martin, Nicole. 2007. "Keep Your Eyes on the Enterprise: Emails, Wikis, Blogs, and Corporate Risk." *EContent* 30, no. 6 (July): 54–59.

Multnomah County Library. 2008. "RSS." Multnomah County Library, October 22. Available: www.multcolib.org/catalog/rss.html/ (accessed July 1, 2009).

National Initiative for a Networked Cultural Heritage. 2002. *Guide to Good Practice in the Digital Representation and Management of Cultural Heritage Materials.* Washington, DC: National Initiative for a Networked Cultural Heritage.

Nicholas Senn High School Library. "Nicholas Senn H.S. Library." Available: http://sennlibrary.blogspot.com/ (accessed July 1, 2009).

Searls, Doc. 2008. "The Live Web." Doc Searls Weblog, September 26. Available: http://blogs.law.harvard.edu/doc/2008/09/26/the-live-web/ (accessed July 1, 2009).

Shanahan, Seanean. "The Library Lady." Available: http://shayanasls.podomatic.com/ (accessed July 1, 2009).

Stephens, Michael. 2007. "Best Practices for Social Software in Libraries." *Library Technology Reports* 43, no. 5 (September): 67–74.

Swanson, Kari. 2007. "Second Life: A Science Library Presence in Virtual Reality." *Science & Technology Libraries* 27, no. 3 (March): 79–86.

W3Schools. "HTML Introduction." Available: www.w3schools.com/html/ html_intro.asp (accessed July 1, 2009).

Wainfan, Lynne, and Paul Davis. 2004. *Challenges in Virtual Collaboration*. Santa Monica, CA: RAND.

WebAIM. "Introduction to Web Accessibility: Principles of Accessible Design." Available: www.webaim.org/intro/#principles. (accessed July 1, 2009).

Chapter 7

Policies and Procedures for Technology Management

Most of this book details the nuts and bolts of managing technology resources: what to get and how to maintain it for its effective use to support the library media program. Know-how. This chapter focuses on the big picture: policies and procedures that impact the effective use of library technology as a system.

POLICIES AND PROCEDURES

Policies may be considered as "doing the right thing." Basically, policies codify decisions so that fair practice can be assured. Policies usually have to be approved by a governing body because the institution as a whole is responsible for the consequences of policy decisions. Most library media center (LMC) policies are approved by the site administrator, but some policies might need to be approved by a school board if those statements impact other functions within the site or district. An example of such a policy would be requiring students to pay the replacement value for any equipment that is damaged or lost. The business office could be impacted, and outstanding bills might jeopardize graduation activities.

In contrast, procedures enable staff to "do things right." Procedures explain how to carry out a policy. As such, they tend to be much more detailed than policies, and they normally do not require approval beyond the LMC. An example of a procedure, building on the previous policy, would consist of the steps for determining a student's responsibility for equipment damage, assessing the cost, writing up the fine, and communicating with the student, business office, and possibly the graduation coordinator.

Generally, library media specialists (LMS) write policies and procedures, with input from the rest of the LMC staff and LMC advisory boards. Certainly, those entities should review document drafts for clarity and accuracy. LMC staff and volunteers who need to follow procedures should test draft versions to make sure that all steps are included and that directions are accurate. Site administrators should be consulted when creating or changing policies in order to make sure that they align with the site's other policies, particularly technology ones, and to keep administrators informed about the LMC's administrative practices. The site administrator can also provide needed support in approving and enforcing those LMC policies. For some examples of various technology policies, see Table 7.1 at the end of the chapter.

Access

Effective technology use requires thoughtful learning and opportunities for practice and application. Therefore, the LMC needs to ensure that the school community has convenient physical access to a variety of technologies. As information central, the LMC can centrally organize the equitable use of technology throughout the school, as access is not limited to the library but is *facilitated* via the library.

Physical Access

Many LMSs utilize LMC technology in day-to-day instruction to support student achievement. In addition, many LMSs are responsible for ordering, distributing, and maintaining audiovisual equipment schoolwide. The LMS must develop clear circulation policies for LMC technology in order to ensure library media program equipment is not lost or stolen. This includes in-library use policies, class use policies, and at-home use policies.

Often, students themselves utilize the technology. For example, students use LMC laptops to access subscription databases, Webcams to create videos, and graphics tablets for an art project. Moreover, students, including those with Individualized Education

Plans (IEPs) that mandate extended time, need the ability to access library media program equipment outside of the class period as projects are completed.

Because many schools serve students from a range of socioeconomic backgrounds, it cannot be expected that all students would have advanced technology at home, so the LMS must ensure that needed resources will be available to all students; to this end, library media programs may have extended LMC hours before or after the school day to ensure equitable access. However, extended hours and student breaks such as lunch represent a more vulnerable time for library media program equipment. Unlike with class visits, there is no clear grouping of students. Students may be constantly coming to and leaving the LMC. After school, many LMCs are abuzz with walk-in tutoring programs. Often, the LMS is busy assisting individual students and checking out LMC materials all while trying to effectively supervise the LMC. In many parts of the country, the LMS runs the LMC without any additional paid support staff. In such circumstances, the LMS needs a simple approach for circulating technology that doesn't require much effort.

Ultimately, for day-to-day technology use, the LMS should investigate all existing practices and policies to ensure that they meet program needs. If time is the scarcest resource, then relaxed policies should be in place, while keeping in mind that citizens expect public schools to be good stewards of public resources. This includes money used to purchase library media program equipment. If money is the scarcest resource, the LMS may need to put more time-consuming procedures in place that work to further protect library media program equipment. As is often the case, both money and time are scarce resources for LMC media programs, forcing the LMS to find a positive balance between the two.

For equipment that is fairly stationary, such as a desktop computer, many LMSs are comfortable with simply allowing students to access the resource without checking it out. This is especially true when appropriate computer security software, discussed in Chapter 5, is in place. Such software helps protect the computer's configuration, leaving theft and vandalism as main concerns. LMSs address these concerns through security hardware, also discussed in Chapter 5, such as video surveillance, lockdown devices, or even fake cameras.

On the other hand, using the circulation program to check out equipment provides valuable statistics, as discussed in Chapter 3. For LMSs who find it difficult to acquire school funds for new technology acquisitions, barcoding and cataloging all equipment can provide valuable circulation statistics to stakeholders, depending on the stability of the circulation program.

While the LMS can bar-code portable equipment for library staff to scan at the circulation desk, not all equipment is portable. Students are not able to bring the computer to the circulation desk to "check out." A common strategy when circulating desktops through the integrated library system is to bar-code a smaller device, such as a small acrylic sign, which is designated for a specific computer number (necessitating that the LMS label each computer, as discussed in Chapter 3). The student checks out the sign and places it on the appropriate computer. A sign holder or Velcro can hold the sign in place. Some LMSs use computer management software (discussed in Chapter 3) to lock the computer until a student checks it out.

LMC laptops warrant special consideration due to their high costs and extreme portability. The LMS should ensure that effective policies are in place for their use. For example, the LMS needs to determine who will use the laptops, where the laptops are used, and when they are used. Will individual students have the ability to use the laptops, or will they be reserved for whole-class use? If used by students, will laptops be available throughout the day, such as during lunch time and other student breaks? Note that when presented a choice, students almost always will choose a laptop over a desktop, even if told the desktop is faster.

Understaffed library media programs may find that for individual use, checking out laptops and supervising their use can impact library staff time and availability to perform other tasks. Depending on the arrangement of facilities, including availability of wall space and location of electrical outlets, the laptop cart storage location may not be close enough to the circulation desk for continual checkouts to be practical. This may lead the LMS to consider reserving laptop use for class visits only. On the other hand, a laptop is ideal for certain tasks; for example, a student who wants to record a podcast can relocate with the laptop to quieter areas of the LMC. Thus, policies should be carefully reviewed for their impact on students' ability to effectively complete instructional projects. Here are some questions to consider when developing such policies:

- Will LMS-managed laptop carts be kept and used solely in the LMC?
- Can laptops be used in classrooms?
- How and when will teachers receive training in using laptop carts?
- Are student aides or other LMC personnel available to provide technical assistance and assist with setup, distribution, and collection of laptops?

Circulation Procedures

Another essential need is a defined procedure for distributing technical equipment. In doing so, LMSs must again balance security needs with needs to maximize instructional time. Schools utilizing block scheduling instead of a traditional bell schedule will find this less of an issue because the time it takes to distribute and return equipment consumes a small percentage of a block class period than for a traditional bell schedule. For example, many LMSs barcode laptops, cataloging that equipment for inclusion in the LMC integrated management system. This practice allows the LMS to circulate and track laptop usage. Other LMSs maintain a checkout sheet or collect student IDs, trading the ID for the laptop. Prior to the end of the period, the laptops must be collected and secured, which unfortunately takes away from instructional time. However, the alternative of waiting until after the dismissal bell rings invites chaos and invites a better opportunity for theft. Even if laptops are collected before the bell rings, theft may still occur.

This scenario shows what can happen. During third period, 20 laptops are distributed to a class of students for in-LMC use. Students take the laptops to tables, but also frequently leave the laptops unattended. For instance, one student goes to the restroom. Several others go to the LMC stacks looking for books for their research. At the end of the period, a laptop is missing. During the same period, several additional students came to the LMC from other classes. These students have now left. Thus, the laptop could still be in the LMC, or a student could have left with it. There is no way to know for sure. Thus, the school cannot justify retaining and searching the remaining students. The school could track down the individual students who used the LMC if the LMS maintained a sign-in sheet. However, even if a student did leave with a laptop, within minutes that student could have passed the laptop off to another student or even stored it in a friend's locker. Thus, again, the school has no clear way to determine who currently possesses the laptop. All the LMS can do is carefully search the LMC in case a student hid the laptop away for later retrieval.

In many school districts where the LMS checks out equipment to specific students, if the item is lost or damaged the student or the student's guardian(s) is (are) liable. However, this brings up several questions:

- Was (were) the guardian(s) notified that their student would be using expensive equipment?
- Did the guardian(s) provide consent for the student to both use this equipment and be liable for its loss?
- If the equipment was required to complete the class activity, did the student have a choice in accepting the liability?
- Does the teacher or library staff bear any responsibility for not providing adequate supervision of the equipment?
- Did the library staff provide the student with a Kensington compatible key lock to secure the laptop, for instance?

Even if the student ultimately is liable, the family might not have the ability to pay. Thus, the need to have the equipment replaced still is not resolved. Anticipating such situations, the LMS can use computer tracking software (described in Chapter 5) to help deter theft. Even then, the occasional lost piece of equipment may be the cost of doing business. If so, effective management must include a regular budget to replace lost or damaged items. Ultimately, policies must balance instructional needs with the management and fiscal needs of each school site.

LMSs need policies for off-campus use of technology in addition to in-library use. Continuing the laptop example, while some LMSs may limit use of laptops to whole classes and other LMSs may allow laptop use on-campus throughout the school day including student breaks, still others may even allow at-home use. The rationale is that students lacking computers at home need the ability to finish technology-dependent assignments. Off-campus use requires special considerations. Once LMC equipment leaves the LMC, the LMS depends on the user to return it. For instance, consider the situation where a student checks out an MP3 player/recorder to complete a podcast assignment. The student "promises" to have it back the following morning. This is important because the LMS needs the item for second period. However, the student forgets the item the following morning, and the student's guardians are unable to bring it to the school for the student. Alternatively, consider the situation where the student suddenly falls sick and doesn't come to school the following day. Thus, allowing off-campus use of equipment needed for class instruction usually is not advisable.

Just as the LMS may designate some books as noncirculating, such as reference books, the LMS can designate technology as circulating and noncirculating. If the library media program needs to have 40 microphones available for class use at all times, the LMS might consider purchasing 50 microphones, with 10 being cataloged as circulating and the other 40 being reserved for class use only. This approach also provides a safety net should one or more microphones in the class set become damaged. The LMS can purchase "Reference" or "Reserve" classification labels from many library supply companies or even order custom labels as a reminder to library staff.

When checking in equipment, especially equipment that students use off-campus, check-in procedures should include equipment inspection, especially for devices with removable parts, such as a camcorder with a removable memory card. For example, if rechargeable AA batteries were included in the device when checked out, the same batteries need to be present when the user returns the item. It would be easy for the user to inadvertently swap out the batteries, especially if the batteries lost their charge, not realizing the old batteries were rechargeable. For a digital camera, if a 1GB removable SD card was included at check out, library staff needs to ensure the same SD card is present. Otherwise, the card could be missing or swapped out with another card of a different capacity.

If there are particular access bays the user should not open, such as the cover to the RAM bay, library staff need to make sure the user did not remove components such as RAM. It is not practical for library staff to unscrew access bays to check for missing components each time a student checks in a device, so attaching a special tamper sticker can solve the problem. This way, if the user removes the cover it will be evident to library staff. Finally, library staff should check items for damage during the check-in process.

For each device, the LMS needs to identify the specific items that the library staff will inspect at check-in. For example, staff should check laptop displays for cracks. A simple solution is to develop a parts diagram and check-in form specific to that device. The LMS can make two columns on the form: one for use at checkout and one for use at check-in. When the user checks out the device, he or she should initial to indicate that all the items are present. Library staff should then file the form nearby so it will be available when the user returns the device; the parts diagram stays with the device to guide the borrower in the device's use. During the check-in process library staff again uses the form to ensure all items for the device are present and in good condition. Because it can be easy to forget specific procedures for these items, which may not be borrowed often, circulation procedures can accompany the item, similar to how stores provide cashier instructions about redeeming coupons.

When a user returns an item with parts missing, the LMS must have clear procedures for handling the situation. Pat Franklin and Claire Stephens, two national board certified LMSs, suggest, "Keep a designated spot in your equipment room for the return of stray parts and pieces of equipment. On a monthly basis, go through the pieces you have collected and return them to their proper set. Items you cannot identify stay in the bin." For many LMSs, the end of the year is the one time when school staff members return all equipment to the LMC, often for safe storage over the summer. This is an excellent time to reconnect pieces separated from their set, to inventory all equipment, and to order missing parts. This ensures all equipment begins the next school year ready to circulate (Franklin and Stephens, 2006).

Teacher or classroom use of library media program technology also requires policies. When a teacher checks out equipment, such as a class set of devices, other teachers are likely to need the equipment as well throughout the school year. Thus, it is important the equipment is well maintained and returned in time for use by the next class. Similar to scheduling the LMC for physical access, the

LMS needs to maintain a calendar for scheduling usage of LMC equipment to avoid conflicts.

When the teacher checks out LMC equipment, the teacher typically becomes responsible for monitoring that equipment. Thus, if equipment is lost or stolen while in the possession of a teacher, is it the teacher's responsibility to replace it? If yes, what about LMC books or other LMC materials or equipment? If such equipment is lost or stolen from the LMC, is it the responsibility of the LMS to replace it? If policies differ according to format, teachers may think that a double standard exists. Furthermore, classroom teachers might rightly wonder if the LMS is held personally fiscally responsible for a book or piece of equipment. In short, LMSs should try to imagine being in the classroom teacher's shoes figuratively before demanding remuneration.

On one hand, the LMS is often faced with scarce resources, and replacing lost LMC equipment probably costs much more than a book. On the other hand, the success of the library media program is dependent on the support of teachers and their willingness to utilize the LMC. While some teachers will volunteer to replace the item, other teachers may consider such losses regrettable but unavoidable given large class sizes and district demands that force classroom teachers to cut corners in order to maximize instructional time. Thus, LMSs must tread carefully. For instance, involving administration in such matters after the fact can be seen by teaching staff as unsupportive and in the long run undermine support for the LMC at the school site. When in doubt, LMSs should refer to and follow district protocols. For instance, many school districts require a police report anytime school equipment is stolen. The LMS should also find out whether the school or district carries insurance that covers such losses.

Scheduling

In addition to developing plans for how the LMC will circulate library media program technology, the LMS must determine how students and staff will access this equipment during the school day. This involves developing policies for how both students and classes access the LMC.

Some library media programs utilize fixed calendaring, with

predefined classes utilizing the LMC on specific dates during specific times. Other library media programs utilize flexible scheduling, with the LMC open for scheduling by teachers as needed to support the classroom curriculum. Still other library media programs utilize a hybrid approach, combining flexible and fixed scheduling. The American Association of School Librarians (AASL) 1991 position statement on flexible scheduling states:

> The integrated library media program philosophy requires that an open schedule must be maintained. Classes cannot be scheduled in the LMC to provide teacher release or preparation time. Students and teachers must be able to come to the center throughout the day to use information sources, to read for pleasure, and to meet and work with other students and teachers.

In addition to access policies, the LMS must create and communicate scheduling procedures and policies. Here are some questions to consider:

- How will teachers know when the LMC is available?
- How will teachers sign their classes up to use the LMC?
- How far in advance can a teacher sign up to use the LMC?
- How long can a teacher sign a class up for use of the LMC?
- Will LMC availability be on a first-come, first-served basis?
- How can the LMS ensure that access to the LMC is equitable?
- For what purposes may teachers sign up to use the LMC?
- Must the teacher supervise his or her class while in the LMC?

An FAQ list can be an effective tool to communicate this information.

Traditionally, LMSs use a paper calendar to manage the LMC schedule. Teachers who wish to reserve time in the LMC call, e-mail, or visit the LMC to check availability and sign up classes for future visits. These methods can be problematic for multiple reasons. If the teacher calls, this requires the library staff to stop and check the calendar, which takes time. Likewise, if the teacher e-mails the LMS or other library staff, this can ultimately lead to a series of e-mails, especially if the LMC is not available for the requested dates/times and alternate dates need to be proposed. While this may seem trivial, over the course of a school year, routine activities can turn into hours spent that otherwise could have been utilized for other library media program needs and goals. If teachers have to walk to the LMC to sign up, this can be a physical barrier to use, as teachers might not be able to come to the LMC at the moment they are contemplating a class visit to the LMC. Indeed, curriculum planning and development outside of the school day has become the norm for many teachers. Where the ideal would be for all LMC visits to be collaboratively planned well in advance, the reality in many schools is that classroom curriculum, including LMC visits, are often planned at the last minute. This is especially true when working with new teachers.

For these reasons, an online calendar can facilitate use of the LMC by providing teachers with a way to check facility availability even when they are off-campus. The LMS can embed or link the online calendar on the LMC Web site. Online calendars can be time-savers by eliminating the need to respond to phone or e-mail inquiries about LMC availability. A Web search using the keywords "online calendar" will yield a number of Web sites that provide online calendaring applications. Wendy Boswell, author for About. com (www.about.com), identifies her "picks" for some of the best calendars on the Web. She includes 30Boxes, Yahoo! Calendar, and Google Calendar (Boswell, accessed 2009).

Furthermore, the LMS can also allow teachers to book their own LMC visits (another time-saver). Management concerns vary, and some LMSs choose not to implement online calendars or allow staff to sign themselves up due to these management concerns. For example, what if one teacher intentionally deletes the sign-up of another staff member? Another concern is that teachers will sign up for inappropriate uses of the LMC or that select teachers will hoard LMC availability. Again, while a potential and valid concern, this is a policies issue rather than a determining factor in the decision to utilize an online calendar. At schools where teachers heavily utilize the LMC, either throughout the year or during peak seasons, the LMS must carefully consider and then enforce LMC equitable scheduling policies. For example, the LMS can monitor the sign-ups and contact an overly ambitious teacher. Ideally, these policies are made with the stakeholders such as a Library Leadership Team. While concerns exist, so do solutions, so LMSs should consider moving ahead with online calendars.

Is advanced scheduling always needed? Some LMSs require

all visits to the LMC to be collaboratively planned in advance and focus on the development of student information literacy skills. While a worthwhile endeavor, it is the opinion of the authors of this book that all visits to the LMC should be encouraged and seen as opportunities for the LMS to highlight the LMC's program and resources. Ultimately, informal visits during one year can lead to more formal, collaboratively planned visits the following year. With such as philosophy, using an online calendar allows teachers to utilize the LMC, even at the last minute.

Connectivity

Between the information source and the information consumer exists a communication channel. At the very least, some kind of equipment is usually needed in order to access the information "package." Increasingly, the information source exists outside of the library wall: from another location on campus, or on the opposite side of the world. The channel itself may be able to handle a few bits of information at a time or a movie in real time, depending on the type of connectivity. As multimedia information is being increasingly pushed via the Internet to more people globally, the robustness and speed of connectivity needs to keep up with these transfers of rich technology.

Web Proxies

A Web proxy is a combination of hardware and software on the network through which outgoing Web traffic is routed. When a user types a Web site address into a browser, the computer sends a request to the server that hosts that particular Web site. The server then sends the Web site content to the computer. When a Web proxy exists on the network, the Web proxy acts as an intermediary between the computer and the requested Web site. Requests are routed to the Web proxy, which in turn requests data from the server hosting the Web site. The Web proxy receives this data and routes it back to the user. This transaction occurs seamlessly in the background.

One use of Web proxies is to improve the speed at which users are able to navigate Web sites. The proxy does this by keeping a cache or storage of frequently accessed sites. After the first computer on the network accesses the requested Web site, the Web proxy maintains a copy of the site in its cache. When additional requests for the same Web site are sent through the proxy, the proxy is able to immediately send the content to the requesting computer without contacting the hosting Web site again. Of course, dynamic Web sites with content that updates frequently should not be configured for caching by the Web proxy as this will prevent users from accessing the most current content available.

Firewalls

In computer terms, a firewall is hardware, software, or a combination thereof used to prevent access to private network resources. Firewalls regulate network traffic. When a firewall is used, computers on the network are configured to access other network resources through the firewall. This routes all traffic through the firewall, which enables the network administrator to enable or disable certain types of network traffic through configuration of the firewall, which helps protect the network from crackers. A cracker is the term for an individual who intentionally tries to bypass security settings such as a firewall to access unauthorized resources.

When utilizing a firewall, resources within the network can be configured into zones. For example, there may be an instructional side and an administrative side to the network, with the firewall used to prevent students from unintentionally or intentionally accessing confidential information typically contained in the school's data systems. At the same time, traffic from one network resource to another network resource within the same zone would be configured to pass through the firewall without being blocked, such as a computer on the instructional side sending a print request to a network printer also on the instructional side.

The most common use of a firewall is to restrict users outside of the network from accessing network resources within the network. This is known as a border firewall. For instance, the LMS may be able to access the Web-based LMC online public access catalog (OPAC) internally while on campus but have no access off campus. In this example, the firewall prevents access to the physical server that runs the OPAC. Every Web site on the Internet is hosted somewhere on a computer that acts as a Web server for that site. If the school's firewall prevents access to on-campus resources from off campus including servers, this action effectively prevents access to the OPAC server. Depending on district or school policy, exceptions can be made to the firewall, with the firewall configured to allow access by off-campus users to specific network resources such as the OPAC server.

Most LMSs find that access to school computers is not available when off campus due to a border firewall. If the LMS has legitimate needs to access certain resources on the network while off campus, the LMS can investigate with the network manager to find out if virtual private network (VPN) is available. VPN allows users to be connected a public network, such as the Internet. When using a VPN client, data is sent encrypted across the Internet, maintaining the privacy of the information.

Human-Technology Interface

Equipment may be available, but if the person cannot access it or does not use it appropriately, then the technology is minimally effective. Forethought is needed to ensure transparent and rightful interaction between the school community and technology. Policies and procedures for purchasing, installation, operations, and instruction need to be enacted in order to facilitate decision making.

Log-on/Authentication

Network security is of utmost importance in order to optimize data integrity and maintain proper computer operations. Without some kind of indication as to who is using a specific system, the network software can identify only the machine and the time. Network administrators need to make sure that the appropriate users are accessing the data. This process is called authentication. Typically, both a log-on/login set of numbers and letters and a password are needed. While it is possible to have students sign in at the circulation desk and be assigned a specific machine, or have students write their names on a sheet by each computer, log-on authentication procedures for each machine are much more convenient and accurate.

Another aspect of authentication is level of access. Sophisticated software can assign different levels of access to different people, based on their responsibility and expertise. This practice is common in integrated library management systems (ILMS) where student aides can circulate materials but cannot override overdues;

only the LMS and maybe the school technology specialist would have full access.

Log-on procedures are also necessary for most subscription licenses, especially those that are based on dynamic IP (Internet protocol) addresses (that is, a person can use any computer in order to access the information). The alternative solution is to limit access to computers within a range of assigned IP addresses. In some cases, the remote user has to log on to access the library portal or server. Once authenticated at that level, then the user can access any product on the server (keeping the appearance of static IP addresses); this practice is called internal authentication. Similarly, the vendor can be provided with a range that includes all of the campus computers, but in either case the library staff have little control over access outside of the library walls (let alone inside the facility when the library is supposedly closed).

Particularly for subscription databases, some libraries institute a single log-on and password, usually a unique combination for each product because vendors may vary on their log-on specifications. While this practice permits remote access (if the license agreement is based on dynamic IP addresses), it does not enable staff to determine which individual is accessing the information. A very poor practice is to post the log-on and password information on the library portal for anyone to see; hundreds of users around the world will be very happy to have that information, but the intended users at the school might not be able to access the site if remote users take up all of the user "slots" in those cases where the license agreement is based on a specific number of simultaneous users. If the library does use a single log-on/password for a database, this information should be provided only in print form: on the machines, on bookmarks, in school family newsletters, or in school planner binders.

Regardless of the process used, one of the main stumbling blocks of log-ons and passwords is forgetfulness. Students forget their locker numbers and their student numbers, so forgetting log-ons and passwords falls into that same category. Increasingly as students and adults have access to technology at home, they may have several accounts, each of which might have a different set of codes. The solution may be the same: whatever the person uses to remember those other numbers can be used for computer access codes. Individuals usually have a planner, be it print or digital, where such codes are kept. Of course, such centralization can be risky if another person can access it readily, but the responsibility has to rest with the owner rather than LMS, although reminders about security measures can be useful (such as not writing the password on a sticky note pasted on the monitor edge or just inside the top desk drawer—truly, people do this, and hackers take advantages of such vulnerable actions). Resending the password, or erasing the old log-on/password and providing a new one, can be laborious, so finding an automated way to do this process is key. Two tricky aspects arise: having someone (or a process) re-authenticate the person and the user having difficulty accessing the sent password if he or she cannot get online. The former issue can be dealt with by asking another security question; the latter might require human intervention.

One other scenario may also occur: a student does not get a log-on/password in the first case, most likely because the family and student do not sign and submit an acceptable use policy for whatever reason (be it forgetfulness, dislike of the policy, or fear of being tracked). The LMS should make sure that the library has the resources needed for the student to complete his assignments. For that reason, the collection should continue to maintain print reference materials and periodicals. The issue transcends the library, however, since all teachers need to make those same accommodations for their students. For this reason, collaboration between the LMS and classroom teacher is a key factor for student success.

Unfortunately, what sometimes happens is that students "borrow" log-ons/passwords from their peers or even their teachers, and occasionally they abuse that privilege by hacking onto the system or doing other inappropriate actions. Amazingly, teachers have been known to be "kind" and give the student their passwords, only to find that their files have been compromised or that the network finds that mischief has been done in the teacher's "name"; those same teachers are horrified to find that they are held responsible for the computer abuse. It is in the LMS's best interest, therefore, to educate the entire school community about authentication and the supporting protocols so that people can be aware of the consequences and learn how to be a good cyber citizen. Here are some good tips on choosing a "strong" (less likely to be hacked) personal password that can be shared when talking about security:

- Choose a password that is easy to remember and easy to type quickly (so others don't see the keystrokes).
- The two most used passwords, and the ones that hackers try first, are "123456" and "password." Avoid them.
- Use a combination of at least eight characters and numbers, preferably including capitals. Sometimes symbols work (_, $, %, #), but sometimes those symbols activate a code line that can interfere with the log-on procedure.
- Choose a word that has personal meaning but is unlikely to be known by acquaintances, such as a grandmother's maiden name.
- Choose a non-English word, an acronym that has personal meaning, or a string of words (such as Ilikepickles).
- Consider using a random password generator, such as the free program www.certtest.com/passgen.html.
- If a password needs to be changed regularly, choose a word that can be easily modified *and* remembered. Here is a good example: 1september, 2eptembers, 3ptemberse (see the pattern?).

Ideally, the library's authentication process should be part of a schoolwide network process with each student and adult having a unique log-on and password. Increasingly, schools provide a unique directory for each user in order to facilitate file transfers. For instance, students and teachers who find pertinent resources doing library research can access those files for their academic subject class. If network access protocols are carefully designed, data can be transferred across applications so that library records can be uploaded from the school's administrative program, and student accounts can include library fines.

Administrative Access

Library staff, particularly the LMS, usually need some kind of administrative access to library computers, at least for the ILMS and one's own computer. Too many little problems crop up, especially at class break time, to have to shut down a system to wait for an already overworked technician to come. Usually, local access can be configured readily. For stand-alone machines, administrative access is normally not a problem unless the school has a configuration process for new equipment that precludes anyone other than the designated personnel making any changes. LMSs should discuss this procedure with decision makers, pointing out the cost-time benefits of having library control. By physically demonstrating competency in installing and troubleshooting equipment, LMSs can back up their argument forcefully. The nature and extent of administrative access can also be negotiated at that time to preclude future situational stumbling blocks.

One benefit of a schoolwide authentication process is that library staff can install and troubleshoot software, interfacing with the instructional server and utilities more easily, rather than wait hours or months for a technician to take care of problems. On the other hand, with access comes responsibility, and a digital mistake can jeopardize operations of the library and possibly other functions. Therefore, LMSs should think carefully—and gain technical expertise—before asking for broader access. Furthermore, tech-savvy LMSs may find themselves spending a disproportionate amount of time dealing with authentication and other networking matters to the detriment of library services. Probably the best solution is to learn about networking protocol, particularly in terms of security and access, in order to talk intelligently with network administrators and be their advocate. A positive working relationship with network specialists can speed up and improve technical service.

Sometimes when the LMS has the reputation of being organized and technically competent, school administrators delegate him or her to coordinate student ID cards and log-on/passwords as well as take charge of acceptable use policies. The LMS thus serves as a digital citizen administrator. This service enables the LMS to meet each student, talk with them about library/Internet use, and establish accurate student library accounts. While this task takes considerable time upon student entry, it can be manageable since the main data seldom changes. Any LMS who has had to suffer the consequences of having student ID cards with the wrong bar coding knows that being in charge of such details from the start can actually take less time than having to deal with inaccurate data later on.

Outside Hardware

Increasingly, users bring their own equipment into the library, be it a mobile device or a laptop. As stand-alone equipment, they usually pose no problem except for theft. It should be noted, though, that some schools still prohibit the possession and use of electronic equipment (even pagers), largely a hark back to times of drug deal connotations and now a distractive element. Library staff need to know and comply with the school policy about the presence of such devices. On the other hand, some students may be required to bring electronic devices as a learning accommodation. Again, library staff need to know which students are affected by such measures.

In any case, outside hardware can pose a problem when it interfaces with the library or school network. Depending on the year that facilities were built or renovated, Internet connectivity might be supported through numerous cable outlets (a "hard" connection) or wifi boxes. To be safe, an authentication process should be built into the network so that the user cannot access any data otherwise. Directions for using outside hardware can be kept at the circulation desk. Particularly since nonschool individuals occasionally cruise neighborhoods to locate free wireless networks that they can piggyback on, schools need to plan carefully when installing and configuring wifi systems. The following announcement, posted on the California State University Long Beach Library's portal (www.csulb.edu/library/guide/wireless.html), demonstrates how library policies can deal with outside hardware. Notice that the library staff are not in the business of computer troubleshooting.

BeachNet, the campus wireless network, is run by CSULB Network Services with support provided by the Campus Technology Help Desk. Network Services has installed antennas for wireless device access in the public areas of the Library (reading rooms). All users of the campus wireless network must authenticate before they may use BeachNet. All devices are scanned for known vulnerabilities and threats before they may use the BeachNet wireless network. Computers found with serious problems are denied access. The owners must correct the problem before they can gain access to BeachNet. Students who are unable to connect should be referred to the Technology Help Desk in the Horn Center. Students who are STOPPED from connecting because their computer has a known vulnerability are responsible for correcting the problem. The Library does not provide configuration or troubleshooting support for personally owned devices. Any staff or faculty that are from other departments who have problems using the wireless network should be referred to their own technical support people in their department. Students who experience problems with weak signals should move and see if another location provides a better connection.

Accessibility

Institutions that receive federal funds (most K–12 schools) need to comply with accessibility regulations such as the Workforce Investment Act, which strengthened Section 508 of the Rehabilitation Act of 1973. At this point, section 508 compliance should be expected for any digital product to be acquired or leased, such as subscription databases, software programs, and CDs/DVDs. The United States Access Board provides guidelines for software applications and operating systems, which can be used as a checklist when considering purchases (www.access-board.gov/sec508/guide/1194.21.htm). Certainly, Web-based resources need to be comparably accessible to individuals with disabilities such as the vision impaired. The following federal Web site details the technical standards: www. section508.gov/index.cfm?FuseAction=Content&ID=12#Web.

When developing digital resources such as a library portal or uploading digital documents, those same standards need to be applied. Fortunately for LMSs who do not want to spend a lot of time designing fancy documents, the plainer the better is the mantra. Designers can omit frames, tables, colorful backgrounds, and animation. All images must be captioned. For once, content really can be king. Some Web design products such as DreamWeaver include an accessibility check that can help address accessibility issues. The following Web sites provide good advice for ensuring that documents are sufficiently accessible.

- U. S. Government Section 508: www.section508.gov
- World Wide Web Consortium Web Accessibility Initiative: www.w3.org/WAI
- Association of Specialized and Cooperative Library Agencies Library Accessibility: www.ala.org/ala/mgrps/divs/ascla/ asclaprotools/accessibilitytipsheets/default.cfm
- California State University Long Beach Accessibility: www. csulb.edu/lats/itss/design/access.html

- University of Wisconsin–Stevens Point Web Accessibility Survey Site: http://library.uwsp.edu/aschmetz/Accessible/websurveys.htm

Interface accessibility also applies to the technology equipment itself. Users need to be able to access, retrieve, and input information physically. The LMC needs to follow existing policy ensuring equitable student access and assurances that students with disabilities will have appropriate accommodations (which is covered by instructional educational plans that follow federal law). Theoretically, every school district has such a policy or refers to a higher governmental level associated policy, which the LMS should locate and have access to. Starting with access devices, here are feasible ways to make accommodations for individual needs:

- **Mouse.** Use the palm to move a track ball without gripping the whole mouse device.
- **Touchpad.** Use fingers along a pad mirroring the screen layout.
- **Joystick.** Move a stick with broader actions than a mouse.
- **Pointers.** Head-mounted pointers and even eye-sensitive pointers can be coordinated with a touch screen or other type of sensitive monitor. This equipment is most likely housed in a center for the severely disabled.
- **Modified keyboard.** Use a keyboard with modifications that include smaller or larger keys, keys with raised letters or braille, single-hand keyboards.
- **Intelligent keyboard.** Create templates (e.g., IntelliTools) to customize keyboards for easy typing.
- **Screen keyboard.** Click on the online keyboard.
- **Tablet PCs.** Write on the computer "screen" using the special stylus.
- **Kurzweil Reader.** Scan documents using the machine and have it read the text aloud. The equipment is quite expensive, so it is likely that a student would be referred to an institution having it, such as a university library.
- **OCR Scanners.** Scan documents with optical character recognition software and upload them onto the computer. Then the computer's narration software can read the scanned

file. While more cumbersome than a Kurzweil Reader, this solution is less expensive. It should be noted that the output from OCR scanning usually requires "touch-ups" because letters might not be recognizable to the software.

- **Monitor modifications.** Read enlarged text on larger monitors. Touch-screen monitors provide another way to input information.
- **Screen modifications.** Use a computer operating system that includes ways to facilitate access, such as cursor modifications, text size and appearance, screen magnifiers, text narration, keyboard character customizations. These changes can be user-specific so that at log-off the system resets to the default settings.
- **Document modifications.** Make document-specific changes for easier use. One of the most interesting customizations is background color; some students' eyes see black-on-white characters as distorted, but another color can minimize that distortion. This change in background can be applied to Web sites as well.
- **Browser modifications.** Change settings specifically for the Internet interface, similarly as with the desktop screen.
- **Screen-reading software.** Have Web pages (usually the source code) read to you aloud. The popular product JAWS is technically a screen-reading Web browser.
- **Voice-recognition software.** Employ a microphone to capture words and "translate" them into text. They require hours of "training" in order to distinguish the voice patterns of each individual.

WestEd in San Francisco lists several good Web sites on access and equity, with particular attention to assistive technology. This Web site is a good starting point: rtecexchange.edgateway. net/cs/rtecp/view/rtec_str/2. A good megasite that deals with issues of special needs, equity, and diversity within K–12 education is www.4teachers.org/profd/index.shtml. Some other good specific Web pages include the following:

- http://abilityhub.com
- www.wid.org/resources/accessibility-assistive-technology

- http://specialed.about.com/od/assistivetechnology/Technology_in_the_Classroom.htm
- www.microsoft.com/enable/at/default.aspx
- www.apple.com/accessibility
- www.itcompany.com/inforetriever/dis_gen.htm

Content Issues

Especially with Internet access, the library program is placed in a vulnerable position because library staff are responsible for the library's collection *and information that is accessible from the library.* The physical collection, including the technology to support it, is controllable, but the Internet itself is hardly controllable by anyone. The issue here is not so much how the information is accessed but the nature of the information, the content, itself. If a pornographic image was physically found in the library, the library staff would need to take action to remove it or else they might be accused of being negligent in their role as loco parentis. With this legal responsibility of taking care of minors, LMCs are held to a higher standard than other types of libraries. Particularly in busy LMCs with open access to the Internet, managing questionable content can be daunting. For this reason, having pro-active policies in place to minimize the likelihood of inappropriate content and procedures to deal with such content that might come to light helps the library staff carry out its mission with fewer headaches.

Just as important, LMSs need to teach students how to be discerning consumers and producers of content. Protecting a child from strangers does not help the child know what to do when confronted by a malicious stranger, so too should LMSs go beyond selection and filtering policies to teach students how to recognize inaccurate, inappropriate, and malicious content, regardless of format. Because technology enables students to have access to so much more information, much of it of questionable value, critical thinking curriculum and instruction procedures need to be a central feature of library programs.

Content Filters and Blocking Software

Most LMSs are more familiar with the use of Web proxies as content filters. Because all Web traffic passes through the Web proxy, a content filter proxy can be used to manage Web traffic, preventing users from accessing specific content. The Children's Internet Protection Act (CIPA) is a federal law "enacted by Congress to address concerns about access to offensive content over the Internet on school and library computers" (Consumer and Governmental Affairs Bureau, 2009).

Passed in 2000, CIPA requires schools to "make efforts to ensure that students cannot access materials that can be classified as 'child pornography, obscenity, and harmful to minors,' and [it] requires that a content-filtering system be put in place" (Johnson, 2007). Schools receiving E-rate funds must comply with CIPA. E-rate is a federal program that provides discounts of 20–90 percent on eligible telecommunications services. Funding is based on both student economic need and whether the district is considered urban or rural. Regardless of location, schools with at least 75 percent of students eligible to participate in the National School Lunch Program are eligible to receive discounts of 90 percent on phone service, Internet service, and hardware such as network switches. Schools receiving funding through the Elementary and Secondary Act (ESEA) must also comply with CIPA.

As most schools receive funding through ESEA or E-rate, most districts have content-filtering Web proxies to block sites that may contain pornography and other content deemed inappropriate for a school setting. This is known as content filtering or Web filtering. Software companies providing content filtering use technology to traverse the Internet and evaluate Web sites for potentially objectionable content. Updated lists of sites companies and institutions might deem undesirable are then provided to users as part of a regular subscription, typically in categories such as pornographic sites or game sites. The network administrator managing the content filter receives these updates and chooses which categories of sites to block.

As additional sites are discovered the network administrator must manually block these sites. Software that is used to block specific sites is known as blocking software. Likewise, when an overzealous content filter blocks appropriate sites such as a site on breast cancer research because of the keyword "breast," the network administrator must manually unblock the site. On a personal use level, many companies also offer content filtering software. These are often used by families and small institutions without an enterprise-level Web proxy. Examples include Net Nanny Parental Controls, CYBERsitter, CyberPatrol, and Norton Parental Controls.

The National Center for Education Statistics in the survey Internet Access in U.S. Public Schools and Classrooms: 1994–1995 found that

> among schools using technologies or procedures to prevent student access to inappropriate material on the Internet in 2005, 99 percent used blocking or filtering software. Ninety-six percent of schools reported that teachers or other staff members monitored student Internet access, 79 percent had a written contract that parents have to sign, 76 percent had a contract that students have to sign, 67 percent used monitoring software, 53 percent had honor codes, and 46 percent allowed access only to their intranet" (National Center For Education Statistics, 2006).

Content filters have their limitations. First, new Web sites are constantly being produced, and immense amounts of content are added to the Web every minute. The pace at which new content is added far outstrips the ability for content filters to keep up with new content that may be objectionable or undesirable. Thus, while content filters may block the known they are unable to effectively block the unknown, which inevitability students will find at the aghast of teachers and LMSs who believe the content filter blocks all objectionable content. Second, no perfect algorithm exists that can consistently block inappropriate Web sites and allow all appropriate ones; eventually, some individual needs to override automatic false determinations.

Bypassing Content Filters

LMSs teach students how to become information literate, which includes teaching students how to effectively utilize research tools to access desired information. For many students, this desired information is available on Web sites such as YouTube (www.youtube.com) or MySpace (www.myspace.com), which are blocked by many school districts across the United States and the world. Thus, utilizing learned Web search strategies, students use Google and other search engines to perform keyword searches, such as "unblock Myspace," "access Myspace school," or "get Myspace school."

With a little research they quickly learn various methods to bypass the content filter. So it should be no surprise when students find ways to bypass content filters.

Using Remote Desktop to access a home computer or another computer on the Internet that is outside of the school network is one method to bypass content filters. With Remote Desktop, a student can access their home computer, which is not blocked by the content filtering software. They can then open Internet Explorer or another Web browser on their home computer and use that computer and its Internet connection to access any Web sites they want.

Another common strategy is to find a Web site that offers a free Web-based proxy service, also known as an online proxy server. As discussed earlier in the chapter, a Web proxy server serves as an intermediary, receiving requests for Web content from network devices such as student computers, retrieving that content and delivering it back to the requesting computer. If the computer asks for content from a specific site that has been identified by the content filter as a site to block, the user is not provided the content and instead is given a message that the site was blocked. To bypass content filters utilizing an online proxy server, the user first types in the Web address of the online proxy server. Once at that site, the user types the desired Web address in a search box on that site. The online proxy server then accesses the site and retrieves the content for the user. The user never leaves the Web-based proxy site, so the content filter is not aware that the user is accessing sites that may normally be blocked by the content filter.

Because of the popularity of online proxy servers, mainly among school age children wanting to bypass proxy filters, there are many available choices, some with very colorful names such as www.cantbustme.com and www.hidemyass.com. In fact, there are an overwhelming number of metasites specializing in Web-based proxy services. A metasite is a directory Web site. Proxy service metasites maintain lists of proxy service sites. Users wishing to bypass content filters simply locate a proxy service metasite and try sites on the list until they find one that works.

In many schools, once a viable online proxy service site is located the Web address is quickly disseminated among students through word of mouth and through social networking sites. Eventually, school staff will discover the Web site, report the site, and the administrator in charge of the content filter subsequently blocks the Web site. As this happens, the content proxy site will see their Web traffic decline, hurting their bottom line. Thus, the online proxy site will change the IP address associated with the Web address for their proxy filter or open up another site. This will allow users to once again reach the site by bypassing the content filter.

Many of these online proxy sites make money through advertisements and are legitimate sites with solid terms of service and privacy policies. However, not all are legitimate, and users of online proxy sites should understand that all data they send is being sent first to the proxy site. In addition, often this is in an unencrypted format. This means that the site is able to record any usernames and passwords provided as well as track Web sites visited. One popular use of online proxy sites is to visit social networking sites where often private information is shared. A malicious site could capture all of this information for use at a later date.

Use

Providing school community access to technology is a goal and responsibility for LMCs, but the appropriate use of that technology is the responsibility of library users. For centuries LMSs have discussed how to use the library, from acceptable ways to handle a book to cleaning up after oneself. Digital technology expands the variety and nature of resources that need to be used appropriately. Library policies can standardize technology use decisions to optimize equitable and fair use and provide agreed on interventions in case of technology abuse. Library orientations and publications need to address technology-related usage upfront, not so much to frighten potential users but to teach them proper care so that technological resources can be kept in good condition for everyone to use when needed. Teaching proper usage of technology may be considered cyber manners.

Acceptable Use Policy (AUP)

An acceptable use policy (AUP) is a set of written rules and policies provided to users regarding access to a particular resource, for instance school computers and network resources. Users should sign the AUP before the school provides those users access to resources covered by the AUP. The National Center for Education Statistics (NCES) provides a sample AUP at nces.ed.gov/pubs2003/ secureweb/a_E1.asp. According to the NCES an AUP should include the following:

- Notice of the rights and responsibilities of computer and network users
- Notice of legal issues, such as copyright and privacy
- Notice of acceptable content and conduct on the network
- Description of behaviors that could result in disciplinary action
- Description of the range of disciplinary options, including the removal of access privileges (National Center for Education Statistics, 2006).

The LMC often contains one of the largest groupings of computers on campus available for student use. Thus, the LMS is involved at many school sites in the enforcement of the AUP. For instance, the LMS should have a process for ensuring that all students who use LMC computers have turned in their AUP. Some schools attach an Internet or AUP sticker to student identification (ID) cards after the student has turned in his or her AUP. Other schools use a special punch to mark the ID card.

In such cases, LMSs can check for this on the ID card. If computers are in the circulation system and the process for computer use is for students to check out computers through the circulation system, library staff can check the ID card during this process. At libraries where students do not check out computers, one strategy is to place acrylic business card holders on the computers. Students can then place their ID card in the holder and library media staff can check the cards as they supervise computer use.

Other schools create a unique log-in for each student. In order to gain access to the Internet, students must first log in to the computer. In order to obtain a username and password, the student must turn in his or her AUP. This saves the library staff valuable time, because the log in process now manages whether AUPs are on file. If this system is in place at the school site, the LMS should ensure that multiple students can not use the same log in simultaneously.

At many school sites, the LMC is responsible for organizing and maintaining AUPs. This includes distributing AUPs to new students, collecting AUPs, alphabetizing and storing AUPs, following up with students who still need to turn in their AUPs, and creating a schoolwide list of students who need their AUP on file.

Many centralized student information systems have a field school staff can mark when students turn in their AUP. The student information system provides built-in reports that allow staff to create reports, such as alphabetized lists of students who still need an AUP on file sorted by homeroom/advisory. If this is available, the LMS can use the centralized student information system to document when students turn in their AUPs.

If this is not an option, the LMS should consider creating a database using Microsoft Access or another database program. With a database, the LMS can create a form for easy entry. For instance, at the beginning of the school year the LMS will have a number of AUPs to enter into the database. The LMS should start by obtaining student names from the school's student information system. The LMS can typically export these names as a comma or tab delimited file and then import these names into the Access database. Using a form containing an alphabetical student list and a Yes/No check box, the LMS will be able to quickly mark off students who turned in their form. Later in the semester, the LMS can use the same form design with one change. This time, the LMS can limit the display of students to those who still have not turned in their AUPs. This again will make data entry easier.

Throughout the year, the LMS will want to generate current lists of students not allowed to use the Internet because those students do not have a valid AUP on file. The LMS can create a report in Access that is for this purpose, updating the list of students each time the LMS runs the report. If the database includes additional data, including student class schedules, the LMS can create a customized report that lists any students without AUP access for any class. Thus, if the LMS is planning a collaborative lesson with a classroom teacher that will require Internet access, the LMS can run the report ahead of time and provide it to the teacher so that the teacher can work to ensure that the students in question turn in a valid AUP or that other accommodations are made so the assignment can be accomplished. Again, the LMS can typically export student schedules from the student information system and import it into his or her Access database.

In addition to a database, the LMS needs a mechanism for physically storing the AUPs. If a student violates the terms of the AUP, the school may need the original signed AUP during the disciplinary process. One strategy is to keep the AUPs organized alphabetically in large three-ring binders. The LMS may want to consider affixing a label to each AUP containing the student's name, as it may be hard to read handwritten entries. The LMS can create a report in the Access database that automatically creates mailing-label sized labels to affix to AUPs the library receives. Affixing labels will make it easier for library staff to identify the proper place to insert new AUPs as the LMC receives them.

At some schools, students must turn in an AUP every school year. At other schools, students need to turn in an AUP only once when they originally register for school. If the latter, the LMS will need to regularly weed the binder, removing students who have left the school, and create a report in Access of those exiting students. This practice facilitates regular pruning of the AUP binders. Likewise, affixing a label on each AUP will make it easier for library staff to identify the proper AUPs to remove.

It must be mentioned that adults might also abuse Internet use. The wisest policy is to require AUPs for the entire school community, including volunteers and substitute teachers. Tippecanoe County Public Library has developed guidelines for library staff computer use (www.tcpl.lib.in.us/admin/scu.htm). Internet use at the workplace has already been determined to be open to supervision and oversight, so the legal basis for mandating AUPs is solid. The more difficult issue is to enforce AUPs. The LMS may be reluctant to confront a parent who is using the Internet inappropriately. However, since the main charge of the school is to provide high-quality education to youth, making sure that the library models digital responsibility and holds users to that standard, the LMS has both the authority and responsibility to ask all users to be responsible themselves. Having AUPs and procedures in place when those practices are not observed helps LMSs carry out their own part in Internet use.

File Transfer

One advantage of an individual school log-on account is that students can transfer files easily. Such accounts can cut down on printing costs and facilitate use of resources for research purposes. However, this benefit can also jeopardize the network if students slip in malicious programs. Furthermore, the popularity of file sharing among youth can result in pirated files being stored on the school server, only to be discovered by some company or government agency who might claim that the school was being negligent about copyright compliance.

The school can cut down on the possible misuse of file storage and transfer by limiting the amount of space available to each person, say to less than 100MG of memory, which should suffice for text files but preclude most multimedia files. A couple of additional preventative measures may be used within the library. Computer stations can be configured so that files can be downloaded only to the desktop or to a designated folder. Then desktop network security programs such as Fortres can erase all those files on user log-out. To save their own work, such as multimedia productions, students can burn single copy CDs.

Social Networking Issues

A 2007 survey by the Pew Internet & American Life Project found that 55 percent of American youth ages 12–17 have online profiles. The survey found that teens do take steps to protect themselves; for instance 66 percent of teens with online sites have profiles to which access is somehow limited. However, it also found that 43 percent of teens using social networking sites reported one or more online contacts by complete strangers, and when contacted, 21 percent interacted with the online stranger to find out more information about that person (Lenhart and Madden, 2007). Other findings included the following:

- 82 percent of profile creators have included their first name in their profiles.
- 79 percent have included photos of themselves.
- 66 percent have included photos of their friends.
- 61 percent have included the name of their city or town.
- 49 percent have included the name of their school.
- 40 percent have included their instant message screen name.
- 40 percent have streamed audio to their profile.
- 39 percent have linked to their blog.

- 29 percent have included their e-mail address.
- 29 percent have included their last names.
- 29 percent have included videos.
- 2 percent have included their cell phone numbers.

LMSs reviewing the data should understand that the majority of their students use social networking sites, and significant percentages provide personal information that puts them at risk. When teaching students how to effectively find information on the Web, LMSs should take this opportunity to teach about Internet safety. For instance, when explaining to students how to use the search command *site:*url keyword (e.g., site:whitehouse.gov cabinet), LMSs can also show students how easy it is to find social networking sites containing keywords such as the school's name (e.g. site:myspace. com school name). Even if Web sites such as MySpace (www. myspace.com) are blocked at the school site, the search results in Google will provide enough information to drive home the point. Once the LMS shows students how easy it is to find profiles, "Remind them that objects such as street signs, school logos, and local businesses can be used to identify locations. Discourage them also from using nicknames that might draw unwanted attention" (Lamb and Johnson, 2007, p. 43).

LMSs need to be aware of social networking issues because LMC computers are often the tool used by students to access social networking sites, even if the district attempts to block sites through content proxies as discussed earlier in this chapter. This is because LMC computers are often the computers students have most access to during school breaks, such as at lunch or after school.

In addition to online actions of students that place them at risk, the LMS needs to be aware of online bullying, which is often perpetrated using social networking tools. Bullying is when an individual or group of individuals intentionally attempts to harm another individual or group of individuals. Cyberbullying is a form of bullying in which the aggressor uses electronic communication to intentionally attempt harm. Electronic communication includes Web sites and blogs, e-mail, chat rooms, and instant messaging services. If cyberbullying is occurring on the school campus, there is a good chance that LMC computers are being used to cyberbully. LMSs need to be aware of the different forms of cyberbullying. The

Center for Safe and Responsible Use of the Internet lists a number of cyberbullying approaches (Willard, 2007):

- Flaming
- Harassment
- Denigration
- Impersonation
- Outing
- Trickery
- Exclusion
- Cyber stalking
- Cyber threats

This knowledge enables LMSs to better identify cyberbullying when it occurs.

In addition, LMSs need to be aware of what the school can and can't do relative to cyberbullying so that the LMS does not accidently violate student rights to free speech. A number of states have passed cyberbullying laws. Most laws differentiate between in-school versus out-of-school cyberbullying. While schools have clear authority over cyberbullying if perpetuated during school hours using school equipment, the same is not true for cyberbullying committed off campus; for instance, when the student is at home using his or her personal computer. In most states, school administrators can discipline students for out-of-school bullying. Arkansas laws allow for schools to discipline students if the cyberbullying has a high likelihood of disrupting school *and* was directed at students or school personnel for the purpose of maliciously disrupting school. Delaware allows school administrators to discipline students for off-campus bullying if there is a school nexus. Iowa allows school administrators to discipline students for off-campus bullying if connected to a school-sponsored activity or function (Jones, 2008). In other states, school administrators have no ability to discipline students for cyberbullying perpetuated off campus. This includes both attacks against students and against teachers, which is disconcerting to school staff victims of such attacks. Likewise, parents of a victimized student may want the school to take action, and hearing that no action can be taken because the attack took place off campus does little to comfort them.

Although the school often cannot take action, in many states parents are financially responsible for the actions of their children. Thus, if a child emotionally injures another child through cyberbullying, the guardian of the injured child can file a civil lawsuit. At a minimum, the threat of a lawsuit can sometimes provide the motivation needed for the cyberbullying to stop. Thus, even if schools do not have the authority to take disciplinary actions, schools should inform the parents of the cyberbullying incident and remind parents of their fiscal responsibility. As Nancy Willard of the Center for Safe and Responsible Use of the Internet writes, "Informing the parents of the cyberbully about this potential is likely the strongest 'motivation' school officials can use to ensure that the cyberbullying stops" (Willard, 2007).

DISASTER PLANNING

Accidents happen. Vandalism happens. Disasters can be caused by water, fire, electric or fuel power, earthquake, weather, hazardous materials, building malfunction, or terrorists. Even though many disasters cannot be predicted, LMSs can prepare for those disasters that *might* happen. To that end, LMSs should take the following actions: assess risks, reduce risks, be prepared for disasters, respond to disasters, and know how to recover from them. Developing a disaster plan is a smart way to consider these actions carefully.

Steps in Planning

Two main factors drive **risk assessment**: the probability of its happening and the extent of its potential damage. Dam failure may be a very low probability, but its consequences could be horrendous, for example. External risks such as storms and riots usually cannot be controlled by the school or library, but steps can be taken to mitigate their impact. On the other hand, internal factors can be identified and corrected in order to prevent possible disasters. The Northeast Document Conservation Center lists these categories of internal risks that can affect technology:

- **Fire:** detection systems, suppression systems, extinguishers, obstructed fire exits, faulty electrical systems

- **Water**: roof condition, poor drainage, leaky skylights, weak foundations, water sources near technology, shelving or computers on the floor, climate control extremes, previous mold infestation (*note*: do not place outlets on the floor because in a flood electrocution might occur)
- **Security**: automated security system, staff supervision, authenticated log-on procedures, secure storage for valuable items, vandalism occurrences
- **Procedures**: backup systems, opening and closing procedures, staff training, building maintenance, insurance.

Once risks are identified, **actions can be taken to prevent or mitigate those risks**, depending on the availability of funding and skilled personnel. In any case, LMSs can gather information about services and vendors, prepare emergency procedures, prioritize recovery efforts, and plan with the rest of the school community. Referring to this list of risks, LMSs can request that water alarms be installed, they can be trained on the use of fire extinguishers, they can supplement security systems with desktop security locks, and they can back up data routinely. Other good preventative measures include routinely upgrading hardware and software to avoid obsolescence, storing files and programs in fireproof cabinets that withstand temperature extremes.

With regard to backup procedures specifically, LMSs have several decisions.

- In what format should backup files be saved: CD, DVD, tape, or Web-based? An automatic tape system offers high-quality convenience; it should be noted that the timing of the backup procedure should not coincide with likely power surge timing, such as midnight, because the computer system might crash from the power overload. Daily backups are recommended at least for new data changes. An easy strategy is to get five tapes, one per week day, so that five recent copies always exist (one of which may be stored weekly at a remote location). Alternatively, data can be "mirrored" (duplicated on another server), thereby automatically maintaining a copy. Still another strategy is to save data on a remote, Web-based server; data is likely to be safer physically but some security may be compromised.

- How important is the data? Perhaps some data need not be saved. Circulation/cataloging programs and data, main software programs, and the operating system are vital, but little-used files (e.g., old monthly reports) might not need long-term saving.
- How long can the library operate without the data? This question may be known as the "recovery time objective." Usually circulation comprises the most time-sensitive data. Most libraries can handle checkout procedures manually for a couple of days, so this procedure needs to be written and available in case of disasters.
- How long until there is too much data to deal with (also known as the "recovery point objective")? At some point, it is easier to re-input the data than to try to compare existing and postdisaster data piecemeal. For example, it may be difficult to maintain an overdue list, so a fines "amnesty" might be a better solution, with a new overdue list being started after recovering data.

To ensure an effective response to disasters, LMSs should have a trained response team, or at least serve on their site's recovery team, managing the library facility. Ideally, each response team should include a coordinator who also serves as a liaison with other response teams, a person in charge of remote operations to get and upload remote files, a person to recover on-site technology, and a troubleshooter. LMSs should also know what disaster procedures exist at the school site as a whole: internal and external communication procedures such as telephone trees and handy lists of service providers, building evaluation plans, salvage priorities, and insurance.

More generally, LMSs should have a disaster plan in place that aligns with the school's disaster plan. Library staff should review and practice the plan at least annually. Here are components of a good library disaster plan (Northeast Document Conservation Center, 2008):

1. Introduction: scope and personnel
2. Actions in case of advance warning
3. First response procedures: first communication contact

personnel, first steps to take, response team members, and duties

4. Emergency procedures by disaster type (e.g., flooding, fire) during the event and at recovery or salvage state
5. Rehabilitation plans for becoming operational again
6. Appendixes: floor plan with evaluation notes, emergency service contacts and functions, telephone tree, alarm procedures, location of keys and remote data, location of supplies, salvage priorities and procedures, insurance information, checklists, and forms

As with other policies and procedures, the library disaster plan should be coordinated by the LMS, with input from all library staff and advisory board members, and reviewed with site administrators. Most schools have a disaster point person who knows the details for effective emergency and disaster planning, so the LMS should discuss plans with that expert. Sample disaster plans and templates are available at: www.nedcc.org/resources/leaflets/3Emergency_Ma nagement/04DisasterPlanWorksheet.php, www.dplan.org, cool-pa-limpsest.stanford.edu/bytopic/disasters/plans/, and www.calpreser-vation.org/disasters/index.html.

With the plan in hand and trained library staff, the LMC should be in good hands when disaster hits and an immediate **response** is called for. The first priority should be human safety, and then a quick scan can provide an initial assessment of possible damage and quick actions to ameliorate problems. For instance, power can be turned off; exits can be closed or opened, depending on the nature of the disaster; and/or vital on-site records can be gathered and removed from the site.

Recovery follows, rehabilitating the salvaged library collection and facility after the disaster. Library operations and services need to function normally, and library staff need to recover their own equilibrium. At the very least, circulation, access to databases, and telecommunications should resume. Some salvage actions need to be taken immediately; for instance, mold can develop within 48 hours on a wet collection, so items need to be removed for quick drying either by air or freeze-dried. Likewise, if flooding occurs, carpets need to be immediately vacuumed to suck up any water. A dehumidifier or fans can also speed up drying. As with other parts of the disaster plan, technology priorities should drive decisions. A CPU and hard drives are more important than a monitor or keyboard, and a server trumps a thin-client station.

Data Storage Issues

Two reasons that libraries migrate from print to online resources is to save space and to save content. At the current cost of digital drive space, most library budgets should be able to handle in-house storage costs of electronic resources, especially text-based ones. The issue is mainly that of retrieval: are files clearly labeled and are servers in good working order? Bandwidth can also be a problem if the school has not upgraded internal cable lines to accommodate multimedia files transfers. Some LMSs are choosing to store documents in remote Web servers to facilitate retrieval, particularly if they use Web-based database generators such as LibraryThing, Delicious, and Rollyo. Remote storage also circumvents any disasters that might destroy data.

Keeping files for years can be problematic because systems crash or upgrade their software and hardware over time. Indeed, the library world may be entering a second Dark Age as new versions of applications and even operating systems might not be backward compatible; files may be unreadable in the future. The result resembles a disaster in slow motion. In some cases, software programs can emulate the older products and "read" the older files, but this approach holds little interest to industry programmers who do not see large profits arising from this effort. Libraries may have to revert to printing out digital files, which is a daunting task, and is in the opposite direction of many libraries that are working hard to preserve irreplaceable documents by digitizing them.

In any case, LMSs need to develop a policy as to what documents to save, the frequency of saving them, where to save them, and when to withdraw them. This policy should support the library program's and school's mission. Normally, the ILMS should be backed up daily, with an archive copy stored off-site in case of disaster. The library portal should also be backed up at least monthly, depending on the frequency of updating. This policy should be reviewed with the site technology specialist, the administrator in charge of technology or documentation (the controller may be a likely candidate), and any other decision-making stakeholder. As with other issues, storage policies can impact other group's work: network architecture, business archives, and vendor agreements.

ETHICAL AND LEGAL ISSUES

Library staff encounters legal and ethical issues daily: providing accurate information, overseeing intellectual property rights, dealing with privacy issues, maintaining confidential relationship with clientele, providing equitable service. In their set of information literacy standards, the American Association of School Librarians (AASL) and Association for Educational Communications and Technology (1998) explicitly address ethical behavior, stating that "the student who contributes positively to the learning community and to society is information literate and practices ethical behavior in regard to information and information technology" (6). In K–12 school settings, which serve as loco parentis, the legal and ethical responsibilities of the LMS surpass the comparable work of librarians in other settings. Dealing with minors adds another layer of legal issues and implies an additional need to model ethical behavior so children will experience and integrate such values.

With the advent of the Internet, legal and ethical issues abound. Technology makes copying practically effortless, so intellectual property rights have to be explained and modeled continuously. Digital rights management has grown dramatically this century. Privacy and confidentiality have become harder to maintain, and students sometimes naively share private information online that can make them very vulnerable. LMSs need to make sure that students do not access pornographic Web sites. For this reason, school libraries need to provide telecommunications filters if they wish to accept federal funding. On a more pro-active level, LMSs try to teach students how to be socially responsible digital citizens.

Intellectual Property

A central aspect of education is intellectual pursuit and the recognition of great minds. Yet teachers bemoan the rise in cheating, which technology facilitates. On their part, students have a more lax attitude about intellectual property. Particularly with Web 2.0, which fosters collaborative knowledge generation, identifying the originator of an idea can be difficult to ascertain.

The publishing world further complicates the intellectual property picture. Reporters are demanding personal credit and remuneration for their contributions. Publishers create copyright agreements to cover authorship rights based on format. Multimedia copyright laws can be very specific, restricting resizing or other image manipulation, or stipulating the length of music or video that can be copied legitimately. Fortunately, education falls under the umbrella of fair use, so restrictions are loosened up a bit in order to support personal research.

LMSs find themselves in the midst of this technological maelstrom being responsible for information resources and their appropriate use. The school community often regards the LMS as the copyright guardian or police. LMSs do need to keep current about intellectual property laws and serve as site experts and instructors. Particularly since schools tend to designate the LMS as the leader in this arena, LMSs can leverage that responsibility and further enhance it in this digital age.

Copyright and Creative Commons

One of the consequences of the LMC's role as Information Center is its high profile relative to copyright issues. In some cases, the only mention of the library in educational administration courses occurs when discussing copyright compliance. In promoting intellectual property, the LMS sometimes feels like the copyright police officer. Particularly when the LMC provides copier service and Internet access, the LMS does have a responsibility to explain the appropriate use of other people's information. For instance, in order to avoid accusations of copyright negligence, the LMS should have a notice on self-service copiers explaining permissible use: "The copyright law of the United States (Title 17, U.S. Code) governs the making of reproductions of copyrighted material. The person using this equipment is liable for any infringement."

Library service may include digital resource downloading or circulation, such as broadcasts. LMSs have to check the distribution license agreement to make sure that their practice complies with the copyright. A teacher may ask the LMS to duplicate a video or software, in which case the copyright permission should be supplied so the LMS is comfortable providing the service. At this point, archival copies of digital resources are usually not permissible, even for software programs, largely because the producers enable legitimate owners of the product to download it from the Internet.

Fortunately, the school community can use information for educational and research purposes, so their practice comes under the umbrella of fair use. Under this stipulation, four general guidelines help educators ascertain if their use of intellectual property complies with copyright.

- Is the purpose and character of the copy for educational use or for profit? Education has more leeway usually.
- What is the nature of the copy? Factual material may be easier to copy than original plays, for instance.
- What extent of the product is being copied? A rule of thumb is 10 percent or less, not including a substantive component such as a key chart summarizing a book.
- Does the copy impact the market value of the product; that is, does the copy deter the person from buying that item?

Nevertheless, schools may be cited and charged for copyright infringement on such works as music scores. Recent court decisions, such as 2001 *The New York Times v. Tasini* Supreme Court case, have addressed the difficulty of efficiently collecting royalties when disseminating articles via subscription databases.

The expansion of digital resource has further complicated copyright laws and fair use. The ease and speed of digital duplication can tempt the most honest user. Especially when software "suites" facilitate repurposing of information (such as turning a PowerPoint into an outline word processed document), it can be difficult to explain how to use digital materials within copyright limits. How does format define information? How does multimedia incorporation change the nature and intellectual property of each information element? These issues can lead to valuable learning moments during which students can understand the nuanced nature of digital information.

In any case, students should be aware of the more important aspects of technology-related copyright laws and regulations. The

1998 Digital Millennium Copyright Law, for instance, limits database company liability and addresses digital preservation. Further complicating matters, different countries have different copyright guidelines, so information accessed from around the world may be subject to conflicting laws; when in doubt, users should be overly conservative. Particularly with the advent of Web 2.0 in which students can produce and disseminate information publicly, copyright applications are stricter. A few examples of technology-relevant copyright practices follow.

- Images should not be resized, cropped, or changed in context without explicit permission.
- Photos of recognizable people require written permission if they are to be broadcast.
- Music and video downloads can be very problematic. It is wisest to use pre-approved sites such as iTunes.
- Slander and libel can occur on social networking sites such as MySpace and Facebook; students may not realize that they can be held legally responsible for their comments and can be even arrested and prosecuted.
- Information about health and legal issues should include a disclaimer so that the author is not held legally responsible in case the reader uses that information and experiences negative results.
- Each database aggregator and disseminator (such as video streaming) has a unique licensing agreement that covers copyright issues. A good rule of thumb is to apply the most conservative guidelines in order to avoid case-by-case decisions.

To help the school community remain in compliance, LMSs should provide in-service training about copyright, include copyright information in the library Web portal, incorporate good copyright practice in instruction, and model copyright compliance in library services. More information about copyright is located at the following Web sites:

- www.copyright.gov
- www2.visalia.k12.ca.us/library/policies/copyright.htm
- http://fairuse.stanford.edu

- www.copyright.columbia.edu/fair-use-checklist#
- www.utsystem.edu/OGC/IntellectualProperty/cprtindx.htm
- www.cetus.org/fairindex.html.

Teachers and administrators also need to know about the 2002 Technology, Education, and Copyright Harmonization (TEACH) Act, which impacts copyright usage in distance education or in cases where digital information is transmitted as a supplement to face-to-face instruction. Displays and performances can be disseminated only for the period of the course and only to those students who are enrolled in the course. Likewise, if teachers copy an article for a face-to-face class, then they can link to the same article online, depending on the magazine database license agreement. A better solution is for the teacher to provide the citation and ask the students to access the article themselves from the library's database collection. However, the teacher should *not* download the whole magazine issue just because it's technically possible; this action probably does not comply with copyright law.

A welcome alternative is the Creative Commons, which enables people to upload and share data with the understanding that any use requires cited acknowledgment, and any changes to the data also need to be uploaded and cited within the Creative Commons. This proactive strategy recognizes the benefits of collaborative knowledge building. LMSs can inform the school community about the Creative Commons (www.creativecommons.org) and encourage individuals to access and use data stored there as well as contribute to that Web site.

Plagiarism

One of the main complaints about technology is the ease with which students can plagiarize now. Students can find information quickly (although the quality of that information might be suspect), cut-and-paste a digital selection into a word processing program, do a few "global replacements" to use synonyms in an effort to avoid straight copying, and reformat the pages to conform to the teacher's instructions. Indeed, many Web sites provide ready-made research papers for students to download for free or for a fee. Because of this situation, teachers may prohibit students from using the Internet, sometimes confusing the "free" Internet with online subscription databases, much to the dismay of LMSs.

Often the problem lies in the nature of the teacher's assignment. Requiring a whole class to "do a three-page report on Leonardo da Vinci" almost dares students to carbon copy write. The central challenge in writing reports used to be locating information, but now it is evaluating the information and manipulating it. Therefore, assignments should emphasize comparing sources, synthesizing findings, and adding to the body of knowledge in original, creative ways. Instead of a three-page report on da Vinci, students could be asked to create a conversation between da Vinci and another artist or a contemporary "celebrity."

In terms of management, LMSs need to take preventative measures to minimize the possibilities of plagiarism, such as the following:

- Require students and teachers to comply with acceptable use policies.
- Build on existing honesty policies. If possible, include students in the creation of antiplagiarism policies.
- Instruct the school community about intellectual property, and show them how to avoid plagiarism.
- Display signs and posters about intellectual property and honest work.
- Set up computer stations to facilitate supervision.
- Consider installing TurnItIn or other plagariasm/copying detection software program into the school's network. It should be noted that the school community needs to use such programs equitably; if one student is asked to submit work to TurnItIn, for instance, then all students in the class need to submit their work to TurnItIn. Furthermore, students need to have an alternative way to submit work if they don't want to use TurnItIn. Teachers should also include a notice about the use of such programs at the beginning of the course to prevent unfair practices. This statement from California State University Long Beach (www.csulb.edu/lats/itss/bb/students/turnitin.html) uses good legal language:

  Instructors may request the submission of course papers to Turnitin.com for the prevention of plagiarism. All submitted papers are included as source documents in the Turnitin.com reference database solely for the purpose of detecting plagiarism of such papers. You may submit your paper in such a way that no identifying information about you is included. Another option is that you may request, in writing to your instructor, that your paper not be submitted to Turnitin.com. However, if you choose this option you will be required to provide documentation to substantiate that your paper is your original work and does not include any plagiarized material.

- Develop a procedure to deal with students who plagiarize and act on it. Unenforced policies are worse than no policy at all because they indicate that the LMS either has no power or does not care enough about the issue or the person to pursue the consequences. Of course, any enforcement efforts need to be documented and communicated with the LMS's supervisor.

Privacy and Confidentiality

When using technology in LMCs, multiple privacy concerns exist. Effective management of library technology includes developing policies regarding privacy. For instance, LMSs use automation systems to circulate library materials. At any time, the LMS can run a report indicating materials currently checked out to one or more users. Many circulation programs provide patron checkout histories. If a parent or guardian comes to the library, wanting to know what books their student currently has checked out or had checked out in the past, how should the LMS respond? What if a fellow teacher or administrator asks for this information? What about paper overdue notices that many library automation programs generate? Often the notice will include the book title. Many LMSs send these notices to classroom teachers for distribution to the students. Is it a violation of student privacy if the teacher sees the titles as they are distributed? What if the teacher announces in front of other students, "Eddie, your book *Love & Sex: 10 Stories of Truth* has been overdue for two months now. I'm tired of getting these notices for you. Take care of it!"

The American Library Association issued in 2003 the document "Principles for the Networked World," with the stated goal "to further discussion within the library community and with the public about the critical information policy issues libraries face." Relating to privacy, this document states, "The rights of anonymity and privacy while people retrieve and communicate information must be protected as an essential element of intellectual freedom" (American Library Association, 2003).

The Family Educational Rights and Privacy Act (FERPA) protects the privacy of student education records. Under FERPA, parents and guardians have the right to review student education records the school maintains. When a student turns 18 or attends a school beyond high school, those rights transfer to the student. Schools must have written permission to release information from a student's educational record. There are a number of exceptions to this privacy, including sharing with other school officials for "legitimate educational interests" and complying with a subpoena or judicial order (U.S. Department of Education, 2008).

Are library circulation records considered part of a student's educational record under FERPA? According to the authors of *Privacy in the 21st Century: Issues for Public, School and Academic Libraries*, the definition of educational records in FERPA does not specifically mention library records. However, it is defined broadly, and, although not specifically mentioned, some read the law to include student library records while others do not. Thus, the answer is unclear, as debate exists and "no court has determined whether school records are 'education records' and thus protected" (Adams et al., 2005, p. 103).

In addition to FERPA, LMSs must be familiar with state laws concerning patron privacy and libraries. According to the American Library Association (ALA), "Forty-eight of 50 states have such laws on the books, but the language varies from state to state." In addition, the District of Columbia has privacy laws, and the two remaining states, Kentucky and Hawaii, have legal opinions written by their state's attorney general on the topic. The ALA Web site provides links to laws by state. Some states have laws specific to LMCs, others are specific to public libraries, and others refer simply to libraries in general (American Library Association, accessed 2009).

Helen Adams, considered an expert by many in library privacy issues, recommends that LMSs create two policies regarding patron privacy. The first policy should cover confidentiality of library records. This policy is directed at anyone who has access to patron records. It should provide an overview of why privacy is important; provide relevant state, federal, and district policies; and have concrete rules and procedures that ensure all library staff work to protect patron records. The second policy should cover privacy within the library. It should clearly outline what expectations patrons can have to privacy within the LMC. Adams recommends LMSs refer to policy statements created by ALA when drafting a privacy policy, including the *Position Statement on the Confidentiality of Library Records* (Adams, 2006).

When creating privacy policies, consider how library technology is currently used and if changes could improve privacy. For instance, for the circulation program, is it possible to password protect reports such as copy history? Does the copy history report list all users who have checked out a particular item? If so, could it be possible to limit the history or otherwise purge the data? What library staff members will have access to the circulation system? If the LMS sends overdue notices to classrooms, consider ways to enhance privacy, such as folding and then stapling closed the notice. Furthermore, consider other technologies, for instance text and e-mail messaging, to deliver overdue notices directly to students (Adams, 2007).

Table 7.1
Sample Technology Policy Reference List

Policy	Where to Find It
Collection Development	
Selection of Instructional Materials	• SMMUSD. 2009. "Selection of Instructional Materials BP 6161." Santa Monica, CA: SMMUSD. • California School Library Association. 2004. "Policy and Procedures Model." Sacramento: CSLA. www.csla.net/pub/freedom/policy_model.pdf.
Media Technology	• SMMUSD. 1978. "Resources for Students BP 6163.5. Santa Monica, CA: SMMUSD.
Purchasing	• SMMUSD. 1999. "Purchasing Procedures." BP 3310. Santa Monica, CA: SMMUSD. • SMMUSD. 1997. "Purchasing Procedures." AR 3310. Santa Monica, CA: SMMUSD.
Gifts	• SMMUSD. 2009. "Acceptance of Gifts." AR 3290. Santa Monica, CA: SMMUSD.
Challenges to Library and Instructional Materials	• SMMUSD. 2009. "Complaints Concerning Instructional Materials." BP 1312.2. Santa Monica, CA: SMMUSD. www.gamutonline.net/DisplayPolicy/581699/1 • SMMUSD. 2009. "Selection and Evaluation of Instructional Materials." BP 6161.1. Santa Monica, CA: SMMUSD. www.gamutonline.net/DisplayPolicy/590973/6. • SMMUSD. 2009. "Selection and Evaluation of Instructional Materials." AR 6161.1. Santa Monica, CA: SMMUSD. www.gamutonline.net/DisplayPolicy/590974/6.
Discarding Library Materials and Hardware	• SMMUSD. 2009. "Sale and Disposal of Books, Equipment and Supplies." BP 3270. Santa Monica, CA: SMMUSD. www.gamutonline.net/DisplayPolicy/581739/3. • California Department of Education. "Weeding the School Library." Sacramento: CDE. www.cde.ca.gov/ci/cr/lb/documents/weedingschlib.pdf (Accessed May 9, 2008).

Table 7.1 *(Continued)*
Sample Technology Policy Reference List

Policy	Where to Find It
Student Use of Technology	
Curriculum and Instruction	• John Adams Middle School. 2007. "Technology." Teacher Handbook 2007–2008. Santa Monica, CA: John Adams Middle School. Available from school office. • SMMUSD. 2002. "Santa Monica-Malibu Schools Technology Use Plan 2008–2011." Santa Monica, CA: SMMUSD. www.smmusd.org/info_services/pdf/TUP2008.pdf (accessed July 3, 2009).
Online services and filtering	• SMMUSD. 2009. "Student Use of Technology." BP 6163.4. Santa Monica, CA: SMMUSD. www.gamutonline.net/DisplayPolicy/590994/6.
Acceptable Use Policy	• SMMUSD. 2009. "Santa Monica-Malibu Unified School District Telecommunications Acceptable Use Policy." BP 6164. Santa Monica, CA: SMMUSD. www.adams2.smmusd.org/Technology/aup.htm (accessed July 3, 2009).
Freedom of Speech/Expression: Publications Code	• SMMUSD. 2009. "Freedom of Speech/Expression." BP 5145.2. Santa Monica, CA: SMMUSD. www.gamutonline.net/DisplayPolicy/599525/5.
Student Information and Privacy	• SMMUSD. 2009. "Student Records." BP 5125. Santa Monica, CA: SMMUSD. www.gamutonline.net/DisplayPolicy/599452/5. • American Library Association. 1999. "ALA Policy 52.4 Confidentiality of Library Records." Chicago: ALA. www.ala.org/ala/aasl/aaslproftools/positionstatements/aaslpositionstatementconfidentiality.htm (accessed May 9, 2008).
Student Conduct	• John Adams Middle School. 2005. "Classroom Behavioral Standards." Student Handbook 2005–2006. Santa Monica, CA: John Adams Middle School. www.adams.smmusd.org/JAMShandbook.pdf (accessed May 8, 2008). • SMMUSD. 2009. "Positive School Climate." BP 5137. Santa Monica, CA: SMMUSD. www.gamutonline.net/DisplayPolicy/599484/5. • SMMUSD. 2009. "Beepers, Pagers, Cellular Phones and Other Electronic Signaling Devices." BP 5131.8. Santa Monica, CA: SMMUSD. www.gamutonline.net/DisplayPolicy/599478/5.

Table 7.1 *(Continued)*
Sample Technology Policy Reference List

Policy	Where to Find It
District and School Websites	• John Adams Middle School. 2008. "Web Page Guidelines for Staff Web Authors." Teacher Handbook 2008–2009. Santa Monica, CA: John Adams Middle School. Available from school office. • SMMUSD. "District And School Web Sites." BP 1113. Santa Monica, CA: SMMUSD. www.tech.smmusd.org/Site%252520Folder/Pages/bp1113.htm (accessed May 8, 2008).
Intellectual Freedom and Property	
Intellectual Freedom	• California School Library Association. 2004. "Policy Statement on Intellectual Freedom." Sacramento, CA: CSLA. www.csla.net/pub/freedom/policy_statement.pdf. • American Library Association. 1996. "Library Bill of Rights." Chicago: ALA. www.ala.org/work/freedom/lbr.html (accessed May 8, 2008).
Intellectual Property	• John Adams Middle School. 2007. "Good Citizenship and Recognition." Student Handbook 2007–2008. Santa Monica, CA: John Adams Middle School. Available from school office. • SMMUSD. 2009. "Use of Copyrighted Materials." BP/AR 6162.6. Santa Monica, CA: SMMUSD. www.gamutonline.net/PolicyCategoryList/2335/6.
Facilities	
LMC Facility Design	• SMMUSD. 1991. "Facilities Accessibility." BP 3030. Santa Monica, CA: SMMUSD. • California School Library Association. 2004. "Standards for School LMC Facilities." Standards and Guidelines for Strong School Libraries. Sacramento, CA: CSLA. • American Library Association. 2008. "Building Libraries and Library Additions." Chicago: ALA. www.ala.org/Template.cfm?Section=libraryfactsheet&Template=/ContentManagement/ContentDisplay.cfm&ContentID=25417 (accessed May 8, 2008).

Table 7.1 *(Continued)*
Sample Technology Policy Reference List

Policy	Where to Find It
Use of Facilities and Collection	• SMMUSD. 2009. "Use of School Facilities." BP 1330. Santa Monica, CA: SMMUSD. www.gamutonline.net/ DisplayPolicy/581710/1. • SMMUSD. 2009. "Keys." BP 3515.8. Santa Monica, CA: SMMUSD. www.gamutonline.net/ DisplayPolicy/581782/3.
Student Use of LMC-- Scheduling Considerations	• California Department of Education. 2002. "Education Code 18103: Libraries Open to Teachers and Pupils." California School Library Laws. Sacramento: CDE. www.leginfo.ca.gov/cgi-bin/displaycode?section=edc&group=18001-19000&file=18100-18104 (accessed May 9, 2008). • American Library Association. 1991. "Position Statement on Flexible Scheduling." Chicago: ALA. www.ala.org/ala/aasl/aaslproftools/positionstatements/aaslpositionstatement.htm (accessed May 9, 2008).
Finances and Budgets	
Library Media Program Budget Allocation	• SMMUSD. 2009. "Budget." BP 3100. Santa Monica, CA: SMMUSD. www.gamutonline.net/ DisplayPolicy/581730/3 • California Department of Education. 2005. "AB 825, Categorical Education Block Grant." Sacramento, CA: CDE. www.cde.ca.gov/fg/aa/ce/ (accessed May 8, 2008).
Personnel	
Professional and Support Staffing	• SMMUSD Library Act Advisory Committee. 2003. "Santa Monica-Malibu Unified School District Library Plan 2003–2005." Santa Monica, CA: SMMUSD. Available from District office and school sites. • California School Library Association. 2004. "Standards and Guidelines for School Library Media Staffing." Standards and Guidelines for Strong School Libraries. Sacramento, CA: CSLA. • American Library Association. 1991. "Position Statement on Appropriate Staffing for School LMCs." Chicago: ALA. www.ala.org/ala/aasl/aaslproftools/positionstatements/aaslpositionstatementappropriate.htm (accessed May 9, 2008).

Table 7.1 *(Continued)*
Sample Technology Policy Reference List

Policy	Where to Find It
Collaboration Opportunities Among Staff	• John Adams Middle School. 2008. "Technology." Teacher Handbook 2008–2009. Santa Monica, CA: John Adams Middle School. Available from school office.
End of Year Teacher Procedures	• SMMUSD. 1982. "Teacher's Annual Report to Principals." BP 6040. Santa Monica, CA: SMMUSD.
Parent Volunteers	• SMMUSD. 1991. "Parent Involvement." BP 1241. Santa Monica, CA: SMMUSD.
Administrative Support	• Bush, Gail. 2000. "The Principal's Manual for Your School Library Media Program." Chicago: ALA. www.ala.org/ala/aasl/aaslpubsandjournals/aaslbooksandprod/principalsmanual.pdf (accessed May 9, 2008). • American Library Association. 2001. "Position Statement on the Role of the School Library Media Specialist in Site-Based Management." Chicago: ALA. www.ala.org/ala/aasl/aaslproftools/positionstatements/aaslpositionstatementroleschool.htm (accessed May 9, 2008).
Evaluation and Assessment	
Assessment of Student Performance	• California School Library Association. 2004. "Standards for Information Literacy Grades K–12." Standards and Guidelines for Strong School Libraries. Sacramento, CA: CSLA. • American Library Association. 1998. "Student Performance Assessment." Information Power: Building Partnerships for Learning. Chicago: ALA.
Assessment of Library Media Program	• American Library Association. 1999. "School Library Media Program Assessment." Information Power: Building Partnerships for Learning. Chicago: ALA.

Source: Used with permission from the author, Jasper Bui (unpublished checklist).

WORKS CITED

Adams, Helen R. 2006. "Protecting the Privacy of Student Patrons." *Library Media Center Media Activities Monthly* 23, no. 4 (December): 37.

Adams, Helen R. 2007. "Conducting a Privacy Audit." *Library Media Center Media Activities Monthly* 23, no. 6 (February): 35.

Adams, Helen R., Robert F. Bocher, Carol A. Gordon, and Elizabeth Barry-Kessler. 2005. *Privacy in the 21st Century: Issues for Public, School and Academic Libraries.* Westport, CT: Libraries Unlimited.

American Association of School Librarians. 1991. "Position Statement on Flexible Scheduling." American Library Association, June. Available: www.ala.org/ala/mgrps/divs/aasl/aaslproftools/ positionstatements/ aaslpositionstatement.cfm (accessed June 9, 2009).

American Association of School Librarians and Association for Educational Communications and Technology. 1998. *Information Power: Building Partnerships for Learning.* Chicago: American Library Association.

American Library Association. 2003. "Principles for the Networked World." ALA, February. Available: www.ala.org/ala/aboutala/offices/ wo/referenceab/principles/principles.pdf (accessed March 29, 2009).

American Library Association. "State Privacy Laws Regarding Library Records." Available: www.ala.org/ala/aboutala/offices/oif/ifgroups/ stateifcchairs/stateifcinaction/stateprivacy.cfm (accessed March 29, 2009).

Boswell, Wendy. "Free Online Calendars: Find a Calendar on the Web." About.com. Available: websearch.about.com/od/dailywebsearchtips/ qt/dnt0424.htm (accessed June 9, 2009).

Consumer and Governmental Affairs Bureau. 2009. "Children's Internet Protection Act." Federal Communications Commission, September. Available: www.fcc.gov/cgb/consumerfacts/cipa.html (accessed March 29, 2009).

Franklin, Pat, and Claire Gatrell Stephens. 2006. "Circulating Equipment: Keeping Track of Everything!" *LMC Media Activities Monthly* 22, no. 7 (March): 42–44.

Johnson, Doug. 2007. "Rules for the Social Web." *Threshold* 7, no. 2 (Summer): 9–12.

Jones, Brent. 2008. "State Action on Cyber-Bullying." *USA Today*, February 6. Available: www.usatoday.com/news/nation/2008-02-06-cyber-bullying-list_N.htm (accessed June 25, 2009).

Lamb, Annette, and Larry Johnson. 2007. "Social Technology and Social

Networks." *Library Media Center Media Activities Monthly* 23, no. 5 (January): 40–44.

Lenhart, Amanda, and Mary Madden. 2007. "Teens, Privacy and Online Social Networks." Pew Internet & American Life Project, April 17. Available: www.pewinternet.org/~/media//Files/Reports/2007/ PIP_Teens_Privacy_SNS_Report_Final.pdf.pdf (accessed March 29, 2009).

National Center for Educational Statistics. 2006. "Internet Access in U.S. Public Schools and Classrooms: 1994–1995." U.S. Department of Education, November. Available: http://nces.ed.gov/pubs2007/2007020. pdf (accessed June 9, 2009).

Northeast Document Conservation Center. 2008. *Preservation Education Curriculum*. 2008. Andover, MA: Northeast Document Conservation Center. Available: www.nedcc.org/curriculum/lesson.introduction. php (accessed March 18, 2010).

U.S. Department of Education. 2008. *Family Educational Rights and Privacy Act*. Washington, DC: U.S. Department of Education. Available: www.ed.gov/policy/gen/guid/fpco/ferpa/index.html (accessed March 29, 2009).

Willard, Nancy. 2007. "Educator's Guide to Cyberbullying and Cyberthreats." Center for Safe and Responsible Use of the Internet, April. Available: www.cyberbully.org/ cyberbully/docs/cbcteducator.pdf (accessed June 25, 2009).

Chapter 8

Technologies for Professional Development

In 1998 the American Association of School Librarians (AASL) in collaboration with the Association for Educational Communication and Technologies (AECT) published *Information Power: Building Partnerships for Learning*. AASL/AECT's *Information Power* continues to be the guiding force for defining the multiple roles an effective library media specialist (LMS) must serve. Fulfilling the information specialist role requires the LMS to serve as the leader and expert on campus, constantly evaluating and incorporating an ever increasing base of technology tools. Technology is constantly evolving. An effective manager of technology understands the need to keep abreast of best practices and to learn from the successes and pitfalls of others. Additionally, effective technology managers continually evaluate existing technology in relation to new and emerging technologies, and they integrate new technologies when the added benefits and costs justify it.

In library schools, future LMSs are exposed to the latest trends and research. Once on the job, LMSs are then faced with the task of continuing to stay current while fulfilling their other roles as teacher, instructional partner, and program administrator. Staying abreast of emerging technologies requires continuous professional development. Many communication technologies, both existing and emerging, can positively support LMSs in their efforts to manage technology resources for their professional growth. This chapter examines how technology can be used as a tool for management-focused professional development to communicate and connect with colleagues worldwide, share best practices, and minimize duplication of effort in synchronous, real-time settings and in asynchronous settings.

HUMAN NETWORKING

In the final analysis, management of information technology is about change, not about technology. It's about people and organizational behavior, not machines. While the lack of technology is a barrier to change, the presence of technology does not guarantee change. Organizational and communication skills together can ensure that technological change can be managed effectively. But because technology keeps changing, LMSs need to keep current about those changes so that they can determine which management approaches will best fit the new situation.

Thinking Locally

Because the LMS is often alone as a librarian professional on site, this personal updating process can seem isolated. Some schools provide a technology curriculum with a computer technology teacher doing the instruction. This person can share technology-related management issues such as lab supervision and resource management. Although such persons are likely to lack some of the formal organizational skills of the LMS, they have an instructional focus that can prove useful to the LMS. Indeed, the technology teacher and LMS can be symbiotic partners for learning and management.

Additionally, school districts are hiring technology specialists to oversee technology, be it administrative or instructional aspects. These experts tend to have more technical expertise, and less instructional experience, than the LMS. However, both need to use management skills to inventory and maintain hardware, software, and the supporting infrastructure. As such, they can draw on each other's expertise and keep each other informed of new developments.

Of course, LMSs can communicate regularly with their peers, either at the district or county level. Monthly meetings, either face-to-face or virtually, provide a systematic way to share concerns and ideas. In between these meetings, LMSs can send news about technology trends, forthcoming products, and services. Ideally, LMSs can create a repository of these documents to optimize their use. In some regions, multitype librarian groups offer a way to cross-fertilize management expertise. In terms of technology management, special librarians may well spearhead initiatives as they work in technology-rich environments. In their part, LMSs work in educational settings that can help students be prepared for those corporate environments, so adopting and applying current technology management practices can help these potential employees.

Professional Organizations

Professional organizations can provide LMSs with excellent support in library technology management. These professional organizations exist on the local, state, regional, national, and international level. Library professional organizations, such as the American Association of School Librarians (AASL), help LMSs develop professionally in all aspects of their job, including the management of technology. Thus, involvement in library professional organizations at all levels clearly can benefit LMSs by providing a source of ongoing professional development.

In addition, LMSs should consider the benefits of non-library-content-specific organizations, such as the National Council for the Social Studies (NCSS). Individuals who belong to these organizations share the same goal of many LMSs, which is to improve student achievement. Most hold annual if not semi-annual conferences, and emerging technology is typically a common thread. LMSs gain insights into technologies innovative educators are using in classrooms. In turn, LMSs may consider integrating these technologies within their library media programs. To reduce the fiscal burden when attending such conferences, LMSs can consider submitting a session proposal related to library technologies, such as effective researching in social studies using subscription databases. Most organizations offer free or reduced registration fees to conference speakers.

A third grouping of professional organizations focuses on issues related to the educational use of computers. This includes the Association for Educational Communications and Technology (AECT), Association for the Advancement of Computing in Education (AACE), and the International Society for Technology in Education (ISTE). Participation in such organizations can improve LMSs' understanding of technology and its role both in the school and specifically in the library media center (LMC). At a minimum, all of the professional organizations listed in this section have Web-based presences. By taking the time to visit these sites, LMSs can use them as an ongoing source of professional development.

Professional Learning Communities

While they have existed informally for centuries, professional learning communities (PLCs) have gained recent attention as a way to optimize mutual learning and improve programs systematically. Usually, a PLC includes both new and veteran members, the idea being that each has unique perspectives and experiences; newer members may have current training or insights garnered from other organizations, and senior members bring a collective history and sagacity about organizational culture. Critical features of a PLC include the following:

- A system of socializing new members to form a group identity
- A "flat" system so that everyone can learn from one another
- Meaningful tasks that draw on group wisdom and challenge members to learn more (Wenger, 1998)

PLCs for technology management offer a cost-effective way to optimize practices because individual LMSs can identify areas for improvement and also provide input about criteria for successful practices. Particularly since some management solutions require substantial costs, such as for integrated library management systems, working with peers can result in optimum solutions and possibly group discounts for purchasing and training.

Increasingly, virtual PLCs are being used to complement, supplement, or replace face-to-face communities for several reasons: to overcome transportation and geographic problems, to provide a mechanism to communicate more often, to archive interactions and documents created by individuals and groups, to provide timely feedback, and to keep members active and engaged (Rheingold,

2000). However, virtual PLCs have disadvantages: sense of isolation, possibly less commitment and accountability, lack of nuanced communication cues (e.g., body language, tone), less spontaneity, and technical limitations (e.g., cost of equipment, software, difficulty of learning the technology) (Lynch, 2002).

COLLABORATIVE TECHNOLOGY TOOLS

Several technology-based tools have been used to foster PLCs and professional development (PD) in general for LMSs. Technology-enhanced PD offers LMSs information on new technology, latest research, and innovative practices. It is not uncommon for PD participants to share ready-made lessons, PowerPoints, booktalks, publicity campaigns, and more. These practices result in more effective time management by building on the successes of others. Telecommunications, for example, provides convenient information, often on request, such as e-mail contacts and online help desks. Online resources such as tutorials, FAQs, and 'casts offer convenient information just in time. Web 2.0 offers a variety of social networking tools to communicate and share documents. Blogs, wikis, and social bookmarking provide asynchronous venues. Real-time online chat offers a way to provide guided group discussion. The chat is recorded and archived, and virtual offices store group documents. Current technologies make it possible for people to video conference from their computer workstations for free with very little technical setup. In short, PD technology tools provide a support network for LMSs, particularly for newer LMSs to access and utilize the time-tested experiences of their more seasoned colleagues. The following are a few of the existing collaborative technology tools that can be harnessed to advance knowledge about technology management issues.

Listservs

A listserv is one such technology resource that can be utilized to support professional growth. Listservs provide the LMS with a mechanism to both maintain and develop relationships with colleagues around the nation and world. A listserv is a discussion group of a specialized nature that is managed electronically through hardware, providing for asynchronous discussions that are, for the most part, automated by the list server. Listservs are asynchronous communication tools because the discussion occurs in stages over time. With synchronous discussion tools, communication occurs at the same time, for instance a chat forum or video conference.

Many LMSs find there is a statewide listserv specializing in school libraries. Examples include CALIBK12 (California), SLMS-NYLA (New York), OASL Listserv (Oregon), ISLAMANET-L (Illinois), and WLMA Listsev (Washington). The originator of the list is known as the list owner. This is the individual or institution that supports the listserv, which includes the physical server and software to process and distribute commands sent to the list. Typically, but not always, the list owner is a related state school library association or a university from within the state. On the national level, LM_NET is a listserv for school LMSs, and INFOLIT is an American Library Association listserv for K–20 school, academic and public librarians, which focuses on collaborative information literacy programs.

Most listservs have list moderators. How the listserv functions and the role the moderator plays depends on how it is set up by the list owner, also known as the list administrator. The list owner has the ability to require moderator approval before allowing individuals to join the listserv or can require message moderation for all messages or only certain messages filtered by the listserv based on keywords identified by the list owner. Most educational listservs are open, allowing any interested party to join the listserv, and do not require moderator approval before messages are sent. In such instances, the moderator of the listserv still plays an important role in monitoring listserv messages to maintain listserv policy and community norms, known as listserv etiquette. For instance, the CALIBK12 listserv serving California LMSs is a noncommercial listserv, and any advertising must be approved in advance by the list moderator. The moderator can also end discussion on any thread. This can be useful if the discussion becomes redundant or off-topic or if community norms are being violated.

Participating in listserv discussions is a great way to manage professional development needs while developing lifelong collegial relationships, especially when appropriate listserv etiquette is followed. This behavior includes using descriptive subject lines, succinct messages, and a "signature" with contact information. Listservs are meant to be information resource centers that ultimately save subscribers time through the collective pooling of resources and information, so any e-mail content should be carefully considered before submitting it to the listserv. Extraneous, off-topic listserv messages waste time and, if received in excess, can camouflage the more pertinent messages. This behavior, in turn, can discourage listserv participation and ultimately undermine the effectiveness of the listserv.

In addition, when drafting replies to listserv messages, discerning whether the message is intended for one individual or the entire listserv helps avoid the common listserv mistake of sending a private message to the entire listserv. Another common mistake in using listservs involves sending command messages, such as *unsubscribe*, to the entire listserv. Unless the goal is to upset strangers, this should be avoided. It is important to understand that any listserv will have at least three associated e-mail addresses:

1. E-mail address for sending commands. The e-mail address used to subscribe to the listserv is also the e-mail address to unsubscribe. These e-mails are sent directly to the list server. Depending on the LISTSERV software, there are a number of possible commands that can be sent to the list server.
2. E-mail address for the listserv owner. This e-mail is used to send a message only to the physical owner of the listserv. Unlike messages sent to the list server, which are processed automatically through the LISTSERV software, these messages will be directed to a human being. The listserv owner e-mail address is used to ask questions about the setup of the listserv.
3. E-mail address for sending messages. A separate e-mail address is used to send a message to all the subscribers of the listserv.

Listserv archives allow subscribers the ability to access past discussion threads. Over the years, these archives can grow to become powerful knowledge databases that are keyword searchable. To access listserv archives, users send a command to the list server.

Newer versions of LISTSERV software provide users with a Web-based interface from which to search listserv archives, simplifying the ability of users to locate past discussion threads.

Listservs keep users informed of upcoming professional development (PD) opportunities as well as serve as an ongoing source of PD through access to a steady stream of resources and best practices. When the LMS needs assistance with a difficult situation, such as a book challenge, a single e-mail to the listserv will almost inevitably lead to a wealth of strategies and tips gleaned from the collective wisdom and experience of colleagues.

The Pull Side of RSS

Chapter 6 discussed the use of RSS feeds to push library media program content to patrons. For professional growth, the LMS switches roles from content producer to content consumer. From this perspective, the feed aggregator is pulling content from the Web, making it available to the user in one central place.

LMSs can use feeds through a feed aggregator as a way to keep current in the field, by subscribing to feeds by library journals and publications. For example, *School Library Journal*'s Web site offers a number of different technology-related feeds, including Digital Resources News, Educational Technology News, Digital Reshift Blog, Gadgets News, Gaming News, and Technology News ("RSS Feeds on *School Library Journal*," accessed 2009). Even better, RSS feeds are now available from various subscription databases, including the Professional Collection from Gale-Cengage Learning, EBSCO Publishing's Professional Development Collection and ProQuest's Professional Education and Education Journals databases.

Setting up an RSS feed from a subscription database requires performing either a basic or advanced search in the database, using any limiters desired. For example, a search can be limited to articles available in full text, limited to particular sources, and limited to particular keywords such as Web 2.0, RSS, or library technology. After performing a search, the user should look for the orange RSS icon. By clicking on this icon and following the prompts, an RSS feed URL will be generated for this search. The feed address is inputted into a personal RSS aggregator to establish the new RSS feed. When new articles are published and available in the electronic database

TECH MOMENT: USING A LISTSERV

To join a listserv, you must know the e-mail address used to send commands to the list server. Next, you typically send an e-mail to the list server, with *subscribe first name last name* in the body of the e-mail. What is important to note is that the message is being sent to hardware, not a human being. Thus, additional text in the e-mail serves no purpose. Some listservs make the sign-up process easier by providing a Web site with an online form that completes this step for you. This means all you have to do is type your name and your e-mail address into the Web-based form. After sending the subscribe request, the list server will respond with an automated e-mail to confirm your request to join. Check your e-mail inbox. You will need to find this e-mail and follow the directions to complete your subscription request. At this point, the list server will welcome you to the group. You will usually receive a second e-mail that will provide you with the listserv posting guidelines, including directions for sending messages to the entire group.

Once subscribed, you will begin receiving messages sent to subscribers of the group. The volume of messages will depend on the number of active subscribers, the time of year and, of course, the content of the current discussions. Most list servers provide subscribers options to manage their subscriptions and the number of e-mails they receive. These options include setting up temporary vacation stops as well as changing a listserv subscription from all e-mails to weekly or daily digest mode, which condenses the content of e-mails sent into one longer message. Third-party software programs like Microsoft Outlook can also be used to effectively manage listserv messages. Within Outlook, users can create rules that are applied to certain items such as all incoming e-mail. For instance, a rule can be set up so that any e-mail coming from the listserv e-mail address is automatically routed from the in-box into another designated folder. This practice has two advantages: first, delivery of listserv messages is not slowed, as occurs in digest mode where the message is not delivered until the end of the day or the end of the week. Second, each message is received in its original format, allowing the subscriber to respond back to the group, thus continuing the discussion thread.

the RSS aggregator will provide the citation information and link to the full article.

Another idea for keeping current is subscribing to blog feeds of LMC service and technology education innovators. For example, many LMSs attend annual conferences where outstanding keynote speakers and workshop presenters provide innovative approaches to LMC organization, instruction, and management. Upon returning from these conferences, an LMS utilizing a feed aggregator such as Google Reader can perform Web searches to locate those speakers utilizing blogs, Delicious, or other Web 2.0 services providing automatic feeds. In addition to regular Google searches, conducting a Google Blogsearch (blogsearch.google.com) enables the LMS to search by keyword for blogs that have been indexed by this search tool. The LMS can then subscribe to any feeds that are found, thus garnering a continual source of professional development that lasts well beyond the physical conference.

Finally, simple Google searches that combine a desired topic with the keyword RSS (e.g., LMC RSS, technology education RSS, Web 2.0 RSS) will generate multiple RSS feeds. For example, LMSs might want to selectively access the blog *iLibrarian* (oedb. org/blogs/ilibrarian/) written by Ellyssa Kroski, author of *Web 2.0 for Librarians and Information Professionals*. Kroski describes her blog as "news and resources on Library 2.0 and the information revolution." Recent blog title postings included "Top Technology Breakthroughs of 2008" and "E-books gaining ground." Windows also assists in finding RSS feeds. With the public release of Windows Internet Explorer version 7.0 in 2006, users were provided with a new button on the toolbar: the Feeds button, which provides automatic feed discovery, lighting up whenever users visit a Web page with available feeds (Thurrott, 2006).

Real-Time Interaction

Online learning communities for educators are another tool for professional development and allow the LMS to communicate and connect with colleagues worldwide.

Tapped In (www.tappedin.org) exemplifies a free virtual community (such as a PLC) where educators can meet to discuss and share best practices. Tapped In, which was established in 1997 through National Science Foundation grant and Sun MicroSystems, is based on the idea that teachers need support groups to grow professionally. Funding is also received by a number of tenants, professional development companies, and organizations that "rent" buildings and rooms in the Tapped In environment, although an educator can become a member of Tapped In for free. Tapped In contains a number of specialized rooms, such as the Cybrarian room. Using the Tapped In calendar (tappedin.org/tappedin/do/ CalendarAction), LMSs can find relevant discussions and events. To start, the LMS can check out a "Tips and Tricks" session, where Tapped In volunteers familiarize users with the Tapped In interface and features. Next, the LMS can try out a few scheduled discussions, including Targeting Librarians!, a monthly discussion on the third Wednesday of each month from 7:30–9:00 p.m. EST. The Tapped In calendar provides more details on the discussion. Through monthly discussions, LMSs receive exposure to current trends in library technology. Equally importantly, LMSs establish connections with other library professionals.

Webcasts enable audio and video files to be broadcast on the Internet. More recently, this technology has become more interactive, blending text and multimedia in group conversational online environments. Typically, the speaker narrates a slide show and then answers questions from the audience via chat, microphone, or telephone. Both commercial and open source programs (such as Elluminate, TalkPoint, Mogulus, ePresence) provide audio and visual tools for real-time collaboration. Increasingly, library associations are offering virtual workshops that use Webcasting as their platform. While end user LMSs can usually participate in Webcasts without buying the underlying software, they should test the Webcast environment ahead of time to make sure that all required plug-ins are downloaded onto their computers and that any audiovisual equipment functions properly; finding out at the last minute that a headphone connector is the wrong size for the port can result in a very frustrating online session.

More recently, videoconferencing (VC) is being used as an online collaborative tool for LMS groups to address some of the limitations of virtual communities. Parties in two or more different locations can use Internet-connected computers, video equipment, and microphones to experience one another virtually. The following features of VC make it a unique and beneficial conduit for PLCs:

- High-resolution video and audio that can accommodate groups of people

- Real-time interaction without high transportation costs
- Multilocation access
- Ability to record sessions
- Ability to incorporate external resources: computer, document stand, whiteboard, telephone link, data conferencing link

Longer-term PLCs sometimes use online course management systems (CMS) to provide a single-entry system that incorporates synchronous and asynchronous communication as well as archived documents. Both professional and higher education entities use this technology to facilitate threaded discussion and a federated building of knowledge. However, CMSs can be more complicated than participants want or need, and they are usually more costly or require additional technology expertise if they use an Open Source model.

Virtual reality environments, such as Second Life, enable participants to assume avatar personas to share and store information. However, these virtual microworlds require high-powered hardware and significant training time. Several professional organizations such as the Special Libraries Association have a Second Life presence, so those LMSs who like this environment may find like-minded peers to exchange ideas.

NEXT STEPS

Technology management requires ongoing vigilance about change: of technology, of the educational community, and of the librarianship profession. These same factors, though, can also help LMSs cope with that change. In the final analysis, management of technology tries to optimize people's ability to use technology, so keeping people central in mind when improving management provides a useful focus in self-development in this arena.

WORKS CITED

Kroski, Ellyssa. "iLibrarian [homepage]." Available: http://oedb.org/blogs/ilibrarian/ (accessed January 3, 2009).

Lynch, M. 2002. *The Online Educator*. London: Routledge.

Rheingold, H. 2000. *The Virtual Community*. Cambridge, MA: MIT Press.

"RSS Feeds on *School Library Journal*." Reed Business Information. Available: www.schoollibraryjournal.com/learnRss (accessed January 2, 2009).

Thurrott, Paul. 2006. "Internet Explorer 7 Review." Paul Thurrott's SuperSite for Windows, October 18. Available: www.winsupersite.com/reviews/ie7.asp/ (accessed January 1, 2009).

Wenger, E. 1998. *Communities of Practice.* Cambridge, UK: Cambridge University Press.

Glossary

action research: Situationally based research that seeks to improve a concrete issue; the research is an active participant in the situation.

ADA: Americans with Disabilities Act.

aggregator: Collector, usually applied to subscription databases that aggregate periodical articles or to RSS feeds that aggregate Web content.

algorithm: A formula or set of instructions.

ambient light: Available or existing light.

antivirus program: A program that detects viruses and attempts to delete or quarantine them to prevent further spread and harm to computers.

assessment: Evaluation of a behavior at one specific time under one specific condition.

AUP: Acceptable use policy.

authentication: The process of identifying an individual, usually based on a username and password.

authoring program: Computer software that enables the user to combine and sequence text, images, sound, and motion, usually presented in a series of "cards" or "screens."

authorization: The process of giving persons access to systems based on their identities.

AVCHD: Advanced video codec high definition.

bandwidth: In computing, the amount of data that can be transmitted in a given period of time.

benchmark: An identified step toward a standard, with a concrete indicator that indicates that a person has progressed to that point.

BIOS: Basic Input/Output System.

blog: Weblog; informally, a Web diary.

brainstorming: Generating many ideas, usually without critiquing them initially.

broadband: Referring to a wide band of frequencies, usually relative to radio or telecommunications.

broadcasting: Sending a message to many people simultaneously.

browser: A software program that allows the user to view and interact with Internet resources.

camcorder: A video camera recorder.

case study: A set of descriptions and information about a specific action or situation.

CAT-5: Category 5 cable, a type of twisted pair wiring used to create Ethernet cables. Ethernet cables are also made out of CAT-5e or CAT-6 wiring.

CC: Carbon copy, also known as courtesy copy.

cognitive: Pertaining to factual knowledge.

collaboration: The process of sharing resources and responsibilities to create shared meaning and attain a common goal; interdependent cooperation.

computer management software: A program that allows for control of computers or printers through a central interface, also known as lab management or classroom management software.

computer security software: A software program that protects a computer from unwanted tampering.

connectivity: The quality of connection between a computer system and the Internet.

consensus: Decision supported by the entire group rather than by a majority.

constructivism: Individual construction of meaning through active interaction with the environment or stimuli.

content analysis: Analysis of a document by classifying, tabulating, and evaluating key themes and ideas.

content filter: Web proxy used to block sites that may contain inappropriate content.

CPU: Central processing unit; the "brains" of the computer that manages data processing.

cracker: An individual who intentionally tires to bypass security settings.

Creative Commons: A nonprofit organization that seeks to make creative work available for others to build on while respecting intellectual property rights.

cyberbullying: A form of bullying in which the aggressor uses electronic communication to intentionally attempt harm.

data projector: A projector that connects to an electronic device (e.g., computer, video player, DVD player).

database: A collection of related information, often used or produced by a computer application program.

demographics: Statistics about human populations.

desktop publishing: Sophisticated word-processing software programs that enable text and graphics to be combined in a publishable format.

DHCP: Dynamic Host Configuration Protocol; a protocol for assigning IP addresses to devices on a network.

differentiated instruction: Instruction that accommodates the varying needs of different individuals.

digital citizenship: Responsible and positive proactive use of technology.

digital resource: Usually an electronic document.

digitization: The process of transforming documents into electronic format.

disk imaging: Ghosting; the process of making an exact data copy onto an image file.

distance education: An educational delivery system that offers remote access; correspondence courses, videotape courses, and online instruction are typical means.

DNS: Domain name system.

drive, flash/portable/thumb/USB: A small portable external drive, usually containing a USB, and sometimes called a memory stick.

DSL: Digital subscriber line.

dynamic: Capable of change; computer-related work done "on the fly" or upon need.

e-book: Electronic book; usually a digitized version of a monograph.

e-group: Electronic group; similar to a listserv, an Internet service that allows groups to share information via telecommunications.

environmental scan: A systematic monitoring of internal and external factors that impact an organization.

firewall: Hardware and software used to restrict data on a network.

flash: Browser independent, vector-graphic animation technology that requires low bandwidth to view.

formatting: The process of preparing a drive for use by the operating system.

FTP: File transfer protocol.

gigabyte: 1,000 megabytes; a unit of measurement for representing data storage capacity.

graphic organizer: A visual structure to organize information, such as a Venn diagram, t-chart, or concept map.

graphics tablet: An electronic device that looks like a flat, oversized PDA that accepts drawing input.

GUI: Graphical user interface.

handheld device: A small electronic device such as a PDA or compact PC, sometimes called a mobile device.

hard drive: A computer storage device that contains ROM, computer programs, and data.

hardware: Computer equipment, such as monitors and computer-processing systems.

HD: High-definition; usually referring to video or other visual formats.

HDMI: High-definition media interface.

HTML: Hypertext markup language; a programming language commonly used to create Web sites.

HTTP: Hypertext transfer protocol.

hypertext: Text that embeds Web links to other texts.

IDF: Intermediate distribution frame.

IM: Instant messaging.

indicator: A specific, concrete behavior or disposition that demonstrates that a person has met a standard.

information literacy: The ability to locate, assess, use, and share information effectively and purposefully.

infrastructure: The technological system to support telecommunications (e.g., facilities, cables, equipment, services, etc.).

in-service: Usually refers to a professional development event for fully employed educators.

instructional design: A systematic analysis of training needs and the development of aligned instruction.

Integrated Library Management System (ILMS): A software program that includes several library management functions: cataloging, inventory, circulation, etc. Replaces the term "automation system."

interactive interface: An electronic display that allows the user to input information and get feedback.

interface: In technology, it often refers to the means by which users interact with a computer system.

intranet: An internal network. Also known as LAN.

IP: Internet protocol.

ISDN: Integrated services digital network; a digital telephone network that carries both data and voice messages.

ISP: Internet service provider.

Java: A platform-independent, object-oriented programming language.

just-in-time training: Training that occurs at the moment of need, usually to solve an immediate, specific problem.

LAN: Local area network. Also known as Intranet.

LCD: Liquid crystal display; usually refers to a monitor that does not use a cathode ray tube.

learning aid: A device or product that helps a person learn, such as a guide sheet, CD-ROM, or manual.

listserv: An Internet service that allows participants to share information via e-mail, usually in a relatively closed environment.

MAN: Metropolitan area network; two LANs in close proximity.

MARC: Machine-readable cataloging.

mass media: Television, movies, radio, newspapers, and other periodicals.

MB: Megabyte. 1,000 kilabytes or 1 million bytes; a unit of measurement for representing data storage capacity.

MDF: Main distribution frame.

media literacy: Information literacy as it applies to communications, particularly mass media.

mentoring: The process whereby experienced, successful practitioners coach and acculturate new practitioners, usually on a one-to-one basis.

metatag: Bibligraphic control data, usually about a digital document.

mobile device: A portable technological piece of equipment, usually with a computer chip or processing unit (e.g., handheld device, laptop, smartphone).

moderator: A facilitator or overseer.

motherboard: The computer's circuit board, which contains several of the electronic components in a computer.

MP3: MPEG-1 (Moving Picture Experts Group) Audio Layer 3; a standard for encoding and compressing audio files.

multimedia: Two or more combined media, usually referring to authoring or presentation tools.

MUVE: Multi-user virtual environment. *See* VIRTUAL REALITY.

navigation tool: Elements that help people find their way and use an electronic resource. Tools may include menu bars, hyperlinks, help buttons, etc.

needs assessment: The process of determining the needs of a targeted population. Typical instruments include observations, surveys and questionnaires, interviews and focus groups, examination of student work, and performance evaluations.

network device: Any device, such as a printer or computer, capable of accessing the Internet or Intranet.

OCR: Optical character recognition; a software program that scans a printed text and digitizes it into machine-readable text.

OPAC: Online public access catalog.

open source: Coding that is freely available to the public, usually applied to software development.

operating system (OS): System software the coordinates hardware device activity and enables users to run software.

outcome: An anticipated or desired result.

PCI: Peripheral component interconnect; a means to attach peripherals to computers.

PDA: Personal digital assistant; a type of handheld device.

peripheral: Devices that can be connected to the computer but are external to the CPU and motherboard.

plug-in: Usually refers to a software program module that adds a specific feature or service to a larger system.

podcast: Broadcast audio files.

POP3: Post Office Protocol version 3.

portal: Web site that functions as an access point to information, especially external resources.

presentation tool: A software application program that is used to present information visually as well as textually. It usually refers to programs such as PowerPoint, HyperStudio, or KidPix.

productivity tool: Typically a software application program that helps one work more productively, such as word processing, databases, and spreadsheets.

professional learning community: A group of people with mutual interests who gather to inform one another and improve their organization.

profile: Computer representation of user information (e.g., desktop settings, file locations).

proxy server: A server that serves as a firewall by screening all incoming and outgoing messages.

publishing tool: In andragogy, a means to share or report information, such as newsprint or overhead transparency.

quality control: A system of activities to ensure quality of a product or process.

RAID: Redundant array of independent disks; computer data storage schemes that divide and copy data among multiple hard drives.

RAM: Random-access memory. Temporary memory that can be used while the computer is on but is erased when the computer is turned off.

rapid prototyping: Developing a product (e.g., software package) by creating, testing, and refining models or prototypes.

realia: Real objects, such as models and artifacts.

refresh cycle: Planned, structured process for replacing computers as they age.

repurpose: Taking the same information used for one purpose and altering it for another purpose; for example, a PowerPoint presentation might be repurposed as a flyer for a different audience and objective.

RFP: Request for proposal; a document that defines the specifications of a product or service that is being requested.

RJ45: A type of connector commonly used with twisted pair wire to create Ethernet cables.

ROM: Read-only memory. Permanent computer memory.

RSS aggregator: Also known as RSS reader, it provides a central place for the user to receive RSS feeds.

RSS feed: Really Simple Syndication or Rich Site Summary; a Web-based means to disseminate (syndicate) content.

rubric: A table or chart that describes the concrete attributes and quality of an indicator (e.g., product or behavior).

scaffolding: Learning aids, cues, and other instructional support to help students understand a concept.

screen dump: Downloading or printing the contents of a monitor screen of information (e.g., a Web page).

screencast: A video recording of a computer screen.

search engine: A software program that indexes Internet sources and enables the user to "search" for specific information.

server: A computer that manages resources on a network and provides a central storage for software programs and data.

SMART Board: An electronic whiteboard.

SMS: Short message service.

SMTP: Simple mail transfer protocol.

sniffer: Network packet analyzer; network software or hardware that seeks and intercepts network traffic.

social network: Social structure consisting of individuals who are connected, usually applied to Web 2.0 environments.

software license: An agreement providing the user the right to install and use specific software.

spam: Unsolicited e-mail or posting, usually advertising a service or product.

spreadsheet: A computer ledger application program.

stakeholder: A significant constituent who has the potential to be impacted by, or can influence, an effort; an invested party.

standard: A basis for comparison.

storyboard: A sequential set of visuals and narrative outlining a media story.

streamed/streaming video: Digital video that is transmitted via the Internet in compressed "chunks" to facilitate downloading and viewing.

subscription database: Collections of resources, usually organized thematically. Also called research databases, electronic databases, and online databases.

synchronize: Copy and delete files in both directions, keeping only the most recent modified copy version.

telecommunications: Systems that transmit messages over a distance electronically (e.g., telephone, Internet).

threaded discussion: Online discussion that follows a topic.

URL: Uniform resource locator; a Web address.

USB: Universal Serial Bus.

utility program: System software that performs a specific task.

virtual chat: An online discussion that occurs in real time.

virtual private network (VPN): A network constructed by using public wires to connect nodes.

virtual reality: Use of a computer to create a simulated environment that resembles a real setting and allows the user to explore and manipulate that environment.

virus: A small software program that is intended to spread among computers and interfere with their operations.

virus definition file: A listing of known viruses, this file is used by antivirus programs to scan for threats on a computer.

vodcast: Broadcast video files.

WAN: Wide area network; two or more LANs connected together.

Web 2.0: Interactive Web; enables people to collaborate and share online.

Web page: Single document on the Internet that users can access via a unique URL.

Web proxy: Combination of hardware and software on the network through which outgoing Web traffic is routed.

Web site: Set of interconnected Web pages, including a homepage.

Webcam: Video camera that can transmit video on the Internet.

Webcast: Web-based broadcast of audio and video files.

Webliography: A Web-based bibliography.

WebQuest: A structured, interactive online learning activity that integrates identified Web sites; it often incorporates cooperative learning and simulations.

wifi: Wireless fidelity; usually refers to wireless, 802.11 networks.

wiki: A Web site that allows for easy creation and editing.

work around: An alternative way to solve a problem.

XML: Extensible markup language.

Resources

The following Web sites provide helpful general guidance for technology management issues. Local resources are more likely to address specific procedures that impact individual schools and districts.

GENERAL

ALA TechSource
www.alatechsource.org
> This unit of the American Library Association publishes *Library Technology Reports, Smart Libraries Newsletter*, and the ALA TechSource Blog.

CaliforniaK12 HighSpeedNetwork
www.k12hsn.org
> Take advantage of this site for technology management, resources, and software.

Council on Library and Information Resources
www.clir.org
> CLIR fosters new approaches to the management of digital and nondigital information resources so that they will be available in the future.

InfoPeople
http://infopeople.org
> This grant-funded organization provides technology-related training and resources for librarians.

Information Technology & Telecommunication Services
www.ala.org/ala/aboutala/offices/itts/index.cfm
> American Library Association's office on technology issues offers

advice and support, and a linked center gives guidance on information technology policy. The Washington, DC, office also focuses on intellectual freedom.

ISTE (International Society for Technology in Education)
www.iste.org
Their journal *Learning & Leading with Technology* has monthly technology comparison reviews as well as technology strategies.

Librarian's Shelf
http://lists.webjunction.org/web4lib
Library Spot's directory links to Web sites about several aspects of librarianship, including technology and management.

Library & Information Technology Association
www.ala.org/ala/mgrps/divs/lita/litahome.cfm
This cutting-edge technology division of the American Library Association provides resources, services, and experts.

NPower
www.npower.org
This nonprofit organization provides technology assistance for other nonprofits.

Resources for School Librarians
www.sldirectory.com
A retired librarian maintains this Web directory, which links to technology and management Web sites.

TechAtlas Tools
http://techatlas.org/tools/features.asp#eventtracker
This planning center offers many technology planning tools for nonprofit organizations.

TICAL: Technology Information Center for Administrative Leadership
www.portical.org
This is where California school administrators go to get info about technology.

Virtual Computer Library
www.computer-and-printer-reviews.com
Maintained by the University of Texas at Austin, this site offers buying and repair advice.

Washington State Library Digital Best Practices
http://digitalwa.statelib.wa.gov/newsite/best.htm
> This Web site guides librarians in planning digital projects.

Web Junction
www.webjunction.org/1
> Now managed by OCLC, this Web site focuses on library technology management, including policies.

Web4Lib Electronic Discussion
http://lists.webjunction.org/web4lib
> The Web4Lib electronic discussion is for the discussion of issues relating to the creation, management, and support of library-based World-Wide Web servers, services, and applications.

ACQUISITIONS

CNET
www.cnet.com
> This commercial Web site is a good starting point for reviewing technology options.

Computer Information Center
www.compinfo-center.com
> This extensive one-stop Web site lists useful source of computer information.

Consumer Reports
www.ConsumerReports.org
> The gold standard for general objective consumer product ratings, their perspective is the average home consumer, not the school site with heavy-handed users.

Consumer Search
www.ConsumerSearch.com
> *New York Times* owns About.Com, which provides this service.

Information Today
www.infotoday.com
> This well-known company focuses on the needs of information professionals and provides product reviews as well as vendor lists.

PC World

http://pcworld.com

> This long-standing magazine (in computer years) is known for its regular thematic and yearly reviews.

DIGITAL RESOURCES

Basics of Library Automation

www.cde.state.co.us/cdelib/technology/atauto.htm

> The Colorado State Library offers guidance on selecting and implementing integrated library management systems.

CERT

www.cert.org

> Carnegie Mellon's University CERT studies Internet security vulnerabilities and develops resources and training to improve security.

Library Technology Guides

www.librarytechnology.org

> This Web site aims to provide comprehensive and objective information related to the field of library automation.

MSDN Library

http://msdn.microsoft.com/en-us/library/default.aspx

> Microsoft Developer Network provides essential information for those using Microsoft tools, products, and technologies.

NERL Licensing Guidelines & NERL Generic License

www.library.yale.edu/NERLpublic/licensingprinciples.html

> This university Web site guides librarians in negotiating licenses.

The Web Developers' Virtual Library

http://wdvl.internet.com

> This is a comprehensive illustrated encyclopedia of Web technology.

MAINTENANCE

Computer Maintenance and Repair 101

www.preventiveguru.com

> Practical advice is given for a variety of issues.

Information Technology Management
www.uwstout.edu/lib/subjects/telecomm.htm
> This directory links to many good Web sites about technology management.

Library Information Technology
www.lib.umich.edu/lit
> This site gives a good idea of how information technology management can be delegated.

MacFixit
www.macfixit.com
> Where do you go to get technical advice about Macs? Here. (Apple has its own site too, but these folks are in the trenches doing the dirty work.)

Microsoft
www.microsoft.com
> This site addresses both hardware and software maintenance.

PC Guide Preventative Maintenance
www.pcguide.com/care/pm.htm
> This site offers many good tips for keeping systems in good order.

POLICIES

Acceptable Use Policies
www.awesomelibrary.org/Classroom/Technology/Integrating_Technology/
Acceptable_Use_Policies.html
> Dr. Adam's "Awesome Library" identifies several good sources of information about this important policy.

Columbia University Libraries/Information Services Copyright Advisory Office
http://copyright.columbia.edu
> This well-respected site is geared to librarians and educators.

Copyright Site
www.benedict.com
> This Web site provides general copyright information for educators, students, and digital resource creators.

Electronic Information Privacy Center
http://epic.org
> EPIC is a public interest research center in Washington, DC, established to focus public attention on emerging civil liberties issues and to protect privacy, the First Amendment, and constitutional values.

LAMA Security Guidelines
www.ala.org/ala/mgrps/divs/llama/lamapublications/librarysecurity.cfm
> Keeping systems secure is a big job, and this ALA division can help.

The USA PATRIOT Act and Patron Privacy on Library Internet Terminals
www.llrx.com/features/usapatriotact.htm
> Law library consultant Mary Minow reviews the implications of the USA PATRIOT Act for libraries and for patron use of the Internet.

Bibliography

4Teachers. 2006. "Technology Glossary." ALTEC. Available: www.4teachers.org/techalong/glossary/ (accessed June 21, 2009).

Absolute Software. "CompuTrace Complete." Absolute Software Corporation, 2010. Available: www.absolute.com/ products/computrace-complete (accessed January 4, 2010).

Adams, Helen R. 2006. "Protecting the Privacy of Student Patrons." *Library Media Center Media Activities Monthly* 23, no. 4 (December): 37.

Adams, Helen R. 2007. "Conducting a Privacy Audit." *Library Media Center Media Activities Monthly* 23, no. 6 (February): 35.

Adams, Helen R., Robert F. Bocher, Carol A. Gordon, and Elizabeth Barry-Kessler. 2005. *Privacy in the 21st Century: Issues for Public, School and Academic Libraries.* Westport, CT: Libraries Unlimited.

Adeona. "Frequently Asked Questions." University of Washington. Available: adeona.cs.washington.edu/faq.html (accessed January 17, 2009).

American Association of School Librarians. 1991. "Position Statement on Flexible Scheduling." American Library Association, June. Available: www.ala.org/ala/mgrps/divs/aasl/aaslproftools/positionstatements/ aaslpositionstatement.cfm (accessed June 9, 2009).

American Association of School Librarians. 1999. *A Planning Guide for Information Power: Building Partnerships for Learning.* Chicago: American Library Association.

American Association of School Librarians. 2007. *Standards for the 21st Century Learner.* Chicago: American Library Association. Available: www.ala.org/aasl/standards/ (accessed July 2, 2009).

American Association of School Librarians and Association for Educational Communications and Technology. 1998. *Information Power: Building Partnerships for Learning.* Chicago: American Library Association.

American Library Association. 2003. "Principles for the Networked

World." ALA, February. Available: www.ala.org/ala/aboutala/offices/
wo/referenceab/principles/principles.pdf (accessed March 29, 2009).

American Library Association. "State Privacy Laws Regarding Library
Records." Available: www.ala.org/ala/aboutala/offices/oif/ifgroups/
stateifcchairs/stateifcinaction/stateprivacy.cfm (accessed March 29,
2009).

Bailey, Gail C., and Jayne E. Moore. 2008. "Buying Power." *T.H.E. Journal*
35, no. 7 (July): 31.

Bates, Naomi. "Booktalk Podcast." Northwest High School. Available:
www.nisdtx.org/120820731141528687/podcasts/browse.asp?A=39
9&BMDRN=2000&BCOB=0&C=70101 (accessed July 3, 2009).

Bing. 2009. "SyncToy 2.0." Microsoft Corporation. Available: www.
microsoft.com/DownLoads/details.aspx?familyid=C26EFA36-98E0-
4EE9-A7C598D0592D8C52&displaylang=en (accessed January 17,
2009).

Bloglines. 2004. "Bloglines Marks Search Milestone of 100 Million Blog
and News Feed Articles." IAC Search & Media, August 12. Available:
www.bloglines.com/about/pr_08122004 (accessed July 1, 2009).

Bobrosky, Mark. 2007. *Walter Reed Middle School Faculty Services Handbook*. Los Angeles: Los Angeles Unified School District. Available:
www.reedmstech.com/library/images/PDF/fac_hndbk.pdf (accessed
January 5, 2009).

Bookwink. 2007. "Video Booktalk Archives." Bookwink.com. Available:
www.bookwink.com/archives.html (accessed June 31, 2009).

Boswell, Wendy. "Free Online Calendars: Find a Calendar on the Web."
About.com. Available: http://websearch.about.com/od/dailyweb-
searchtips/qt/dnt0424.htm (accessed June 9, 2009).

Breeding, Marshall. 2006. "Web 2.0? Let's Get to Web 1.0 First." *The
Systems Librarian* (May): 30–33.

Breeding, Marshall. 2007. "Introduction." *Library Technology Reports*
43, no. 4 (July/August): 5–14.

Brown, M. 2005. "Learning Spaces." In *Educating the Net Gen*, edited by
D. Oblinger and J. Oblinger, 12.1–12.22. Boulder, CO: Educause.

Buechner, Maryanne Murray. 2004. "50 Coolest Websites." *Time*. Available: www.time.com/time/techtime/200406/ (accessed January 1,
2009).

California Library Association. 2005. *Technology Core Competencies for
California Library Workers*. Sacramento, CA: California Library Association. Available: www.cla-net.org/included/docs/tech_core_com-
petencies.pdf (accessed June 30, 2009).

Cannon, R. 1988. "Learning Environment." In *Encyclopedia of Educa-*

tional Media Communications and Technology, edited by D. Unwin and R. McAlees, 342–358. New York: Greenwood Press.

Carheden, Andrew. 2005. "Disk Imaging Tools: Install, Clone, Manage." Windows ITPro, May. Available: http://windowsitpro.com/article/ articleid/45890/disk-imaging-tools-install-clone%20manage.html (accessed January 16, 2009).

Clark, Laura, and Denise Davis. 2009. "Findings from Site Visits." *Library Technology Reports* 45, no. 1 (January): 28–30.

Computer Refresh Committee. 2008. *Computer Refresh Program*. Farmington, UT: Davis School District. Available: www.davis.k12.ut.us/ district/ets/sts/files/F4098BFBB691467885ED0E9EACF83CC3.pdf (accessed June 21, 2009).

Consumer and Governmental Affairs Bureau. 2009. "Children's Internet Protection Act." Federal Communications Commission, September. Available: www.fcc.gov/cgb/consumerfacts/cipa.html (accessed March 29, 2009).

Coombs, Karen A. 2007. "Building a Library Web Site on the Pillars of Web 2.0." *Computers in Libraries* 27, no. 1 (January): 16–20.

CoreCollections.net. "SchoolLibraries.net: Web Pages Created by School Librarians." H.W. Wilson. Available: www.school-libraries.net (accessed July 1, 2009).

Cunningham, Ward. 2003. "Correspondence on the Etymology of Wiki." Available: http://c2.com/doc/etymology.html (accessed July 1, 2009).

Czarnecki, Kelly, and Matt Gullett. 2007. "Meet the New You." *School Library Journal* 53, no. 1: 36–39.

Dewey, John. 1933. *How We Think*. New York: D. C. Heath.

Edmondson, Ray. 2004. *Audiovisual Archiving: Philosophy and Principles*. Paris: UNESCO.

Ertl, Bernard, Franz Fischer, and Heinz Mandl. 2006. "Conceptual and Socio-Cognitive Support for Collaborative Learning in Videoconferencing Environments." *Computers & Education* 47, no. 3 (November): 298–315.

Farb, S., and A. Riggio. 2004. "Medium or Message? A New Look at Standards, Structures and Schemata for Managing Electronic Resources." *Library Hi Tech* 22, no. 2 (February): 144–152.

Federal Trade Commission. 2007. *FTC Factors for Consumers*. Washington, DC: Federal Trade Commission. Available: www.ftc.gov/ bcp/edu/pubs/consumer/tech/tec03.pdf (accessed February 3, 2010).

Florida Center for Instructional Technology. "Ideas for Podcasting in the Classroom: Book Talks." Available: http://fcit.usf.edu/podcasts/ book_talks.html (accessed January 3, 2009).

Franklin, Pat, and Claire Gatrell Stephens. 2006. "Circulating Equipment:

Keeping Track of Everything!" *School Library Media Activities Monthly* 22, no. 7 (June): 42–44.

Griffith, Eric. 2009. "Make the Most of Your New PC: Follow This Simple 12-Step Program to Guarantee Maximum Performance, Security, and Ease of Use. Plus, Decide How to Deal with All Your Old Stuff." *PC Magazine* (January). Available: www.pcmag.com/article2/0,2817,2337550,00.asp (accessed June 27, 2009).

Henke, Karen Greenwood. 2007. "How Fast Is Fast Enough? The Question of Adequate Bandwidth Is Increasingly the Issue of the Day." *Technology & Learning* 28, no. 3 (October): 16–20.

Henning, J. 2005. "Final Report." Available: jhenning.law.uvic.ca/final_report.html (accessed August 16, 2009).

Horrigan, John B. 2008. "Home Broadband Adoption 2008." Pew Internet & American Life Project, July. Available: www.pewInternet.org/pdfs/PIP_Broadband_2008.pdf (accessed January 8, 2009).

Intel. 2009. "Intel Processors." Available: www.intel.com/consumer/learn/processors/ (accessed June 21, 2009).

International Digital Publishing Forum. "Wholesale E-book Sales Statistics." Available: www.idpf.org/doc_library/industrystats.htm (accessed March 30, 2009).

International Society for Technology in Education. 2007. *National Educational Technology Standards for Students.* Eugene, OR: International Society for Technology in Education. Available: www.iste.org/Content/NavigationMenu/NETS/ForStudents/2007Standards/NETS_for_Students_2007_Standards.pdf (accessed July 2, 2009).

International Technology Education Association. 2003. *Advancing Excellence in Technological Literacy: Student Assessment, Professional Development, and Program Standards.* Reston, VA: International Technology Education Association. Available: www.iteaconnect.org/TAA/PDFs/AETL.pdf (accessed July 2, 2009).

Internet Corporation for Assigned Names and Numbers. 2005. "Abuse Issues and IP Addresses." IANA, October 17. Available: www.iana.org/abuse/faq.html (accessed January 16, 2009).

Johnson, Doug. 2007. "Rules for the Social Web." *Threshold* 7, no. 2 (Summer): 9–12.

Joint Information Systems Committee Development Group. 2006. *Designing Spaces for Effective Learning.* Bristol, England: University of Bristol. Available: www.jisc.ac.uk/media/documents/publications/learningspaces.pdf (accessed June 11, 2009).

Jones, Brent. 2008. "State Action on Cyber-Bullying." *USA Today*, February 6. Available: www.usatoday.com/news/nation/2008-02-06-cyber-bullying-list_N.htm (accessed June 25, 2009).

Kaplan, S., and R. Kaplan. 1982. *Cognition and Environment: Functioning in an Uncertain World.* New York: Praeger.

Keane, Nancy. "Booktalks Quick and Simple." Available: www.nancykeane.com/booktalks/ (accessed July 1, 2009).

King, David Lee. 2007. "Inviting Participation, Part 4: Specific Tools—Blogs," January 17. Available: www.davidleeking.com/2007/01/17/inviting-participation-part-4-specific-tools-blogs/ (accessed July 1, 2009).

Kioskea.net. 2008. "Random Access Memory (RAM or PC Memory)." Kioskea.net, October 16. Available: http://en.kioskea.net/contents/pc/ram.php3 (accessed January 10, 2009).

Kroski, Ellyssa. "iLibrarian [homepage]." Available: http://oedb.org/blogs/ilibrarian/ (accessed January 3, 2009).

Lamb, Annette, and Larry Johnson. 2007. "Social Technology and Social Networks." *Library Media Center Media Activities Monthly* 23, no. 5 (January): 40–44.

Lamb, Annette, and Larry Johnson. 2008. "The Virtual Teacher-Librarian." *Teacher Librarian* 35, no. 4 (April): 69–71.

Lemke, C., and E. Coughlin. 1998. *Technology in American Schools: Seven Dimensions of Progress, An Educator's Guide.* Santa Monica, CA: Milken Family Foundation. Available: www.mff.org/edtech (accessed July 2, 2009).

Lenhart, Amanda, and Mary Madden. 2007. "Teens, Privacy and Online Social Networks." Pew Internet & American Life Project, April 17. Available: www.pewinternet.org/~/media//Files/Reports/2007/PIP_Teens_Privacy_SNS_Report_Final.pdf.pdf (accessed March 29, 2009).

Library of Congress. 2002. *Preservation: Cylinder, Disc and Tape Care in a Nutshell.* Washington, DC: Library of Congress. Available: www.loc.gov/preserv/care/record.html#Storage (accessed July 7, 2009).

Los Angeles Unified School District. 2006. "Educational Technology Plan." Los Angeles Unified School District, July 1. Available: http://notebook.lausd.net/pls/ptl/ptl_apps.elib_item.show_item?p_item_id=259499 (accessed January 15, 2009).

Lynch, M. 2002. *The Online Educator.* London: Routledge.

Martin, Nicole. 2007. "Keep Your Eyes on the Enterprise: Emails, Wikis, Blogs, and Corporate Risk." *EContent* 30, no. 6 (July): 54–59.

Massachusetts School Library Media Association. 2003. "Facilities Standard." Massachusetts School Library Media Association, April. Available: www.mslma.org/MediaForum/Apr2003/Facilities.html (accessed March 28, 2009).

Microsoft Security. 2008. "What Is a Computer Virus?" Microsoft Cor-

poration, November 18. Available: www.microsoft.com/protect/
computer/basics/virus.mspx (accessed March 23, 2009).

Milne, A. 2007. "Entering the Interactive Age." *Educause* (January):
13–31.

Mitchell, Bradley. "Connect Two Home Computers for File Sharing."
About.com. Available: http://compnetworking.about.com/od/
homenetworking/a/connecttwocomp.htm (accessed January 9, 2009).

Multnomah County Library. 2008. "RSS." Multnomah County Library,
October 22. Available: www.multcolib.org/catalog/rss.html/ (accessed July 1, 2009).

Nadel, Brian. "Better than Buying." Scholastic. Available: http://content.
scholastic.com/browse/article.jsp?id=11645 (accessed June 21, 2009).

National Board for Professional Teaching Standards. 2001. *NBPTS Library
Media Standards*. Arlington, VA: National Board for Professional
Teaching Standards. Available: www.nbpts.org/the_standards/stan-
dards_by_cert? ID=19&x=52&y=8 (accessed June 30, 2009).

National Center for Educational Statistics. 2006. "Internet Access in U.S.
Public Schools and Classrooms: 1994–1995." U.S. Department of Education, November. Available: http://nces.ed.gov/pubs2007/2007020.
pdf (accessed June 9, 2009).

National Center for Education Statistics. "Safeguarding Your Technology:
Practical Guidelines for Electronic Education Information Security."
U.S. Department of Education. Available: http://nces.ed.gov/pubs98/
safetech/ (accessed January 25, 2009).

National Initiative for a Networked Cultural Heritage. 2002. *Guide to
Good Practice in the Digital Representation and Management of
Cultural Heritage Materials*. Washington, DC: National Initiative
for a Networked Cultural Heritage.

Nicholas Senn High School Library. "Nicholas Senn H.S. Library." Available: http://sennlibrary.blogspot.com/ (accessed July 1, 2009).

Northeast Document Conservation Center. 2008. *Preservation Education
Curriculum*. Andover, MA: Northeast Document Conservation Center. Available: www.nedcc.org/curriculum/lesson.introduction.php.

Oblinger, D. 2006. *Learning Spaces*. Boulder, CO: Educause.

Oliver, James. 1997. "10 'Must Ask' Questions When Developing a
Technology Plan." American Association of School Administrators,
April. Available: www.aasa.org/publications/saarticledetail.cfm?mn
itemnumber=&tnitemnumber=&itemnumber=4797 (accessed June
21, 2009).

Penrod, Lee. 2008. "What Is PCI Express?" *Directron*, August 13. Available: www.directron.com/expressguide.html (accessed June 21,
2009).

Pinnacle Systems. "Pinnacle Studio." Pinnacle Systems Inc. Available: www.pinnaclesys.com (accessed June 28, 2009).

Powers, Deborah. 2008. "Accelerated Reader: Motivation and Engagement of Students and Teachers." Master's thesis, California State University, Long Beach, California.

Rheingold, H. 2000. *The Virtual Community*. Cambridge, MA: MIT Press.

Rhoades, Gale. 2007. "Tips for a Healthy PC." *Key Words* 15, no. 2 (April/June): 53–55.

"RSS Feeds on *School Library Journal*." Reed Business Information. Available: www.schoollibraryjournal.com/learnRss (accessed January 2, 2009).

Schmid, Patrick. 2007. "Analysis: Vista's Ready Boost Is No Match for RAM." *Tom's Hardware*, February 8. Available: www.tomshardware.com/reviews/analysis-vista-ready-boost,1891.html (accessed June 21, 2009).

Scott-Webber, L. 2004. *In Sync: Environmental Behavior Research and the Design of Learning Spaces*. Ann Arbor, MI: Society for College and University Planning.

Searls, Doc. 2008. "The Live Web." Doc Searls Weblog, September 26. Available: http://blogs.law.harvard.edu/doc/2008/09/26/the-live-web/ (accessed July 1, 2009).

Shade, Daniel D. 1996. "Care and Cleaning of Your Computer." *Computers and Young Children* 23, no. 1 (March): 165–168.

Shanahan, Seanean. "The Library Lady." Available: http://shayanasls.podomatic.com/ (accessed July 1, 2009).

Shankland, Stephen. 2005. "Sun and Google Shake Hands." CBS Interactive, October 4. Available: http://news.cnet.com/Sun-and-Google-shake-hands/2100-1014_35888701.html?tag=mncol;txt (accessed January 10, 2009).

Smith, Ivan. 2008. "Cost of Hard Drive Storage Space," January 21. Available: www.alts.net/ns1625/winchest.html (accessed June 21, 2009).

St. Sauver, Joe. 2001. "What's IPv6 . . . and Why Is It Gaining Ground?" *University of Oregon Computing News* 16, no. 3 (Spring): 14–16.

Stephens, Michael. 2007. "Best Practices for Social Software in Libraries." *Library Technology Reports* 43, no. 5 (September): 67–74.

Swanson, Kari. 2007. "Second Life: A Science Library Presence in Virtual Reality." *Science & Technology Libraries* 27, no. 3 (March): 79–86.

Thurrott, Paul. 2006. "Internet Explorer 7 Review." Paul Thurrott's SuperSite for Windows, October 18. Available: www.winsupersite.com/reviews/ie7.asp/ (accessed January 1, 2009).

Tortorice, Anthony. 2008. "IT Desktop Computer Maintenance and Support." Los Angeles Unified School District, May 30. Available:

http://notebook.lausd.net/pls/ptl/docs/PAGE/CA_LAUSD/FLDR_ ORGANIZATIONS/FLDR_INFOTECH/REF%201657%202%20 IT%20COMPUTER%20AND%20PERIPHERAL%20MAINT%20 AND%20SUPPORT%20V16.PDF (accessed June 21, 2009).

U.S. Department of Education. 2004. *Toward a Golden Age in American Education.* Washington, DC: U.S. Department of Education. Available: www.ed.gov/about/offices/list/os/technology/plan/2004/site/ theplan/NETP_Final.pdf (accessed July 2, 2009).

U.S. Department of Education. 2008. *Family Educational Rights and Privacy Act.* Washington, DC: U.S. Department of Education. Available: www.ed.gov/policy/gen/guid/fpco/ferpa/index.html (accessed March 29, 2009).

W3Schools. "HTML Introduction." www.w3schools.com/html/html_in-tro.asp (accessed July 1, 2009).

Wainfan, Lynne, and Paul Davis. 2004. *Challenges in Virtual Collaboration.* Santa Monica, CA: RAND.

Wayne, Richard. 2005. "PC Management Software." *Computers in Libraries* 25, no. 2 (February): 37–45.

WebAIM. "Introduction to Web Accessibility: Principles of Accessible Design." Available: www.webaim.org/intro/#principles. (accessed July 1, 2009).

Wenger, E. 1998. *Communities of Practice.* Cambridge, UK: Cambridge University Press.

Wikipedia. 2009. s.v. "Techie." Available: http://en.wikipedia.org/wiki/ Techie (accessed June 21, 2009).

Willard, Nancy. 2007. "Educator's Guide to Cyberbullying and Cyber-threats." Center for Safe and Responsible Use of the Internet, April. Available: www.cyberbully.org/ cyberbully/docs/cbcteducator.pdf (accessed June 25, 2009).

Windows. 2008. "What Is Windows SteadyState?" Microsoft Corporation. Available: www.microsoft.com/windows/products/winfamily/ sharedaccess/whatis/default.mspx (accessed January 9, 2009).

Index